CHRISTIAN SOLAR SYMBOLISM AND JESUS THE SUN OF JUSTICE

CHRISTIAN SOLAR SYMBOLISM AND JESUS THE SUN OF JUSTICE

Kevin Duffy SM

LONDON • NEW YORK • OXFORD • NEW DELHI • SYDNEY

T&T Clark
Bloomsbury Publishing Plc
50 Bedford Square, London, WC1B 3DP, UK
1385 Broadway, New York, NY 10018, USA
29 Earlsfort Terrace, Dublin 2, Ireland

BLOOMSBURY, T&T CLARK and the T&T Clark logo are
trademarks of Bloomsbury Publishing Plc

First published in Great Britain 2022
Paperback editon published 2023

Copyright © Kevin Duffy, 2022

Kevin Duffy has asserted his right under the Copyright, Designs and
Patents Act, 1988, to be identified as Author of this work.

For legal purposes the Acknowledgements on pp. xiii–xiv constitute an
extension of this copyright page.

Cover image: Tim Gainey / Alamy Stock Photo

All rights reserved. No part of this publication may be reproduced or transmitted
in any form or by any means, electronic or mechanical, including photocopying,
recording, or any information storage or retrieval system, without prior
permission in writing from the publishers.

Bloomsbury Publishing Plc does not have any control over, or responsibility for,
any third-party websites referred to or in this book. All internet addresses given
in this book were correct at the time of going to press. The author and publisher
regret any inconvenience caused if addresses have changed or sites have ceased
to exist, but can accept no responsibility for any such changes.

A catalogue record for this book is available from the British Library.

Library of Congress Cataloging-in-Publication Data
Names: Duffy, Kevin, (Theologian), author.
Title: Christian solar symbolism and Jesus the Sun of justice / Kevin Duffy, SM.
Description: London ; New York : T&T Clark, 2022. |
Includes bibliographical references and index. |
Identifiers: LCCN 2021035268 (print) | LCCN 2021035269 (ebook) |
ISBN 9780567700100 (hb) | ISBN 9780567701756 (paperback) |
ISBN 9780567700117 (epdf) | ISBN 9780567700124 (epub)
Subjects: LCSH: Jesus Christ–Name. | Sun–Religious aspects–Christianity. |
Light–Religious aspects–Christianity. | Christian art and symbolism.
Classification: LCC BT590.N2 D84 2022 (print) |
LCC BT590.N2 (ebook) | DDC 232–dc23
LC record available at https://lccn.loc.gov/2021035268
LC ebook record available at https://lccn.loc.gov/2021035269

ISBN: HB: 978-0-5677-0010-0
PB: 978-0-5677-0175-6
ePDF: 978-0-5677-0011-7
eBook: 978-0-5677-0012-4

Typeset by Integra Software Services Pvt. Ltd.

To find out more about our authors and books visit www.bloomsbury.com
and sign up for our newsletters.

O oriens, splendor lucis aeternae et sol justitiae

O Rising Sun, splendour of eternal light and Sun of Justice

Vespers, 21 December

CONTENTS

Acknowledgements	xiii
Copyright Acknowledgements	xiv
Abbreviations	xv
Introduction	1
Notes	2

Part I
RETRIEVAL

Chapter 1
SCRIPTURE — 5
- Light and darkness — 5
  - The light of the sun — 5
  - Two varieties of darkness — 6
- God and the sun — 6
  - Sun worship — 6
  - Yahweh and solar motifs — 7
- The Sun of Justice (Malachi 4.2) — 7
  - Sun and justice — 7
  - Justice and healing — 9
- Christ, light and sun — 9
  - A light shining in the darkness — 9
  - Christ the Rising Sun — 10
  - The shining face of Christ — 11
- Beyond the sun — 12
- Conclusion — 12
- Notes — 13

Chapter 2
THE EARLY CHURCH — 15
- Christian solar motifs — 15
  - Jesus Christ and the sun — 15
  - Rhythms of daily prayer — 15
  - Solar themes and inculturation — 16
  - Christ as a ray of sunlight? — 17
  - The sun metaphor and the divinity of Christ — 17
- The Egyptian connection: Alexandria — 18
  - The *Physiologus* — 18

Clement of Alexandria	18
Origen	19
Constantine and the sun	21
The emperor and the Unconquered Sun	21
The Day of the Sun	22
The cult of Mithras/Sol	22
Visual culture after Constantine	23
Christ as a solar emperor?	23
Art and architecture	24
Early church light	24
Two theologians of good darkness	25
Gregory of Nyssa	25
Dionysius the Areopagite	26
Conclusion	26
Notes	27

Chapter 3
THE LATIN WEST — 32

Ambrose	32
Augustine	33
Solar metaphors	33
His rejection of Manicheism	33
An interior light	34
Light rather than sun	34
Eucherius	34
Leo the Great	35
Fighting Manicheism	35
A warning to Christians	35
A fading interest in the cosmos	36
Gregory the Great	36
Contemplation and the sun	36
Chinks of light	36
'A distant region of the world': Insular Christianity	37
Two Romano-Britons: Patrick and Gildas	37
High crosses	38
Irish light	39
Conclusion	40
Notes	41

Chapter 4
THE MIDDLE AGES — 45

Light and its symbolism	45
Solar symbolism	45
The study of physical light	46
Medieval church light	47

Architecture and light	47
Ornate style	47
Plain style	48
Three German women	49
Hildegard of Bingen	49
Mechthild of Magdeburg	50
Gertrude the Great of Helfta	50
Francis of Assisi	51
The *Canticle of Brother Sun*	51
Creator and creation	52
A call to conversion and praise	52
Thomas Aquinas	52
Transmitting solar tradition	52
Downgrading metaphor	53
The language of light	53
Conclusion	54
Notes	54

Chapter 5
INTO THE MODERN ERA

	58
The birth of the modern era	58
Michelangelo's *The Last Judgment*	58
Renaissance and Reformation	58
Tommaso Campanella	59
The rise of modern science	60
Christian solar symbolism in a new era	60
New devotional possibilities	60
Pierre de Bérulle	61
The Society of Jesus and a modern solar emblem	61
Sun and eucharist	62
Solar symbolism in the new world	63
An Aztec solar Christ	63
The 'Sacramented Sun'	64
The Virgin of Guadalupe	64
Sor Juana Inés de la Cruz	64
John of the Cross and the discovery of night	65
A cultural shift	65
A poet of the night	66
Night and sun	66
Thomas Traherne	67
A theological aesthetic	67
'Things strange yet common'	68
Solar practices	68
Conclusion	69
Notes	70

Part II
REVIVAL

Chapter 6
REVIVING SOLAR SYMBOLISM — 77
  Towards a natural theology of sunlight — 77
    Reading the Book of Nature — 77
    Natural theology — 78
  East and West — 78
    A church breathing with two lungs — 78
    A recent work in the Western tradition — 79
  Sense experience and spiritual perception — 80
    'Spiritual senses' — 80
    Hans Urs von Balthasar — 80
    Idolatry and the esoteric — 81
  Metaphors of light and sun — 82
    Light and darkness — 82
    An interior sun — 82
  How metaphor works — 83
    An illuminating fiction — 83
    Meaning and truth — 83
    A different logic — 83
    Plasticity and discipline — 84
  Conclusion — 85
  Notes — 85

Chapter 7
RESOURCES FOR RECASTING — 89
  Science and technology: Challenges and opportunities — 89
    Astronomy — 89
    Chronobiology — 90
    Ray Bradbury, *Fahrenheit 451* — 90
    Dietrich Bonhoeffer — 90
  Pope Benedict XVI — 91
    Theology of light: Joseph Ratzinger — 91
    Pope Benedict — 92
  Pope Francis — 92
    Laudato si: Sir Brother Sun — 92
    The Book of Nature — 93
    The sun shines in the city: Carlos María Galli — 93
  A selection of hymns — 94
    Ancient and Modern — 94
    George Matheson — 95
    'Dayspring of Eternity' — 96
  Catholics and pagans — 97

Carthusian monks	97
Thomas Merton (1915–68)	98
Paul Murray (1947–)	99
Conclusion	99
Notes	100

Chapter 8
SACRED DIRECTION: ARE CHRISTIANS TO PRAY TOWARDS THE SUN? — 103

Varieties of sacred direction	103
Ad orientem	103
The direction of graves	103
Praying upwards	104
Oriented prayer	105
The early church	105
The Western church	106
Orientation in liturgy and church buildings	107
The early church	107
The Middle Ages and beyond	108
An unstable symbolism	108
Solar metaphors and interiority	109
The Western church	109
The Eastern church	110
Conclusion	111
Notes	112

Chapter 9
LIGHT, SUN AND LITURGY — 115

The incarnation	115
Epiphany: A feast of light	115
Christmas and the winter solstice	116
The paschal mystery	117
Baptism	117
Good Friday	118
Holy Saturday	118
Easter	120
Light and sun in the current liturgy	121
The Roman Missal	121
The Liturgy of the Hours	123
Conclusion	124
Notes	124

Chapter 10
JESUS THE SUN OF JUSTICE IN A SUNLESS AGE — 128

A sunless age	128
Friedrich Nietzsche and Thérèse of Lisieux	128

Philip Larkin	129
'A wintry season'	130
The Sun of Justice	131
Dusk and dawn	132
Jesus and the sun	132
Holistic justice	133
Justice in the church	133
Restoring cosmic order	134
Healing and conversion	135
Conclusion	137
Notes	137
Conclusions	**140**
Christian solar symbolism	140
Where it came from	140
Why it weakened	140
How it can be revived	141
Five strategies for revival	141
The Book of Scripture	141
The Book of Nature	142
Liturgy and prayer	143
The natural theology of sunlight	143
Jesus Christ the Sun of Justice	144
Notes	144
Bibliography	**145**
Biblical Reference Index	**166**
Index	**168**

ACKNOWLEDGEMENTS

When I went on about solar symbolism in recent years, confreres in several Marist communities listened patiently with a generous interest that went well beyond the call of duty.

The community at Mt Eden and Good Shepherd College, Auckland, New Zealand were generous hosts for a sabbatical period, while the community at Mount St Mary's, Milltown, Dublin and the librarians at the Milltown Jesuit Institute offered a welcome for several working holidays.

I am sure I will have left out some but I would like to thank various people who helped with advice, or ideas or by reading over portions of text: Pedro Alarcon, Gerald Arbuckle, Fritz Arnold, Barbara Dando, Brendan Duffy, Larry Duffy, Merv Duffy, Rocio Figueroa, Paul Gifford, John Hannan, Little Sister Kathleen of Jesus, Patricia Larkin, Bill Matthews, John McAllister, Jimmy McElroy, Paolo Mancinelli, Declan Marmion, Yvan Matthieu, Marian Monaghan, Gerard Moore, Michael Mullins, Paul Murray, Tom O'Loughlin, Eileen Plunkett, Iakonos Potamiamos, Susan K. Roll, Anne-Marie Salgo, John Sullivan, Justin Taylor, Beáta Tóth, Dilys Wadman, Anthony Ward and Christina Anjey Wase.

COPYRIGHT ACKNOWLEDGEMENTS

Excerpts from *That They May Face the Rising Sun* by John McGahern (Copyright © John McGahern, 2009) used by permission of Faber & Faber Ltd.

USA: Excerpt(s) from *By The Lake* by John McGahern, copyright © 2002 by John McGahern. Used by permission of Alfred A. Knopf, an imprint of the Knopf Doubleday Publishing Group, a division of Penguin Random House LLC. All rights reserved.

Canada: *That They May Face the Rising Sun* by John McGahern (Copyright © John McGahern, 2009). Reprinted by permission of A.M. Heath & Co Ltd.

'Final Soliloquy of the Interior Paramour', copyright 1951 by Wallace Stevens; and 'Notes toward a Supreme Fiction', copyright 1942 by Wallace Stevens; from *The Collected Poems of Wallace Stevens* by Wallace Stevens. Used by permission of Alfred A. Knopf, an imprint of the Knopf Doubleday Publishing Group, a division of Penguin Random House LLC. All rights preserved.

Excerpts of Wallace Stevens, *Selected Poems* (London: Faber & Faber, 2010) used by permission of Faber & Faber Ltd.

Excerpts from Kenneth Jackson, *Studies in Early Celtic Nature Poetry* (© Cambridge University Press, 1935). Reproduced with permission of the Licensor through PLSclear.

Excerpts from Hildegard of Bingen, *Scivias* (trans. Columba Hart, Jane Bishop, Classics of Western Spirituality Series), ©1990 by the Abbey of Regina Laudis: Benedictine Congregation Regina Laudis of the Strict Observance, Inc. Used with permission of Paulist Press. Permission conveyed through Copyright Clearance Center, Inc.

From *The Complete Poems of Philip Larkin* by Philip Larkin, edited Archie Burnette. Copyright © 2012 by The Estate of Philip Larkin. Introduction copyright by Archie Burnett. Reprinted by permission of Faber & Faber and Farrar, Straus and Giroux. All rights reserved.

ABBREVIATIONS

ANF *Ante-Nicene Fathers: The Writings of the Fathers down to A.D. 325* (eds Alexander Roberts and James Donaldson; revised A. Cleveland Coxe (New York: Christian Literature Publishing Co., 1885).

CCL *Corpus Christianorum, Series Latina* (Turnhout: Brepols, 1953–).

CSEL *Corpus Scriptorum Ecclesiasticorum Latinorum* (Vienna: Hoelder-Pichler-Tempsky, 1866–).

ET English Translation

FC Fathers of the Church

NPNF *Nicene and Post-Nicene Fathers* (eds Philip Schaf and Henry Wallace; Second Series; New York: The Christian Literature Company; Oxford and London: Parker and Company, 1893).

PG J.-P. Migne (ed.), *Patrologiae Cursus Completus, Series Graeca* (166 vols.; Paris: J.-P. Migne, 1857–83).

PL J.-P. Migne (ed.), *Patrologiae Cursus Completus, Series Latina* (221 vols.; Paris: J.-P. Migne, 1844–65).

SC Sources Chrétiennes

ST Summa Theologica

Unless otherwise noted, all scripture quotations are from the New Revised English Standard Version.

INTRODUCTION

The present work started with a remark about Muslims. I mentioned how impressive it was to see Muslims lay down their mats and pray facing Mecca in Abidjan airport in West Africa. A confrere replied that if early Christians came to earth today, they might well make the initial mistake of identifying Muslims as their coreligionists, since early Christians prostrated themselves and faced eastwards when they prayed. I started exploring what seemed a potent symbol, collecting related ideas such as Christ returning from the east, and the eastern location of the garden of Eden, only to discover that a list of such related ideas was drawn up by St John Damascene in the eighth century, and was readily available on Eastern Orthodox websites.[1] It also became clear that Christian sun symbolism has deeper roots in the Bible and in tradition than orientation to the east, and yet solar motifs hardly figure in recent Catholic theology and spirituality. Then, at the conclave where he was elected pope, Francis declared that the church had forgotten the patristic symbol of a lunar church that receives its light from the sun.[2] I could find no general book on Christ and the light of the sun. Hence this work.

In *That They May Face the Rising Sun,* John McGahern places a complex of Christian sun symbolism at the heart of a novel set in rural Catholic Ireland. A twilight graveyard scene where several of the principal characters in the book are assembled gives the work its name. They are digging a fresh grave in an ancient graveyard, bordering a ruined abbey, when Patrick Ryan notices that they have dug the grave in the wrong direction. The head is in the east. 'I kind of knew as soon as we saw the bones.' When the fault is put right one of the others asks him whether it makes any difference that the deceased's head now lies in the west. 'It makes every difference, lad, or it makes no difference.' He explains:

> 'He sleeps with his head in the west … So that when he wakes he may face the rising sun.' Looking from face to face and drawing himself to his full height, Patrick Ryan stretched his arm dramatically towards the east. 'We look to the resurrection of the dead.'
>
> The shadow from the abbey now stretched beyond the open grave, but the rose-window in the west pulsed with light, sending out wave after wave of carved shapes of light towards that part of the sky where the sun would rise.
>
> 'You never lost it, Patrick', Jamesie said.

'You never lost it, Patrick' plays at two levels – the character's theatrical gifts and the persistence of the past. The final word is given to another gravedigger, John Quinn: 'It'd nearly make you start to think.'[3] Where did this Christian sun symbolism come from? How did it weaken without disappearing? In Part I, we address these two questions. In Part II, we ask: how can we re-activate a largely dormant pattern of symbols in a technological and urban world quite different from the world we see disappearing in John McGahern's elegiac novel?

Notes

1. For example, *Orthodoxprayer*. Available online: https://www.orthodoxprayer.org/Facing%20East.html (accessed 28 December 2020).
2. Gerard O'Connell, *The Election of Pope Francis: An Inside Account of the Conclave That Changed History* (Maryknoll, NY: Orbis, 2019), p. 154.
3. John McGahern, *That They May Face the Rising Sun* (London: Faber and Faber, 2009), pp. 296–7.

Part I

RETRIEVAL

Chapter 1

SCRIPTURE

Light and darkness

The light of the sun

> In the beginning when God created the heavens and the earth, the earth was a formless void and the darkness covered the face of the deep, while a wind from God swept over the face of the waters. Then God said, 'Let there be light'; and there was light. And God saw that the light was good; and God separated the light from the darkness. God called the light Day, and the darkness he called Night. And there was evening and there was morning, the first day.
> (Gen. 1.1-5)

> God made the two great lights – the greater light to rule the day and the lesser light to rule the night – and the stars … And God saw that it was good. And there was evening and there was morning, the fourth day.
> (Gen. 1.16-19)

In these passages from Genesis, and in the Old Testament in general, light and sun are good and created by God. They are intimately connected without being identical. Light is daylight – 'God called the light Day' – and comes from the sun – 'Why is one day more important than another, when all the daylight in the year is from the sun' (Ecclus 33.7)? All the same, the Genesis account has the sun created three days later than light, probably to rule out idolatrous sun worship. The sun is not divine but a creature serving God's purposes as 'the greater light to rule the day' determining the diurnal rhythms that mark the lives of humans and animals (Ps. 104.20-23).

In possibly the first writing of the New Testament, Paul encourages his readers in the Greek port city of Thessalonica: 'You are all children of light and children of the day; we are not of the night or of darkness' (1 Thess. 5.5). His readers were mostly recent Greek converts, and Paul was not presuming that they had a deep knowledge of the Hebrew scriptures. There are no parallels in Greek texts for Paul's expression 'children of the day'[1] which seems to be an expression he coined meaning 'day people' or 'children of daylight'.[2] His Greek readers will have understood it in terms of their daily experience of daylight and sparkling created sunlight. According to Paul, for Christians to avoid wrongdoing is, metaphorically, to live in daylight (Rom. 13.13) and to wake up into daylight is to cultivate joy and thankfulness (1 Thess. 5.16-18), with the risen Christ shining on them (Eph. 5.14). For the peoples of the ancient Middle East, the sky was fascinating, populated with heavenly bodies seen as living beings and often as gods. By New Testament times, however, the divinity of the sun was not an issue for the Jewish world the converts of Thessalonica had entered, and when the Jewish Christians addressed by James looked upwards at the sky, they saw the sun and other 'lights' as changing, created things in contrast to the unchanging 'Father of lights' (Jas 1.17).

Two varieties of darkness

In the Genesis narrative, light is brought into existence from the primaeval chaos; like darkness, it is part of creation.[3] Both light and darkness provided metaphors to talk about God with light the dominant motif. God wears light like a piece of clothing (Ps. 104.2), light dwells with him (Dan. 2.22), and his brightness is 'like the sun' (Hab. 3.4). While light is positive, darkness has two connotations, one positive and the other negative. Moses draws near to the thick darkness where God is (Exod. 20.21) and God speaks from a cloud (Exod. 24.16). 'Clouds and thick darkness are all around him; righteousness and justice are the foundations of his throne' (Ps. 97.2). This positive darkness complements the primary symbolism of light. It was not a major theme in the New Testament, but was taken up in Christian theology, in Origen for instance, who would talk about a 'good darkness', and in Dionysius the Areopagite and John of the Cross. A second metaphor is of darkness as evil and ignorance: 'The way of the wicked is like deep darkness' (Prov. 4.19). 'The wise have eyes in their head, but fools walk in darkness' (Eccl. 2.14). This negative darkness is the primary metaphor of darkness in the New Testament, where created light is a metaphor to express the very nature of God who 'dwells in unapproachable light' (1 Tim. 6.16) and in whom 'there is no darkness at all' (1 Jn 1.5).

God and the sun

Sun worship

The Old Testament expresses belief established at the time of the Babylonian captivity, after 598 BCE, in Yahweh as the only God, the Creator we see in Genesis. This belief was the result of a long process of development through various forms of polytheism. Yahweh was not identified with the physical sun[4] which is itself to offer worship: 'Praise him, sun and moon;/praise him, all you shining stars' (Ps. 148.3). When Joshua gives the sun orders – 'Sun, stand still at Gibeon, and Moon, in the valley of Aijalon' (Josh. 10.12-13) – it obeys. Sun worship was, nevertheless, an issue. For Jeremiah, the bones of practitioners should be exhumed and scattered like dung to bake under the sun they have worshipped (Jer. 8.1-2), while Ezekiel inveighs against those who turn their backs to the Temple to prostrate themselves before the rising sun (Ezek. 8.16-18). Heavenly bodies were so fascinating that they could be a source of temptation: 'And when you look up to the heavens and see the sun, the moon, and the stars, all the host of heaven, do not be led astray and bow down to them and serve them' (Deut. 4.19). Examining his conscience, Job asks himself: 'If I have looked at the sun / when it shone, / or the moon moving in splendour, / and my heart has been secretly enticed, / and my mouth has kissed my hand' (Job 31.26-27).

Yahweh and solar motifs

Sometimes, however, God seems to be identified with the sun: 'The Lord came from Sinai, / And dawned from Seir upon us; / He shone forth from Mount Paran' (Deut. 33.2). Israel gradually took over motifs from various cults, including solar cults, and applied them to Yahweh. Shamash, a Mesopotamian sun god, was a source of light, warmth and justice. In the Babylonian Shamash Hymn, he is the all-seeing eye and the guardian of justice whose 'beams are ever mastering secrets': 'The meek, the weak, the oppressed, the submissive,/ Daily, ever, and always come before you.'[5] Israel transferred solar epithets and images from Shamash to Yahweh, without identifying the two deities. The result is a God of justice who is not literally solar, but who is described figuratively using the light and sun he created – 'For the Lord God is a sun and shield' (Ps. 84.11). The glory of the sun was a source of wonder. In Psalm 19, the sun is a marvel that 'comes out like a bridegroom from his wedding canopy, and like a strongman runs its course with joy' (Ps. 19.5). The people of Israel in turn can shine with reflected light: 'Arise, shine; for your light has come, and the glory of the Lord has risen upon you' (Isa. 60.1).

This solar religiosity was part of the general culture of the Middle East, from the late Bronze Age (*c.* 1600–1200 BCE) when solar language for monarchs and for divinities spread from New Kingdom Egypt to other areas including Israel.[6] There were solar themes in both Canaanite and Mesopotamian cults. Probably, they were applied first to human rulers; the just ruler 'is like the light of morning, like the sun rising on a cloudless morning, gleaming from the rain on the grassy land' (2 Sam. 23.3b-4). In a second step, they were applied to pagan deities, and eventually to Yahweh[7]: 'Restore us, O God of hosts; let your face shine, that we may be saved' (Ps. 80.7). There may have been a solar cult in the Jerusalem Temple itself (see 2 Kgs 23.5, 11 and Ezek. 8.16). Perhaps the sun was reverenced as a being in the host of heaven or even for a time with parallel cults of Shamash and Yahweh in the Temple.[8] Whatever the details of the process, the result was a non-solar Yahweh described with appropriated sun metaphors.

The Sun of Justice (Malachi 4.2)

Sun and justice

'But for you who revere my name the sun of righteousness [justice] shall rise, with healing in his wings. You shall go out leaping like calves from the stall' (Mal. 4.2).[9] This verse from the sixth-century prophet Malachi was taken up with enthusiasm by early Christians, at the latest from the third century, and applied to Jesus the Messiah. Now, sometimes expressions come loose from their moorings in a literary text and take on a life of their own, as with 'the slings and arrows of outrageous fortune' in Shakespeare's *Hamlet*.[10] A biblical example is Yahweh treading the winepress in anger in Isa. 63.3 which detached itself from its original context and lodged in the American consciousness figuring, for example, in the Battle Hymn of the Republic and in John Steinbeck's novel *The Grapes of Wrath*. Did something similar happen to Mal. 4.2 since, in its original meaning, the verse was not messianic? It seems not. Christians were tapping into a vibrant visual tradition and into Old Testament currents of thought where God is associated with a holistic or connective conception of justice, establishing and defending right order in areas as diverse as law, wisdom, nature, cult and kingship.[11] Israel used solar symbolism to link law with light, in such a way that divine judging and saving were two sides of a single coin. Christians turned to Malachi's 'Sun of Justice', with its rich symbolic connections, to express a messianic eschatology of God breaking into the present world healing and transforming it.

To understand these symbolic connections, we look to Egypt. Many of the psalms are close to Egyptian beliefs that spread throughout the ancient Middle East, that God promotes justice, intervening against enemies. Ps. 104.20-30 shares features with the Egyptian Great Hymn to Aten.[12] In the Egyptian worldview, human flourishing, and indeed cosmic order, was tied to the sun's successful completion of its daily course. The Egyptian pharaoh was the priest of Ra, the sun god, and Ra's power was expressed in the setting and the rising of the sun. In Exod. 10.21 a darkness descends on Pharaoh's Egypt. A modern comparison might be an oil slick or a black hole where light is not simply absent but eaten up.[13] In the middle of the fourteenth century BCE, the Pharaoh Akhenaten introduced a dramatic but ill-fated reform. Instead of being one god among others, the sun god was effectively the only God, exercising his power over everything through light and time. He is, however, completely outside worldly processes, with nothing to do with justice, and wholly unaffected by human rituals. It is easy to see why the reform was rejected – more than half of the many hymns that we have from ancient Egypt are hymns to the sun. The fear was not just that at some point during the day the sun would stop, but that the fundamental structure of reality would fall apart. The ancient Egyptians saw the world in terms of cosmic solidarity. Ma'at – justice or righteousness – was personified as a goddess who goes forth from the sun god and fills the world with life and light. In Psalm 85 righteousness will appear from on high and walk before Yahweh, just as the goddess Ma'at walks in front of the Egyptian sun god (Ps. 85.11-13).[14] While Israel inherited a link between the cosmic and the personal that originated in Egypt, a striking difference between the religion of Israel and that of Egypt, Babylon, or Persia is that Israel had little interest in detailed cosmological speculations.[15] Israel's interest was intensely inter-personal. This is something that marked its whole engagement with the symbolism of sun and light.

Another influence on Mal. 4.2 coming originally from Egypt was the winged solar disc.[16] This object combined the imagery of a bird (an eagle or falcon) and the sun, looming large in Akhenaten's solar religiosity.[17] It arrived in Syria in the eighteenth century BCE, subsequently spreading throughout the Near East.[18] There is clear archaeological evidence of the disc in Israel and no evidence of opposition to it. As is often the case with material culture, the symbol is polyvalent. The translation of Mal. 4.2 can read 'in his wings' or 'in his rays'. 'Rays' underscores the solar character of the symbol, while 'wings' expresses the movement and speed evoked by the image, and in the Bible wings are generally seen as protective: 'Guard me as the apple of the eye; hide me in the shadow of your wings' (Ps. 17.8).

Justice and healing

Although the expression 'sun of justice/righteousness' is unique to Malachi, he was employing symbolism familiar to his audience. 'Healing' meant promoting cosmic, bodily, social and religious well-being.[19] The word-picture of the solar disc also expressed an association of the morning sun with healing in an epiphany of God as the just vindicator of the innocent: 'Then your light shall break forth like the dawn, / and your healing shall spring up quickly; / your vindicator shall go before you, / the glory of the Lord shall be your rearguard' (Isa. 58.8). Whether Malachi wanted the sun to refer primarily to God himself or to his intervention on the Day of the Lord is unclear.[20] While he was not referring to a messianic figure, he looked forward to a dramatic reversal of present circumstances, when the moral mist would clear, and the People of the Covenant would be gloriously vindicated: 'You shall go out leaping like calves from the stall.' In one of the Dead Sea Scrolls, written in New Testament times, there are the same connections between sun and justice and final triumph: 'As smoke disappears, and no longer exists, so will evil disappear for ever. And justice will be revealed like a sun which regulates the world.'[21] When, 200 years later, Egyptian Christians in Alexandria sensed evocative potential in Malachi's 'Sun of Justice', they were tapping into a symbol with a deep past and probably multiple continuing connections to their contemporary culture.

Christ, light and sun

A light shining in the darkness

In the Fourth Gospel, there is an interplay between the symbols of light and darkness and motifs of wisdom, word and glory. While for the later Gnostics the created world is a zone of evil darkness from which they sought deliverance, for John there is no such disjunction between creation and salvation. He was probably close to the thought-world of the Essenes who produced the Qumran scrolls, where light and darkness symbolize two opposed moral realms of good and evil.[22] For John, and for the New Testament in general, darkness is not a symbol for the mystery of God, as it was in the darkness in Exodus, nor for creation as such, but for sin and ignorance. The created world is good and natural light is good but in Jesus we are in the presence of a higher divine light that demands a personal response, a radical conversion of life seen as turning away from darkness. To be in his presence is to be faced with urgent choices – 'The light is with you for a little longer. Walk while you have the light, so that the darkness may not overtake you. If you walk in the darkness, you do not know where you are going' (Jn 12.35). When John narrates the healing of the man born blind, a model of a believer opening to the Light, the Feast of Tabernacles is in the background (Jn 9.1-41).[23] In this feast of water and light, for seven days four seven-branched candlesticks illuminated the Court of the Women in the Temple for dancing and hymn-singing throughout the night till daybreak. Paul speaks with the same urgency as John, with a metaphor of darkness fading as dawn approaches: 'Night is far gone, the day is near. Let us then lay aside the works of darkness and put on the armour of light; let us live honourably as in the day' (Rom. 13.12-13). John's and Paul's readers will have understood light with reference to their experience of daylight and nocturnal darkness.

In the Old Testament sapiential tradition, Wisdom is a personified female figure expressing poetically attributes of the one God reflecting the eternal light of God (Wis. 7.26) opening a way for humans with a light that is superior to natural light: 'She is more beautiful than the sun, / and excels every constellation of the stars. / Compared with the light she is found to be superior, / for it is succeeded by the night, / but against wisdom evil does not prevail' (Wis. 7.29-30). John applies this Wisdom symbol to the person of Jesus of Nazareth who is the Light.[24] The Fourth Gospel starts in parallel with the account of creation in Genesis – 'In the beginning was the Word.'[25] Just as God created light, his Son comes as the light of the world (Jn 8.12; 9.5) with the glory of the eternal God shining forth in his own person. Christ shines or radiates majestically, not in an episode as in the synoptic accounts of the Transfiguration but globally throughout his ministry.[26] John claims that 'we have seen his glory' (Jn 1.14), a glory Ezekiel compares to the sun rising and illuminating the world: 'And there, the glory of the God of Israel was coming from the east; the sound was like the sound of mighty waters; and the earth shone with his glory' (Ezek. 43.2).

Christ the Rising Sun

In the New Testament the metaphor of the sun is secondary. Light symbolism abounds while there are only a few, admittedly striking, instances of solar symbolism. Some verses from Luke's *Benedictus* canticle are particularly evocative: 'By the tender mercy of our God, / the dawn [*anatole*] from on high will break upon us / to give light to those who sit in / darkness and in the shadow of death, / to guide our feet into the way of peace' (Lk. 1.78-79). Luke has Zechariah refer to Jesus the Messiah as ἀνατολή (*anatole*) in Greek, a word which can be translated as rising sun, dawn or east. Its basic meaning was 'rising', and in astronomy and geography it referred to the rising of the sun. The two senses of the dawn and the east were intertwined, with the precise meaning fluctuating. For example, in the Septuagint the usual meaning of *anatole* is 'east'. In Zech. 3.8, 6.12, and in the rabbinic literature, *anatole* refers to the Messiah. This usage was based on a secondary meaning of the term in Greek as indicating growth or springing up: 'Here is a man whose name is Branch [*Anatole*]: for he shall branch out in his place, and he shall build the temple of the Lord' (Zech. 6.12). Even in the Hebrew text before it was translated into Greek, the idea of shining was present alongside that of sprouting or growing.[27] In Luke's text the messianic and the solar are integrated. The Messiah is described as coming from on high, from God's dwelling place. The result is a paradoxical solar image of a sun rising from above.[28] The genre of the *Benedictus*, a poetic mosaic of interwoven allusions to biblical and intertestamental imagery, provides a biblical warrant for multiple meanings in Lk. 1.78-79, based on an indefinitely large range of biblical references.[29] Sun, dawn, light, morning, illumination, newness, freshness, night, day, and darkness all inevitably figure in the reader's response to the canticle. Whenever there is Christian solar symbolism, Lk. 1.78-79 is, as often as not, somewhere in the background.

The shining face of Christ

The author of Ephesians quotes what was probably a very early Christian hymn: 'Sleeper, awake! Rise from the dead, and Christ will shine on you' (Eph. 5.14). The Old Testament trope of God's shining face is in the background as well as daily sunshine. Those who sang the hymn lived in more intimate connection with diurnal rhythms of light and darkness than we do living in our technological world. When Paul defends the authenticity of his apostolic ministry in 2 Corinthians, he claims he has received an illumination that outstrips the manifestations of divine glory in the Old Testament. God is at work in his experience with the same divine power he used to create light in the beginning: 'For it is the God who said, "Let light shine out of darkness", who has shone in our hearts to give the light of the knowledge of the glory of God in the face of Jesus Christ' (2 Cor. 4.5-6). His light experience on the road to Damascus is probably somewhere in the background, but Paul is not talking about a literal vision of Jesus.[30] Verse 6 evokes the blessing of Num. 6.24-26: 'The Lord make his face to shine upon you and be gracious to you. / The Lord lift up his countenance upon you, and give you peace.'

The shining face of God figures as well in the Transfiguration accounts in the synoptic gospels (Mk 9.2-8; Mt. 17.1-9; Lk. 9.28-36): 'Six days later, Jesus took with him Peter and James and his brother John and led them up a high mountain, by themselves. And he was transfigured before them, and his face shone like the sun, and his clothes became dazzling white' (Mt. 17.1-2). Whatever experience on the part of an inner group of apostles may lie behind Matthew's text, it is not a historical narrative like the passion narratives nor modelled on resurrection appearances. Matthew (v. 9) calls the experience of the apostles a 'vision', but it is not apocalyptic like Daniel or the Book of Revelation. The accounts are best seen as presenting a symbolic theology of Jesus's identity, modelled on Exodus chapters 24 and 34 where Moses goes up Mount Sinai. The parallels are evident. The glory of God shows itself; there is a voice coming from a cloud (the theme of a positive darkness is not, then, wholly absent) and awe among the onlookers. The face of Moses shone with reflected light, but in the synoptic narratives Jesus shines with his own light. As in Luke, Matthew has light radiating from the face of Jesus, but he specifies that the light was shining 'like the sun' (v. 2). Matthew is asserting that Jesus is a new Moses[31] but his solar emphasis is part of a wider pattern. When Jesus starts his public ministry in Capernaum, a light has risen or dawned – that is, the sun has dawned – on a people sitting in darkness (Mt. 4.16; Isa. 9.2). 'And when the Kingdom comes the righteous too will shine like the sun in God's kingdom' (Mt. 13.43).

Beyond the sun

At the beginning of the Book of Revelation, the seer perceives one like the Son of Man: 'And his face was like the sun shining with full force. When I saw him, I fell at his feet as though dead. But he placed his right hand on me, saying, "Do not be afraid; I am the first and the last, and the living one"' (Rev. 1.16b-17). The mortal human who cannot see God and live becomes immortal when face to face with the glorified Christ shining like the sun. His servants will worship him and 'they will see his face, and his name will be on their foreheads' (Rev. 22.4). At the same time, there is no night, and the sun is redundant 'for the glory of God is its light, and its lamp is the Lamb' (Rev. 21.23).[32] They have reached a place of safety where 'the sun will not strike them' (Rev. 7.16). Sun and day, darkness and night are temporary features of a passing world: 'And there will be no more night; they need no light of lamp or sun, for the Lord God will be their light, and they will reign for ever and ever' (Rev. 22.5).

Conclusion

In the Bible, God is not a sun god and sun worship is firmly rejected. Nevertheless, the invisible God is said to shine, and he is described in solar metaphors often borrowed from Israel's pagan environment. In the visual culture of the authors of the Hebrew scriptures, created light and sun were not identical but were more closely associated than is the case for us in our world of twenty-four hours a day illumination. Solar motifs are also closely linked with a broad holistic concept of justice, at once judgment and mercy. The prophet Malachi encapsulated these traditions in the image of the Sun of Justice who would come with healing in his wings, an image taken up later with enthusiasm by early Christians.

The few theologically significant solar texts in the New Testament are dense with meaning (for instance, Jesus referred to as the *anatole* – the rising sun – in Lk. 1.78-79), evoking a web of associations from the Old Testament. Descriptions of Christ as shining or radiant had an intense solar resonance for a culture where Paul called Christians 'children of daylight'. Nevertheless, in the New Testament, it is the symbolism of light that is paramount and solar symbolism is secondary. Darkness, the opposite of light, is negative, symbolizing sin, evil and ignorance. The minor motif of positive divine darkness in Exodus only appears in a secondary, implicit way, as in the image of the cloud at the Transfiguration. In sum, the motifs of good darkness and of sun are ancillary metaphors alongside the primary New Testament symbolism of light.

When biblical texts are read alongside other texts in scripture, they take on new meanings and, down the centuries, readers ask what they mean for their time. Throughout history, the church opts for some biblical voices rather than others and combines different voices in different ways. As we will see in later chapters, modern Western theology and spirituality have given a great deal of attention to the ancillary Old Testament metaphors of positive divine darkness and cloud, and relatively little to those of daylight and sun. Listening to neglected biblical voices can help modify exaggerations and imbalances.[33] Equally, if we want to appreciate anew what the biblical authors meant by saying that Christ is the light, the natural phenomenon of sunlight merits particular attention. In the chapters that follow, we will take soundings in the history of how Christians developed a rich tradition of solar metaphor as they engaged with solar texts in the Bible, and with the daily experience of light and darkness, and go on to sketch what solar metaphors and Malachi's Sun of Justice can mean for us today.

Notes

1. Camille Focant, 'Les fils du jour (1 Thes 5,5)', in *The Thessalonian Correspondence* (ed. Raymond F. Collins; Leuven: Leuven University Press, 1990), pp. 348–55.
2. Andy Johnson, *1 and 2 Thessalonians* (Grand Rapids, MI: Eerdmans, 2016), p. 140.
3. Elizabeth R. Achtemeier, 'Jesus Christ, the Light of the World: The Biblical Understanding of Light and Darkness', *Interpretation* 7.4 (1963), pp. 439–49.
4. For a minority view that Yahweh was literally identified with the sun, see J. Glen Taylor, *Yahweh and the Sun: Biblical and Archaeological Evidence for Sun Worship in Ancient Israel* (Sheffield: Sheffield Academic Press, 1993).
5. 'The Shamash Hymn (1.117)', trans. Benjamin R. Foster, in *The Context of Scripture, vol. 1: Canonical Compositions from the Biblical World* (ed. William W. Hallo; Leiden, New York and Cologne: Brill, 1997), pp. 418–9.
6. Mark S. Smith, 'The Near Eastern Background of Solar Language for Yahweh', *Journal of Biblical Literature* 109.1 (1990), pp. 29–39 (35–6).
7. Mark S. Smith, *The Early History of God: Yahweh and the Other Deities in Ancient Israel* (Grand Rapids, MI and Cambridge, UK: Eerdmans, 2002), pp. 152–3.
8. John Day, *Yahweh and the Gods and Goddesses of Canaan* (Sheffield: Sheffield Academic Press, 2000), p. 158. Thomas Römer, *The Invention of God* (trans. Raymond Guess; Cambridge, MA and London: Harvard University Press, 2015), pp. 97–103.
9. This solar title is translated 'Sun of Justice' or 'Sun of Righteousness'. The reference is sometimes given as Mal. 3.20 following the Vulgate.
10. Northrop Frye, *The Great Code: The Bible and Literature* (Cambridge, MA: Harvard University Press, 1982), pp. 217–18.
11. Bernd Janowski, *Konfliktgespräche mit Gott: Eine Anthropologie der Psalmen* (Neukirchen: Neukirchener Theologie, 2013), p. 138.
12. Bernd U. Schipper, 'Egyptian Background to the Psalms', in *Oxford Handbook of the Psalms* (ed. William P. Brown; New York: Oxford University Press, 2014), pp. 57–75. Some scholars argue for a direct influence: James K. Hoffmeier, *Akhenaten and the Origins of Monotheism* (Oxford: Oxford University Press, 2015), pp. 247–56; for a different view, see John Day, 'Psalm 104 and Akhenaten's Hymn to the Sun', in *Jewish and Christian Approaches to the Psalms: Conflict and Convergence* (ed. Susan Gillingham; Oxford: Oxford University Press, 2013), pp. 211–28.

13 Thomas B. Dozeman, *Exodus* (Grand Rapids, MI and Cambridge, UK: Eerdmans, 2009), p. 246.
14 Römer, *The Invention of God*, pp. 129–30.
15 Schipper, 'Egyptian Background to the Psalms', p. 72.
16 Joel M. LeMon, *Yahweh's Winged Form in the Psalms: Exploring Congruent Iconography and Texts* (Fribourg: Academic Press and Göttingen: Vandenhoeck and Ruprecht, 2010), pp. 187–94.
17 'The representation of the sun disk in the art of the period soon becomes extremely original, and makes it clear that it was *precisely* the disk, depicted with rays terminating in helpful little hands, that was the object of Akhenaten's worship.' Giulio Magli, *Architecture, Astronomy and Sacred Landscape in Ancient Egypt* (Cambridge: Cambridge University Press, 2013), p. 207. Emphasis original.
18 Felix Blocher, 'Sonne und Sonnengottheiten im alten Vorderasien', in *Sonne: Brennpunkt der Kulturen der Welt* (ed. Andrea Bärnreuther; Neu-Isenburg: Edition Minerva, 2009), pp. 40–53 (45).
19 Pieter A. Verhoef, *The Books of Haggai and Malachi* (Grand Rapids, MI: Eerdmans, 1987), pp. 329–30.
20 Andrew E. Hill, *Haggai, Zechariah and Malachi: An Introduction and Commentary* (Downers Grove, IL: InterVarsity Press, 2012), pp. 358–9.
21 Prophecy, 1QMysteries (1Q27 [1QMyst]). ET *The Dead Sea Scrolls Translated: The Qumran Texts in English* (ed. Florentino García Martínez; trans. Wilfred G. E. Watson; Leiden, New York and Cologne: E. J. Brill and Grand Rapids, MI: William B. Eerdmans, 2nd edn, 1996), p. 399.
22 John Ashton, *Understanding the Fourth Gospel* (Oxford: Clarendon Press, 1991), pp. 208–14.
23 Andrew T. Lincoln, *The Gospel According to St John* (Grand Rapids, MI: Baker Academic, 2013), pp. 241–2, 277–90.
24 Raymond E. Brown, *An Introduction to the Gospel of John* (ed., updated, introduced and concluded by Francis J. Moloney, SDB; New York: Doubleday, 2003), pp. 259–65.
25 Raymond E. Brown, *The Gospel According to John (i–xii)* (London: Geoffrey Chapman, 1971), pp. 26–7.
26 Craig S. Keener, '"We Beheld His Glory!" (John 1:14)', in *John, Jesus, and History, vol. 2: Aspects of Historicity in the Fourth Gospel* (eds Paul N. Anderson, Felix Just, SJ and Tom Thatcher; Atlanta: Society of Biblical Literature, 2009), pp. 15–25.
27 Daniel Grossberg, 'The Dual Glow/Grow Motif', *Biblica* 67.4 (1986), pp. 547–54.
28 Simon J. Gathercole, 'The Heavenly ἀνατολή (Luke:78–9)', *Journal of Theological Studies NS* 56.2 (2005), pp. 471–88 (482).
29 For example, for v. 78: Isa. 60.1; Mal. 4.2; Num. 24.17. For v. 79: Isa. 9.2b; Isa. 42.6-7; Ps. 107.10-14.
30 Mark A. Seifrid, *The Second Letter to the Corinthians* (Grand Rapids, MI and Cambridge, UK: Eerdmans, 2014), p. 204.
31 Raymond E. Brown, *An Introduction to the New Testament* (New York: Doubleday, 1997), pp. 139, 190.
32 James L. Resseguie, *The Revelation of John: A Narrative Commentary* (Grand Rapids, MI: Baker Academic, 2009), pp. 256–8.
33 Brown, *An Introduction to the New Testament*, pp. 41–6. For a fuller account of this hermeneutical approach, taken essentially from Raymond E. Brown, see Donald Senior, CP, *Raymond E. Brown and the Catholic Biblical Renewal* (New York and Mahwah, NJ: Paulist Press, 2018), pp. 59–75.

Chapter 2

THE EARLY CHURCH

Christian solar motifs

Jesus Christ and the sun

Christians were quick to use solar vocabulary. In *The Odes of Solomon*, probably written around 100 CE, the author declares: 'As the sun is the joy to them who seek its daybreak, so is my joy the Lord; / Because He is my Sun, / And His rays have lifted me up; / and His light has dismissed all darkness from my face.'[1] Ignatius of Antioch, martyred in Rome in the middle of the second century or earlier, has wordplays around the verb 'to rise', the root of *anatole*, referring to Christ, to the resurrection and to Ignatius's imminent martyrdom: 'How good it is to be sinking down below the world's horizon towards God, to rise again into the dawn of his presence.'[2] For Justin Martyr (100–165), *Anatole* was already a title for Christ. He insists that, while no sun worshiper has ever given his life for the sun, Christians are willing to die for the *Anatole*: 'For His word of truth and wisdom is more blazing and bright than the might of the sun, … And Zacharias affirms: "The East is His Name."'[3] Christians read biblical texts together charging them with new meaning: Hippolytus (170–235) combines Christ extending his arms on the cross, Malachi's Sun of Justice (Mal. 4.2) and Christ as a hen gathering its young (Mt. 23.37; Lk. 13.34):

> Jesus Christ, who, in stretching forth His holy hands on the holy tree, unfolded two wings, the right and the left, and called to Him all who believed in Him, and covered them as a hen her chickens. For by the mouth of Malachi He also says: 'Unto you that fear my name shall the Sun of righteousness [justice] arise with healing in His wings.'[4]

The expression Sun of Justice employed by Hippolytus here, and by Clement of Alexandria and Origen in the third century, would become a standard Christological title.[5]

Rhythms of daily prayer

Along with intertextual biblical exegesis, links were made with the daily experience of sunlight. By the time of Eusebius of Caesarea (*c.* 260–*c.* 339), a widespread pattern had developed: 'Throughout the whole world in the churches of God at the morning rising of the sun and at the evening hours, hymns, praises and truly divine delights are offered to God.'[6] Earlier, Cyprian of Carthage (210–58) presents Christ as figuratively Sun and Day:

> For we must also pray in the morning, that the resurrection of the Lord may be celebrated by morning prayer ... Likewise at the setting of the sun and at the end of the day necessarily there must again be prayer. For since Christ is the true Sun and the true Day, as the sun and the day of the world recede, when we pray and petition that the light come upon us again, we pray for the coming of Christ to provide us with the grace of eternal light.[7]

Ambrose of Milan (*c.* 340–397) urges early rising for Christians:

> It would indeed be a shame if the first ray of the sun should find you lazing shamelessly in your bed, and if its lovely light should fall upon eyes still closed in heavy sleep ... Or do you not know, my friend, that you owe the first fruits of your heart and voice to God? Every day you gather a harvest for yourself, every day there is fruit. Run, therefore, to meet the rising sun, so that when day dawns it may find you ready. May the dawn's glorious light never rouse eyes that are heavy and drunken with sleep.[8]

The earliest extant Christian hymn in Greek written after the Bible is the *Phos Hilaron*, or Joyous Light, used for prayer when the lamps were lit at sunset.[9] Already old when Basil of Caesarea quoted it in the fourth century, it may date from the late second century, and as a genre if not in the wording, to the New Testament era.[10] Egeria, a fourth-century Spanish pilgrim, quotes the *Phos Hilaron* as sung in Jerusalem: 'Joyous Light of the holy glory of the immortal Father, / Heavenly, holy, blessed Jesus Christ: / Coming to the setting of the sun, seeing the evening light.'[11]

Another factor that influenced the daily experience of light and darkness was a custom the first Christians inherited from the wider culture: prayer facing east. The custom was given different interpretations such as turning towards the Garden of Eden, or towards the location of Christ's Second Coming. But to face east was, most immediately, to look to where the sun rises. We will examine oriented prayer in greater detail in Chapter 8.

Solar themes and inculturation

Christianity spread in a world with an intense solar interest. The Emperor Julian 'the Apostate' (330–63) penned a hymn to the divine sun. 'From my childhood, an extraordinary longing for the rays of the god penetrated deep into my soul.'[12] When Theophilus of Antioch (*c.* 120–*c.* 190) insisted that if we cannot bear to look at the sun, a mere creature, then no mere mortal can look at God, he was stating a truism shared by Christians and non-Christians.[13] Symbols from the surrounding culture were exploited and in what little pre-Constantinian Christian art survives,

Jesus is sometimes depicted with the face and body type typical of Apollo (a sun god), without being identified with him.[14] An early-third-century lamp with a central image of the Good Shepherd has in the background the sun god Sol,[15] while a Christian mosaic from around 300 in the Vatican necropolis almost certainly depicts Christ as a Helios/Sol figure, with a halo and a garland of rays, and riding a horse-driven chariot from the east to the west, all solar motifs.[16] Christians were using visual tropes transferred from other cults, essentially the same process we saw with Israelites transferring solar motifs from Shamash to Yahweh.

Within the Christian tradition, the use of solar metaphors was guided by pointers emerging from scripture, such as an association of the rising sun with Christ, and a rejection of sun worship. More generally, we can contrast the Christian and the 'pagan' view of nature:

> Though not "sacred" in the way it was for pagans, the world as God's creation continued to have a "sacramental" quality. The delicate prescription was thus neither to deny the beauty of the natural world (which would ungratefully disparage God's work), nor to rest in any adoring appreciation of that beauty (which would be a form of idolatry), but rather to appreciate natural beauty while looking beyond it to its source in the Creator.[17]

Christ as a ray of sunlight?

Solar symbolism was more significant theologically in the early church than its relative absence in histories of Christology would suggest.[18] Could Christ be compared to a sunbeam radiating from the Father, who is compared to the sun itself? Before the Council of Nicaea (325), this image was used both by Sabellius who downplayed the distinction between the three divine persons in the one God, and by Tertullian who wanted to emphasize the distinction.[19] In the event, Nicaea opted for the formula 'Light from light' still recited in the Nicene Creed today. The sunray comparison fell out of favour but it did not disappear; in the current Office of Readings, Gregory of Nazianzen (329–90) affirms that his readers are receiving 'the One Ray from the one Godhead in Christ Jesus our Lord'.[20]

The sun metaphor and the divinity of Christ

Athanasius (296–373) used light to express the divinity of Jesus against the Arians who denied it and saw Christ as merely a superior creature.[21] For Athanasius, not accepting Christ is like denying the existence of the sun on a cloudy day while wondering where all the light is coming from.[22] Even a blind person can sense the sun from the warmth they feel, and even non-believers can sense the warmth of the witness of Christian martyrs, even if they cannot see the truth of the martyrs' creed.[23] For Arians, however, the sun was an uncomfortable metaphor. We have no evidence of an Arian preacher comparing Christ to the sun.[24] This is in striking contrast with preachers like Maximus of Turin, an early-fifth-century adherent of Nicaea's positions. Maximus seized upon the feast of Christmas to combine a Christianized idea of the *Sol Invictus*, and the biblical Sun of Justice in a single celebration.[25] In his Christmas sermon of 400, he exploits the pagan expression 'the new sun' that referred to the winter solstice:

> Well it is that people frequently call this day of the Lord's birth 'the new sun' and assert it with such force that even the Jews and pagans agree to the name. This should willingly be accepted by us, since with the rising of the Savior there is salvation not only for the human race, but even the brilliance of the sun itself is renewed ... We have discovered that nothing is new but Christ the Lord, of whom it is written: 'The sun of justice will rise upon you.'[26]

The Egyptian connection: Alexandria

The Physiologus

The cosmopolitan and religiously diverse city of Alexandria[27] hosted some rich early Christian engagement with solar symbolism. The *Physiologus*, an anonymous Greek text probably from the late second century, is a bestiary, describing animals real and imaginary.[28] Its mixture of folklore and spiritual instruction proved a popular genre in the Middle Ages, with the *Physiologus* itself translated into numerous languages. The sun-lizard is given as an image of the Christian turning to Christ:

> There is a beast called the sun-lizard, that is, the sun-eel. When this animal grows old, he is hampered by [weakening of] his two eyes. No longer being able to perceive the sunlight, he goes blind. What does he do? Moved by his good nature, he finds a wall facing east, enters a crack in that wall, and gazes eastward. His eyes are then opened by the eastern sun and made new again.
>
> And you, O man, ... see that, when the eyes of your heart are clouded, you seek out the intelligible eastern sun who is Jesus Christ and whose name is 'the east' [cf. Zech. 3.8 and 12; Lk. 1.78].[29]

Clement of Alexandria

Clement of Alexandria (*c.* 150–*c.* 215), a convert to Christianity, saw sun worship as something positive, the highest step on the way to true religion, and refers approvingly to the orientation of ancient pagan temples.[30] God gave human beings the sun and other heavenly bodies so that by reverencing them they could be led to him. Although often unsystematic and ambiguous, his use of solar symbolism anticipated several later developments.[31] In the Alexandria of Clement, two centuries earlier, the Jewish thinker Philo (*c.* 20 BCE–*c.* 50 CE) had developed a sophisticated Platonic theology. Clement applied Philo's metaphorical language of solar divinity to Christ. Christ is metaphorically the Sun, though infinitely superior to the physical sun. Christ is the 'Sun of Justice', the 'Sun of the Soul', the 'Sun of the

Resurrection'. Later, in the fourth century, Christian writers would regularly refer to Christ as the Sun of Justice. According to Robert Taft, when Clement writes, 'awake, sleeper, rise from the dead and Christ will shine upon you, the Sun of the Resurrection, the one born before the morning star, whose beams bestow life', he could be giving the original of the early Christian hymn or poem quoted in Ephesians 5.14.[32] By the 'Sun of the Resurrection' Clement probably means the one who raises human beings from the dead.[33]

In his *Protrepticus*, or *Exhortation to the Heathen*, a work that aimed to win over pagan thinkers to Christianity, Clement presents Christ's victory in a light-filled creation, combining symbolism from the Fourth Gospel, Mal. 4.2, and the darkness and the shadow of death of Lk. 1.79. The text quotes the dramatist Aeschylus, 'Hail, O light!'; the Sun of Justice/Righteousness rides the Greco-Roman chariot of the sun; the morning dew is an image of dawn radiance and freshness; there is symbolism of night and day, of east and west, of death as sunset and resurrection as sunrise:

> Hail, O light! For in us, buried in darkness, shut up in the shadow of death, light has shone forth from heaven, purer than the sun, sweeter than life here below. That light is eternal life; and whatever partakes of it lives. But night fears the light, and hiding itself in terror, gives place to the day of the Lord. Sleepless light is now over all, and the west has given credence to the east. For this was the end of the new creation. For "the Sun of Righteousness," who drives His chariot over all, pervades equally all humanity, like "His Father, who makes His sun to rise on all men," and distils on them the dew of the truth. He has changed sunset into sunrise, and through the cross brought death to life.[34]

Despite his positive view of paganism, Clement takes issue with the dramatist Menander: worshipping the sun does not give access to the divine. Only the Sun of the soul, the healing Word, can illuminate the eye of the soul, as he rises in its depths. Clement looks inwards, to his own soul, where the Sun of Justice shines interiorly: 'For the sun never could show me the true God; but that healthful Word, that is the Sun of the soul, by whom alone, when He arises in the depths of the soul, the eye of the soul itself is irradiated.'[35] This is a metaphor we will return to.

Origen

Origen (*c.* 186–*c.* 253) left a decisive mark on Christian light and sun symbolism, distinguishing between the physical sun and the spiritual Sun, a distinction that would become standard in the fourth and fifth centuries. The pagan Celsus accused him of showing contempt for the physical sun and the moon; Origen replies: 'We do not wish to express contempt for these glorious works of God or to say with Anaxagoras that sun, moon and stars are nothing more than fiery lumps of matter; we speak as we do because we know that the inexpressible majesty and greatness of God and of his only-begotten Son surpasses everything else.'[36]

Origen brought different biblical voices into conversation with each other in innovative ways. Christ's face shining like the sun at the Transfiguration is linked to various texts of Paul including 1 Thess. 5.4-5:

'His face' shall shine 'as the sun' so that it may be found shining on the sons 'of light' who 'have stripped themselves of the works of darkness and put on the armour of light,' and are no longer 'sons of darkness and night,' but have become sons 'of God' and walk 'honourably as in the day', and when he has been made manifest he will shine on them not simply 'as the sun,' but they see him to be sun 'of justice.'[37]

He links Zech. 6.12 and Mal. 4.2:

But do not take the statement that 'he sprinkles to the east' as superfluous. From the east came atonement for you; for from there is the man whose name is 'East,' who became 'a mediator between God and man.' Therefore, you are invited by this to look always 'to the east' whence 'the Sun of Righteousness' arises for you, whence a light is born for you; that you never 'walk in darkness'.[38]

Elsewhere, he brings both Zech. 6.12 and Mal. 4.2 to bear on the terse comment in the Gospel of John when Judas leaves the Last Supper to betray Christ: 'And it was night' (13.30):

When Judas received the morsel [and] went out immediately, night was present in him at the time he went out, for the man whose name is 'Sunrise' was not present with him because he left 'the sun of justice' behind when he went out.[39]

This notion of night and darkness is, in Johannine symbolism, the evil and ignorance that oppose divine light. The distinct secondary notion of darkness in Exodus becomes for Origen a concept of 'good' darkness, a concept with a notable future in Christian spirituality:

We must observe that not every time something is named 'darkness' is it taken in a bad sense; there are times when it has also been used in a good sense … Darkness, storm clouds, and thunderstorms are said to surround God in Exodus and in Ps. 17 it says, God 'made darkness his hiding-place, his tent around him, dark water in the clouds of the air'.[40]

Employing the image of a sunray, Origen connects Johannine light symbolism with Heb. 1.3 where Christ is described as 'the reflection of God's glory and the exact imprint of God's very being': 'According to John, God is light. The only-begotten Son, therefore, is the glory of this light, proceeding inseparably from (God) Himself, as brightness does from light.' This splendour shines 'gently and softly' on the weak eyes of mortals and gradually accustoms them to the light.[41] Christ enables creatures to contemplate God, the Sun humans cannot look at.

Earlier in the same work, Origen gives the concrete example of light shining through a window or small aperture, yet another image with a future in Christian solar symbolism:

> Our eyes frequently cannot look upon the nature of the light itself – that is, upon the substance of the sun; when we behold his splendour or his rays pouring in, perhaps, through windows or some small openings to admit the light, we can reflect how great is the supply and source of the light of the body.[42]

Believers receive light from Christ, just as the moon gets its light from the sun: 'For just as the moon is said to receive light from the sun so that the night likewise can be illuminated by it, so also the church, when the light of Christ has been received, illuminates all those who live in the night of ignorance.'[43] This symbol became a standard one in the patristic and medieval eras,[44] and is being revived today in the teaching of Pope Francis.[45]

Constantine and the sun

The emperor and the Unconquered Sun

With the Edict of Milan (313), the Emperor Constantine legalized Christianity and went on to give it a favoured place in his empire but he also promoted the cult of the Unconquered Sun, the *Sol Invictus*. His combined imperial ideology and Christian commitment was complex.[46] The cult of the *Sol Invictus* had been instituted by the Emperor Aurelian (270–75) who had tried to use sun worship to unite the Empire. Constantine inherited the cult and identified himself with the Unconquered Sun. His ecclesiastical biographer, Eusebius of Caesarea, could go along with this solar imperialism only because he could, at the same time, emphasize the creaturely status of the physical sun.[47] While the later traditional Christian account of a dramatic conversion prompted by a vision of the cross at the Battle at the Milvian Bridge in 312 does not square with the first accounts of the vision issuing from the imperial court,[48] Constantine did have some genuine Christian commitment – a Christogram in a fresco of the Lateran imperial palace, for example, has been dated to 315.[49]

From the first years of his reign (306–37), Constantine promoted the worship of the sun god and Christianity, and to promote the religious unity of his empire, he intervened in the Arian controversy, convening the Council of Nicaea (325). He took measures against polytheism and the attendant ritual sacrifices, but not against the sun cult. He promoted one Caesar, one empire and one God and, while Christianity was a major part of this programme, so was the sun cult. At his new capital, Constantinople, he erected a statue of himself that was a reworked version of a statue of the sun god Apollo. When he died, his statue was placed in a mausoleum with that of Christ in the circle of the apostles only to be subsequently relocated. By the middle of the fifth century, however, believers were reverencing it with incense and candles.[50] Such polyvalence and ambiguity were inevitable in the large-scale process of inculturating Christian faith in Greco-Roman culture after Constantine.[51] In the Byzantine Hippodrome in Constantinople, in a fluid pattern of symbolism, chariots and charioteers came to evoke variously Christ, the emperor and the sun-god.[52] Such a fusion of a martial cult of the personality, Christianity and solar religiosity probably reflects the ambitions of a leader Martin Wallraff describes as a fourth-century *Roi-Soleil*. It was, however, the Christian church's cult of the *Sol Justitiae* that ultimately prevailed rather than Constantine's *Sol Invictus*.[53]

The Day of the Sun

On 7 March 321, Constantine declared the venerable Day of the Sun a day of rest. In Christianity, from the beginning, the first day of the Jewish week was celebrated as the day Christ rose from the dead. The week as we know it now is the fusion of two cycles: the Jewish, and subsequently Christian, week beginning on Sunday, and the planetary week, originally beginning on the day of Saturn – Saturday.[54] The pagan practice of assigning the names of planetary deities to the different days of the week spread throughout the ancient world at the same time as Christianity did. From around the middle of the second century, the pagan week was also starting on the day after the day of Saturn, and this first day of the week was called the *dies solis*, the Day of the Sun. The church found this link between Sunday and the sun a mixed blessing.[55] For simple Christians, it was all too easy to see Christ as the sun god with his special day, just as the other days belonged to the Moon, Mars, Mercury, Jupiter, Venus and Saturn. Augustine could not bring himself to use the expression *dies solis*. Christian and pagan cycles were in competition, and where the church's influence was strongest, Christianity won out.[56] In the Latin languages of southern Europe (and in Greek), the word for Sunday is The Lord's Day – *domenica* in Italian, *domingo* in Spanish. In northern Europe, the first day of the week is Sun-Day – Sunday in English, and in German *Sonntag*. Some northern Celtic languages were particularly resistant, and the seven planetary names continued in Welsh, Cornish and Breton.

The fact that up till 321 the Day of the Sun had been a day of work may have contributed to celebrations of the eucharist at dawn on the Lord's Day, as noted for example by the Roman writer Pliny.[57] The fact that Sunday became a day of rest freed up the day for celebrations at other times of the day and may have weakened any perception of a solar aspect to eucharistic celebration at dawn.

The cult of Mithras/Sol

The Mithras cult flourished in late antiquity.[58] It was an all-male movement popular largely among the non-commissioned officers of the Roman army, and there are remains of temples dedicated to Mithras in various sites where the imperial army was stationed, such as at Carrawburgh, Northumberland in northern England, where soldiers defending Hadrian's Wall assembled for the cult.[59] Constantine did not promote it and it gradually died out. Devotions focused on a bull figure with solar aspects that became more pronounced as time went on. The 'Mithraism' we see in the Christian era in the West was to all intents and purposes a cult created there, essentially a new religion assembled out of some older elements.[60] In that, it resembled some recent English-speaking forms of paganism such as Wicca.

The South African poet Roy Campbell was fascinated by the figure of Mithras, for him a pagan Isaiah. In his poem 'Death of the Bull' the poet has Mithras sacrificing a bull: 'Those horns, the envy of the moon, / now, targeting the sun, have set:/the eyes are cinders of regret / that were the tinder of the noon.'[61] Mithraic motifs were not, however, expropriated for Christian use. Jerome was typical of Christian attitudes when, in 403, he wrote to one of the women he was directing in Rome:

> Did not your own kinsman Gracchus whose name betokens his patrician origin, when a few years back he held the prefecture of the City, overthrow, break in pieces, and shake to pieces the grotto of Mithras and all the dreadful images therein? Those I mean by which the worshippers were initiated as Raven, Bridegroom, Soldier, Lion, Perseus, Sun, Crab, and Father?[62]

Visual culture after Constantine

Christ as a solar emperor?

According to the 'imperial style theory', associated with Ernst Kantorowicz and André Grabar, after Constantine the Christian faith was closely interwoven with an imperial ideology.[63] Christ became a cosmic emperor, and the *Sol Invictus* became the *Pantokrator*. For Thomas F. Mathews, on the other hand, Christianity competed with other cults, adopting motifs associated with Jupiter rather than the emperor and applying them to Christ. 'His rightful place is among the gods of the ancient world. It is with them that he is engaged in deadly combat, and it is from them that he wrested his most potent attributes.'[64] There is truth in both approaches. Christian enthusiasm for the empire was certainly not unqualified. In the late fourth century, Martin of Tours has a vision where Christ promises to reveal the date of the Second Coming. Realizing the person in front of him is dressed as the emperor, he concludes that it is not Christ but the devil.[65] Nevertheless, imperial solar imagery was transferred to Christ: the halo (a round patch of light around the head); the mandorla (almond-shaped zones of light surrounding the whole body); a garland or crown of rays.[66] The halo was used for royal persons such as Justinian, and even Herod. Gradually it came to be used for saints and prophets, and for Christ during his ministry, emphasizing Christ as ruler. Christian art opted for the halo over the garland or crown, perhaps because the latter was more intimately linked to the person of the emperor (Nero was depicted with a crown of rays during his own lifetime). Another reason to opt for the halo was its association with Apollo, the sun-god, and we see Christ depicted as shining and all-seeing like

Apollo in the apse of the basilica of Santa Pudenziana and the Mausoleum of Santa Constanza in Rome, both of which are from the fourth century.[67] In Constantine's statue in Constantinople he has a garland of rays, while in the triumphal floor mosaic in the Roman Basilica of St Paul Outside the Walls, Christ is depicted with both a halo and a sun garland.

Art and architecture

In Italy, a rich iconographic tradition developed of a blue heaven with golden stars and a golden cross. The rounded shape of apses, vaults and cupolas, for example, in the baptistery of San Giovanni in Fonte in Naples or the Mausoleum of Galla Placidia in Ravenna, would have suggested sky and sunrise.[68] These designs, with their strong eschatological strain, were among the most common images of the first millennium.[69] Lamb and sun are linked in Revelation 21.23 where the Lamb is the light of the eternal city. For Eusebius, Christ is the Lamb and the Sun of Justice.[70] A lamb appearing in a circle would come to evoke the Second Coming, at least subliminally. There was probably such a figure in the façade of St Peter's basilica at the time of Leo the Great, and it would be a common motif, for example, in Italian rose windows of the twelfth and thirteenth centuries.

The Transfiguration apse mosaic in the church of Sant'Apollinare in Classe, near Ravenna, has multiple layers of theological symbolism. The Sun of Justice leads the onlooker to paradise, against a background of a sky with horizontal strata of red dawn clouds. There is the same background in the Basilicas of Santa Pudenziana and of Cosma e Damiano in Rome where the Second Coming of Christ is represented as the rising of the sun. In the apse mosaic of St Catherine's Monastery at Mount Sinai, constructed by the Emperor Justinian in the sixth century, the Transfiguration is juxtaposed with the Mosaic theophany on Mount Sinai and with the Second Coming. The Sun of Justice is depicted as shining on the whole of humanity living and dead. All this is condensed in a complex visual message, one feature of which is the sun as a circle with eight rays or as an eight-pointed star.[71] This image, which became common in later centuries, stretches back through ancient art, possibly even to prehistoric northern Europe. The different apse designs in Italy and elsewhere, with their notable solar motifs, are exercises in intertextual exegesis of the Bible as we saw it practised by Clement of Alexandria and Origen but executed visually.

Early church light

After Constantine, the Christian church developed the existing form of the basilica.[72] In the first Christian centuries, worship had been generally conducted under an open sky,[73] and in late antiquity the aim was to bring light in, a contrast with buildings like the Roman Basilica of Maxentius that had a windowless apse housing a huge statue of the emperor.[74] Caesarius of Arles (470–542) indicates how his listeners favoured airy light-filled interiors for their places of worship: 'As often as we come to church, we ought to prepare our souls to be such as we want to find in church. You want to find the church shining; do not defile your soul with the filth of sin. If you want a church to be full of light, God also wants your soul not to be in darkness.'[75] The sophisticated light effects in Justinian's sixth-century Hagia Sophia cathedral in Istanbul continue to astonish the visitor.[76]

Radiant light was part of the Christian experience of worship. Usually, services were held with the doors open giving a view of the sky. Ambrose says that a good Christian should be like the undivided space of a church building where the window to the east is open so that the eyes of the Lord can look in.[77] Pope Symmachus (pope 498–514) wrote an inscription at the dedication of St Peter's indicating that everything should sparkle in a space filled with light,[78] while, according to Prudentius, gold-leaf was used in St Paul Outside the Walls in Rome so that the interior light would be golden like the dawn sun.[79] Again, an inscription in the ancient Archbishop's chapel in Ravenna reads: 'Either light was born here or, captured, it reigns here in freedom.'[80]

Sometimes light was orchestrated to serve a theological programme, as it had been in pagan temples. In the temple of Serapis in Alexandria, on the feast day of the god, a ray of sunshine came through a window and shone on the mouth of the statue – the sun was greeting Serapis with a kiss.[81] In the Christian Basilica A in the Syrian town of Resafa there is an oculus with light shining on a cross, and in Sant'Apollinare in Classe light shines through a window on to the cross in the apse mosaic. Sometimes different spaces within Christian churches were lighted differently. In the baptistery in Albenga in Northern Italy (fifth century), there are concentric zones with the density of light increasing towards the centre, while in early medieval Ireland windows were sometimes positioned for light to shine on the altar.[82]

Two theologians of good darkness

Gregory of Nyssa

Gregory of Nyssa (*c*. 335–*c*. 395) developed Origen's approach, combining the imagery of darkness in Exodus with Platonism, especially Plato's parable of the sun shining into the cave in the seventh chapter of his *Republic*. In an initial conversion, Moses sees God in a luminous burning bush: 'At high noon a light brighter than the sunlight dazzled his eyes. Astonished at the strange sight, he looks up at the mountain and sees a bush from which this light is flaming up like a fire.'[83] Growing in knowledge, he ascends the mountain where God is in cloud and darkness: 'He declared that he had seen God in the darkness, that is, that he had then come to know that what is divine is beyond all knowledge and comprehension.'[84] Darkness expresses the mystery and incomprehensibility of God who is seen in a 'luminous darkness'.[85] To understand Gregory, we do not need to imagine visual phenomena. He is not positing three chronologically distinct experiences of light, cloud and darkness, and his metaphors of light and darkness are more theological than psychological.[86]

Dionysius the Areopagite

Dionysius was a fifth- to sixth-century Syrian monk who wrote under the pseudonym of the Athenian disciple of St Paul mentioned in the Acts of the Apostles (Acts 17.34). He compares the beatific vision to the Transfiguration: 'In a way we cannot know, we shall be united with him and, our understanding carried away, blessedly happy, we shall be struck by his blazing light.'[87] He shared the solar enthusiasm of his age. The sun impacts on all things: 'It renews them, nourishes them, protects them and perfects them. It establishes the differences between them and it unifies them. It warms them and makes them fruitful. It makes them exist, grow, change, take root, burst forth.'[88] Even so, the sun is infinitely surpassed by the Divine Goodness, of which it is only a 'dull image'.[89] Dionysius uses the symbol of a sun ray to describe how the invisible God is seen. Having noted that the Bible says that God is invisible and incomprehensible, he speaks of 'a firm, transcendent beam, granting enlightenments proportionate to each being'.[90] It shines everywhere while losing none of its power. If it fails to shine anywhere, the fault is to be found in a defect in the receiving object.

For Dionysius, the symbol of darkness and cloud is not an evocation of dark moods or night-time experiences, as we might easily think, but an aspect of knowing God as light, most particularly in the liturgy. 'The divine darkness is that "inaccessible light" where God is said to live.'[91] As Joseph Ratzinger put it, when Dionysius talks about light and darkness, the symbols are negated and then re-used in a *Hypersymbolik* that is beyond consciousness.[92] Denys Turner talks about Dionysian 'self-subverting symbolism' in a mystical theology that is not essentially a description of experiences.[93] On both these accounts, the symbolism of light and darkness does not refer to states of consciousness or putative mental images accessed by introspection. Rather, we are dealing with a theology of what it is to know God.

Conclusion

We now have an answer to the first question in the Introduction: where did Christian solar symbolism come from? It emerges that the main sources were the Bible and the natural phenomena of sunlight and darkness. Starting with the first generations of Christians, biblical solar motifs were used to express the Christian faith, most particularly in expressions applied to Christ such as 'Rising Sun' and 'Sun of Justice'. Christians read different biblical texts together, generating new patterns of meaning, and quickly developed practices that integrated prayer with the diurnal rhythms of night and day. Pagan solar tropes were harnessed in a visual inculturation of the Christian faith in the Greco-Roman world. Given the significance of Egypt for the development of solar religiosity in ancient Israel, it is perhaps no accident that Alexandria hosted a creative Christian engagement with solar symbolism, particularly in the persons of Clement and Origen. The reign of the Emperor Constantine in the fourth century was a watershed in the history of the church, with his promotion of Christianity in the Roman Empire. Mass conversions would present a challenge for maintaining the integrity of Christian teaching, as we will see in the next chapter. But neither Constantine's promotion of the cult of the Unconquered Sun, nor his institution of Sunday as a day of rest, nor the cult of Mithras/Sol, seems to have marked deeply the character of Christian solar religiosity. The main sources for the solar symbolism of the post-Constantinian church continue to be biblical tradition and the concrete realities of physical light and darkness, in a shared general culture marked by a notable interest in the sun. At the same time, in their theologies of light, Origen, Gregory of Nyssa and Dionysius the Areopagite exploited the secondary positive darkness described in Exodus. As we will see, this secondary darkness would be an object of particular interest in the modern West, but without a countervailing attention to the sun symbolism that was so prominent in earlier eras.

Notes

1. Ode 15.1–2. ET James Hamilton Charlesworth (ed. and trans.), *The Odes of Solomon* (Oxford: Clarendon Press, 1973), p. 67.
2. Ignatius of Antioch, *Letter to the Romans* 2.2. PG 5. 688. ET *Early Christian Writings: The Apostolic Fathers* (trans. Maxwell Staniforth; Harmondsworth: Penguin, 1968), p. 104. See Martin Wallraff, *Christus Verus Sol: Sonnenverehrung und Christentum in der Spätantike* (Münster: Aschendorff, 2001), pp. 25, 48.
3. Justin Martyr, *Dialogus cum Tryphone Judaeo* 126.1. PG 6. 769. ET *St Justin Martyr Dialogue with Trypho* (trans. Thomas B. Falls; revised and with a new introduction by Thomas P. Halton; FC, 3; Washington, DC: Catholic University of America Press, 2003), p. 189.
4. Hippolytus, *De Christo et Antichristo* 61. PG 10. 781. ET *ANF* 5, p. 217. English modified.
5. Martin Wallraff, '"Sonne der Gerechtigkeit" Christus und die Sonne in der Spätantike', in *Sonne: Brennpunkt der Kulturen der Welt* (ed. Andrea Bärnreuther; Neu-Isenburg: Edition Minerva, 2009), pp. 75–85.
6. Eusebius of Caesarea, *In Finem, Psalmus Cantici David* 64. PG 23. 630. ET Robert Taft, *Liturgy of the Hours in East and West: The Origin of the Divine Office and Its Meaning for Today* (Collegeville, MN: Liturgical Press, 1993), p. 33.
7. Cyprian of Carthage, *Liber De Oratione Dominica* 35. PL 4. 541–2. ET *Saint Cyprian Treatises* (ed. and trans. Roy J. Deferrari; FC, 36; repr., Washington, DC: Catholic University of America Press, 1981), pp. 157–8.
8. Ambrose of Milan, *Sermo* 119.22. *Homilies of Saint Ambrose on Psalm 118 (119)* (trans. Íde Ní Riain; Dublin: Halcyon Press, 1998), p. 278.
9. Antonia Tripolitis, 'ΦΩΣ ΙΛΑΡΟΝ: Ancient Hymn and Modern Enigma', *Vigiliae Christianae* 24 (1970), pp. 189–96.
10. Basil of Caesarea, *De Spiritu Sancto* 29.73. PG 32. 205. Peter Plank, *ΦΩΣ ΙΛΑΡΟΝ: Christushymnus und Lichtdanksagung der frühen Christenheit* (Bonn: Borengässer, 2001), pp. 63–5.

11 Andrew B. McGowan, *Ancient Christian Worship: Early Church Practices in Social, Historical, and Theological Perspective* (Grand Rapids, MI: Baker Academic, 2014), p. 126.
12 Julian, 'Hymn to King Helios Dedicated to Sallust', in *The Works of the Emperor Julian, vol. 1* (trans. Wilmer Cave Wright; Loeb Classical Library, London: Heinemann and New York: Macmillan, 1913), p. 353.
13 Theophilus of Antioch, *Ad Autolycum* 1.5. PG 6. 1032.
14 Robin M. Jensen, 'Towards a Christian Material Culture', in *The Cambridge History of Christianity, vol. 1: Origins to Constantine* (eds Margaret M. Mitchell and Frances M. Young; Cambridge: Cambridge University Press, 2006), pp. 568–85 (579–80).
15 Wallraff, '"Sonne der Gerechtigkeit" Christus und die Sonne in der Spätantike', p. 79.
16 Jocelyn Toynbee and John Ward Perkins, *The Shrine of St Peter and the Vatican Excavations* (London: Longmans Green & Co, 1956), pp. 116–17.
17 Steven D. Smith, *Pagans and Christians in the City: Culture Wars from the Tiber to the Potomac* (Grand Rapids, MI: Eerdmans, 2018), p. 116.
18 Wallraff, *Christus Verus Sol*, p. 44, n. 12.
19 Ibid., p. 45.
20 Gregory of Nazianzen, *Oratio* 39.20. PG 36. 360. ET Catholic Church, Roman Rite, *The Divine Office: The Liturgy of the Hours According to the Roman Rite, vol. 1: Advent, Christmastide & Weeks 1–9 of the Year* (London: Collins, 1974), p. 380.
21 Jaroslav Pelikan, *The Light of the World: A Basic Image of Early Christian Thought* (New York: Harper, 1962), p. 78.
22 Athanasius of Alexandria, *Contra Gentes* 1. PG 25. 5.
23 Athanasius of Alexandria, *De Incarnatione* 32. PG 25. 152.
24 Andreas Merkt, *Maximus I. von Turin: Der Verkündigung eines Bischofs der frühen Reichskirche im zeitgeschichtlichen, gesellschaftlichen und liturgischen Kontext* (Leiden, New York and Cologne: Brill, 1997), p. 180.
25 Ibid., p. 181, n. 226.
26 Maximus of Turin, *Sermon* 62.1,2. CCL 23, pp. 261–2. ET *The Sermons of St. Maximus of Turin* (trans. Boniface Ramsey, OP; New York and Mahwah: Newman Press, 1989), pp. 152–3.
27 Christopher A. Beeley, *The Unity of Christ: Continuity and Conflict in Patristic Tradition* (New Haven and London: Yale University Press, 2012), pp. 3–5.
28 Wallraff, *Christus Verus Sol*, p. 84, n. 106.
29 *Physiologus* (trans. Michael J. Curley; Austin and London: University of Texas Press, 1979), pp. 66–7.
30 Clement of Alexandria, *Stromata* 7.7. PG 9. 461–4.
31 Wallraff, *Christus Verus Sol*, pp. 48–51. Michel Cambe, *Avenir solaire et angélique des justes: le psaume 19 (18) commenté par Clément d'Alexandrie* (Strasbourg: Université de Strasbourg, 2009), pp.130–46.
32 Clement of Alexandria, *Protrepticus* 9. PG 8. 196. ET *ANF* 2, p. 196 (text modified). Robert Taft, *Beyond East and West: Problems in Liturgical Understanding* (Washington, DC: The Pastoral Press, 1984), p. 138.
33 Wallraff, *Christus Verus Sol*, pp. 112–13.
34 Clement, *Protrepticus* 11. PG 8. 232. ET *ANF* 2, p. 203.
35 Clement, *Protrepticus* 6. PG 8. 173. ET *ANF* 2, p. 191.

36 Origen, *Contra Celsum* 5.11. PG 11. 1197. ET Hugo Rahner, *Greek Myths and Christian Mystery* (New York: Harper and Row, 1963), p. 97.
37 Origen, *In Evangelium Matthaei* 12.37. PG 13. 1069. ET *The Commentary of Origen on the Gospel of Matthew, vol. 2* (trans. Ronald E. Heine; Oxford: Oxford University Press, 2018), p. 392.
38 Origen, *In Leviticum Homilia* 9.10. PG 12. 523. ET Origen, *Homilies on Leviticus 1–16* (trans. Gary Wayne Barkley; FC, 83; Washington, DC: Catholic University of America Press, 1990), p. 199.
39 Origen, *Commentarium in Joannem* 32.16. PG 14. 811. ET Origen, *Commentary on the Gospel According to John Books 13–32* (trans. Ronald E. Heine; FC, 89; Washington, DC: Catholic University of America Press, 1993), p. 401.
40 Origen, *Commentarium in Joannem* 2.171–2. PG 14. 161. ET Origen, *Commentary on the Gospel According to John Books 1–10* (trans. Ronald E. Heine; FC, 80; Washington, DC: Catholic University of America Press, 1989), pp. 140–1.
41 Origen, *De Principiis* 1.7. PG 11. 135–6. ET *ANF* 4, p. 248.
42 Ibid., 1.6. PG 11. 124. ET *ANF* 4, p. 243.
43 Origen, *Homilia in Genesim* 1.5. PG 12. 150. ET Origen, *Homilies on Genesis and Exodus* (trans. Ronald E. Heine; FC, 71; Washington, DC: Catholic University of America Press, 1981), p. 54.
44 Rahner, *Greek Myths and Christian Mystery*, pp. 154–76.
45 Pope Francis, Homily Epiphany 2016. Available online: http://w2.vatican.va/content/francesco/en/homilies/2016/documents/papa-francesco_20160106_omelia-epifania.html (accessed 29 April 2020). Gerard O'Connell, *The Election of Pope Francis: An Inside Account of the Conclave that Changed History* (Maryknoll, NY: Orbis, 2019), p. 154.
46 Wallraff, *Christus Verus Sol*, pp. 126–43.
47 Ibid., pp. 138–9.
48 Martin Wallraff, '*In Quo Signo Vicit?* Una rilettura della visione e ascesa al potere di Costantino', in *Costantino prima e dopo Costantino Constantine before and after Constantine* (eds Giorgio Bonamente, et al.; Bari: Edipuglia, 2012), pp. 133–44 (143).
49 Ibid., p. 130, n. 23.
50 Martin Wallraff, 'Constantine's Devotion to the Sun after 324', *Studia Patristica* 34 (2001), pp. 256–69 (261–2).
51 James J. O'Donnell, *Pagans: The End of Traditional Religion and the Rise of Christianity* (New York: Ecco HarperCollins, 2016), p. 157.
52 Dean A. Miller, *Imperial Constantinople* (New York: John Wiley and Sons, 1969), p. 127.
53 Martin Wallraff, *Sonnenkönig der Spätantike: die Religionspolitik Konstantins des Grossen* (Freiburg im Breisgau: Herder, 2013), pp. 165–84.
54 Leofranc Holford-Strevens, *The History of Time: A Very Short Introduction* (New York: Oxford University Press, 2005), pp. 64–73.
55 Wallraff, *Christus Verus Sol*, pp. 89–109.
56 Justo L. González, *A Brief History of Sunday: From the New Testament to the New Creation* (Grand Rapids, MI: Eerdmans, 2017).
57 Pliny, *Letters* 10. 96-97. Available online: Pliny: Letters – Book 10 (b) (attalus.org) (accessed 14 December 2020).
58 Larry W. Hurtado, *Destroyer of the Gods: Early Christian Distinctiveness in the Roman World* (Waco, TX: Baylor University Press, 2016), pp. 83–4.

59　English Heritage, *Carrawburgh Roman Fort and Temple of Mithras – Hadrian's Wall*. Available online: http://www.English-Heritage.Org.Uk/Visit/Places/Temple-Of-Mithras-Carrawburgh-Hadrians-Wall/ (accessed 16 April 2020).
60　The cult was varied, even within the West: Philippa Adrych, et al., *Images of Mithra* (Oxford: Oxford University Press, 2017), pp. 169–71.
61　Roy Campbell, *Mithraic Emblems* (London: Boriswood, 1936), p. 31.
62　Jerome, *Epistola* 107.2. PL 22. 868–9. ET Philip Schaff and Henry Wallace (eds), *Nicene and Post-Nicene Fathers, Second Series, vol. 6* (New York: The Christian Literature Company; Oxford and London: Parker and Company, 1893), p. 190.
63　Ernst Grabar, *Christian Iconography: A Study of Its Origins* (repr., Princeton, NJ: Princeton University Press, 1981). Ernst H. Kantorowicz, *The King's Two Bodies* (repr., Princeton, NJ: Princeton University Press, 2016).
64　Thomas F. Mathews, *The Clash of Gods: A Reinterpretation of Early Christian Art* (Princeton, NJ: Princeton University Press, 1993), p. 179.
65　Ibid., p. 178.
66　Johannes G. Deckers, 'Constantine the Great and Early Christian Art', in *Picturing the Bible: The Earliest Christian Art* (ed. Jeffrey Spier, with contributions by Herbert L. Kessler, et al.; New Haven and London: Yale University Press, 2008), pp. 87–109 (108). See also Wallraff, *Christus Verus Sol*, pp. 144–51.
67　Joan E. Taylor, *What Did Jesus Look Like?* (London: Bloomsbury T&T Clark, 2018), pp. 72, 79.
68　Ibid., pp. 153, 172.
69　Jerzy Mizioloek, 'When Our Sun is Risen: Observations on Eschatological Visions in the Art of the First Millennium – II', *Arte Christiana* 83.766 (1995), pp. 3–22 (13).
70　Eusebius of Caesarea, *De Solemnitate Paschali* 3. PG 24. 697.
71　Jerzy Miziolek, '*Transfiguratio Domini* in the apse at Mount Sinai and the Symbolism of Light', *Journal of the Warburg and Courtauld Institutes* 53 (1990), pp. 42–60 (46).
72　McGowan, *Ancient Christian Worship*, pp. 59–60.
73　Martin Wallraff, 'Die Ursprünge der christlichen Gebetsostung', *Zeitschrift für Kirchengeschichte* 111 (2000), pp. 169–84 (178–9).
74　Sible De Blaauw, 'In vista della luce: un principio dimenticato nell'orientamento dell'edificio di culto paleocristiano', in *Arte medievale: le vie dello spazio liturgico* (ed. Paolo Piva; Milan: Jaca Book, 2012), pp. 19–48 (38).
75　Caesarius of Arles, *Sermo* 229.3. CCL 104, pp. 907–8. ET *Saint Caesarius of Arles, Sermons, vol. 3 (187–238)* (trans. Sister Mary Magdeleine Mueller, OSF; FC, 66; Washington, DC: Catholic University of America Press, 2nd edn, 1973), p. 175.
76　Nadine Schibelle, *Hagia Sophia and the Byzantine Aesthetic Experience* (London: Routledge, 2016), pp. 65–70. Wassim Jabi and Iakonos Potamianos, 'Geometry, Light, and Cosmology in the Church of Hagia Sophia', *International Journal of Architectural Computing* 5.2 (2007), pp. 303–19.
77　Ambrose of Milan, *Expositio psalmi CXVIII*, 6.19. CSEL 62, p. 118.
78　Martin Wallraff, 'Licht', in *Reallexikon für Antike und Christentum, vol. 23* (ed. Georg Schöllgen; Stuttgart: Anton Hiersemann, 2010), pp. 100–37 (116).
79　De Blaauw, 'In vista della luce', p. 37.
80　Wallraff, 'Licht', p. 117.
81　Ibid.
82　Tomás Ó'Carragáin, *Churches in Early Medieval Ireland: Architecture, Ritual and Memory* (New Haven and London: Yale University Press, 2010), p. 177.

83 Gregory of Nyssa, *Life of Moses* 20. ET Gregory of Nyssa, *The Life of Moses* (trans. Abraham J. Malherbe and Everett Ferguson; New York, Ramsey and Toronto: Paulist Press, 1978), p. 34.
84 Ibid. 164. *The Life of Moses*, p. 95.
85 Ibid. 163. *The Life of Moses*, p. 95.
86 Andrew Louth, *The Origins of the Christian Mystical Tradition: From Plato to Denys* (Oxford: Clarendon Press, 1981), p. 86.
87 Dionysius the Areopagite, *De Divinis Nominibus* 1.4. PG 3. 592. ET *Pseudo-Dionysius: The Complete Works* (trans. Colm Luibheid; New York and Mahwah: Paulist Press, 1987), pp. 52–3.
88 Ibid. 5.8. PG 3. 824. *Complete Works*, pp. 101–2.
89 Ibid. 4.1. PG 3. 693. *Complete Works*, p. 72.
90 Ibid. 1.2. PG 3. 588. *Complete Works*, p. 50.
91 Dionysius the Areopagite, *Epistola V Dorotheo Ministro*. PG 3. 1073. *Complete Works*, p. 265.
92 Joseph Ratzinger, 'Licht', in *Handbuch der Theologischen Grundbegriffe* (ed. Heinrich Fries; Munich: Kösel, 1963), pp. 44–54 (52).
93 Denys Turner, *The Darkness of God: Negativity in Christian Mysticism* (Cambridge: Cambridge University Press, 1998), p. 45.

Chapter 3

THE LATIN WEST

In this chapter we trace the beginnings of a process where solar symbolism continues but weakens in the Western church. We examine four well-known Western churchmen – Ambrose, Augustine, Leo the Great and Gregory the Great – and one lesser-known figure, Eucherius of Lyons. We then turn to the church in Britain and Ireland when the ancient world was coming to an end and the Middle Ages were beginning.

Ambrose

Ambrose of Milan (340–97) has had a lasting influence in the Western church, through his disciple Augustine and through his own writings. Quoting a pagan philosopher Secundus, Ambrose describes marvelling at the beauty of the sun, adding that beyond it he sees the Sun of Justice:

> It is true that it is the eye of the world, the joy of the day, the beauty of the heavens, the charm of nature and the most conspicuous object in creation. When you behold it, reflect on its Author, when you admire it, give praise to its Creator.
> If the sun as consort or participant in nature is so pleasing, how much goodness is there to be found in that 'Sun of Justice'?[1]

In Ambrose's hymns, which are still in use, he exploits the perception of light and sun at the service of spiritual renewal.[2] In two of these hymns, 'Splendor paternae gloriae' and 'Deus Creator omnium', Ambrose focuses on morning and evening light, respectively. The second strophe of 'Splendor paternae gloriae' asks Christ to irradiate our sense experience: 'And true sun, descend, / gleam with everlasting glow; / and pour the Holy Spirit's / beam into our senses.'[3] According to Jacques Fontaine, 'Deus Creator omnium' is 'an instrument for the spiritual metamorphosis of religious life in the mere experience of light'[4]: 'That, when night's deep gloom / has shuttered up the day, / faith may know no shadows, / and night may shimmer with the faith.'[5] For Ambrose's disciple Augustine, those who sing this hymn can praise the visible light without being ensnared by its temptations. 'I want to be like them; I resist the seduction of my eyes and I lift my invisible eyes to You.'[6]

Augustine

Solar metaphors

Augustine of Hippo (354–430) developed Christian solar symbolism but in a way that weakened it. When he was baptized by Ambrose in Milan, the North African Augustine learnt to call Christ 'Sun of Justice', 'Spiritual Sun' and 'True Sun'. Sensitive to the beauties of light, he remarked on the beauty of the rising sun gradually illuminating a valley, and of African sunlight, the queen of all colours, pouring down over everything.[7] All this experience is open to everyone: 'Only the literate can read the books, but even the illiterate can read the book of the world.'[8] Spiritual conversion involves learning a different way of looking at the world. The unredeemed person is, metaphorically, a figure bent over (*incurvatus in se*), head bowed, with hands covering the eyes because the light is too intense.[9] For believers, there follows a process of healing and conversion that is intellectual (being freed, for example, from the materialist philosophy of Augustine's youth), moral and religious. Augustine felt that he was still viewing sunlight with unconverted eyes. A process of conversion is figuratively moving from seeing sunlight shining on a wall or on fabric, then on gold or silver, and then looking at a bright sky or dawn light. Eventually, we will come to delight in seeing the sun directly without flinching.[10] This is to see the face of God: 'The angelic choir makes an eternal holiday: the presence of God's face, joy that never fails. This is a holiday of such a kind as neither to be opened by any dawn, nor terminated by any evening.'[11]

His rejection of Manicheism

At the same time, Augustine insists on the dangers of sun metaphors:

> But again, don't suppose that the reason why God is not the sun is that the sun is like a kind of wheel, not a boundless space of light; and so you say to yourself, 'God is infinite and boundless light,' and you stretch the sun, as it were, and make it have no limits, neither this way nor that, neither upward nor downward – and you put it to yourself that this boundless light is what God is. God is not that either. God indeed *dwells in light inaccessible* (1Tm 6:16). But such light does not rotate, nor can it be perceived with the eyes in your head.[12]

He speaks like this because, before becoming a Christian, he was a Manichee and prayed four times a day: 'I worship and glorify the great Light-givers, both sun and moon and the virtuous powers in them.'[13] This background left Augustine wary, even recoiling from calling the first day of the week the 'Day of the Sun'. When debating with the Manichee Fortunatus, he says there were only two things he would fault in the services he attended as a Manichee 'hearer': attacking the Catholic Church and prayer facing the sun.[14]

An interior light

In the summer of 386, in Milan, Augustine had had an inner experience of God as a brilliant light. He was subsequently baptized, and he came to see himself as having turned inwards to 'taste' an inner light, while the Manichees turned outwards towards the physical sun. In his *Confessions,* he emphasizes the distinction between the interior light and exterior light, especially the sun:

> I entered, and with the eye of my soul, such as it was, I saw Your unchangeable Light shining over the same eye of my soul, over my mind. It was not the light of everyday ... Your light was not that, but other, altogether other than all such lights.[15]

When asked by a priest Simplicianus about the best posture for prayer, he stressed the Christian freedom to choose whatever posture felt best. It is the interior state of the soul that matters, and the mind can be unaware which way it is facing or of the body's position.[16] While it is natural for people who cannot yet imagine immaterial reality to reverence God in the sun, 'when they eventually come to realise that the dignity of the soul surpasses even that of the heavenly body [the sun], they search for him more in the soul than in the heavenly body'.[17]

Light rather than sun

Alert to the implications of his own personal history, he proclaims: 'Some people are so mad that when they hear, "The sun represents Christ," they think it a proper object for adoration. Worship a rock too, then, since that represents Christ!'[18] Augustine preferred the more abstract notion of light,[19] not a metaphor, but a general concept within which he distinguished between uncreated and created light, and within created light between intellectual or intelligible light and physical light. He remains faced with a mystery, however, asking himself how a creature can say, as he himself had, that he had entered and, with the eye of his soul, had seen God's unchangeable light.[20] In this perspective, the physical sun does not cease to be a Christian symbol, but its significance is qualified.

Eucherius

Building on Augustine's hermeneutic, Eucherius of Lyons (c. 381–93 to c. 449–56) wrote an accessible handbook, his *Formulae spiritalis intelligentiae,* which was a standard manual for biblical interpretation throughout the Latin West till around 1100.[21] Bible and cosmos are systems of interrelated signs with multiple meanings that Eucherius aims to simplify and standardize.[22] Physical phenomena are coded signs of invisible realities. For instance, 'day and night are righteousness and iniquity'.[23] This hermeneutic of propositional decoding devalued physical phenomena as symbolically significant in themselves and helped prepare the way for mediaeval scholasticism with its focus on literal propositions and apodictic proof. He continued traditional solar symbolism: 'The sun is Lord Jesus Christ, who shines on the earth.'[24] However, 'Sun of Justice' and '*Oriens*' are two expressions among hundreds in lists that range from candlesticks to frogs, from pomegranates to bundles of hay, and many of his interpretations seem farfetched – mud, for instance, is to be read as a sign for gluttony.[25] By this approach, the symbolic status of solar expressions was inevitably compromised. Eucherius's *Formulae* is one of the reasons why we have inherited a weakened solar symbolism.[26]

Leo the Great

Fighting Manicheism

With a positive view of the religious significance of light and a determined opposition to the Manichees and sun worship, Leo (pope 440–61) continued emphases of Augustine who died ten years before Leo became pope. In his Christmas homily in 450, Leo links physical sunlight and divine mystery: 'With a new light radiating even in the atoms themselves, no day more than today impresses the entire splendour of this amazing mystery upon our senses.'[27] He fought hard against the Manichees for whom incarnation in a human body implied contamination by matter. The purity of sunlight counts against such a view: 'For if … the bright rays of the Sun – which is certainly a material creation – are not spoiled by any dirty or muddy places, is there anything of any quality whatsoever that could contaminate the essence of that Light that is eternal and immaterial (sc. Christ)?'[28]

A warning to Christians

Sometimes Leo targeted sun worship directly, probably the Hellenistic sun cult, rather than specifically the Roman cult of the *Sol Invictus*. In another Christmas sermon, he criticizes Christians for pausing at the entrance to the Basilica of St Peter, which faced the east, to reverence the sun. They may be in good faith, but it is dangerous:

> This behavior, partly due to the vice of ignorance and partly to the spirit of paganism, upsets and saddens us very much. Even if some of them do worship the Creator of that beautiful light rather than the light itself, which is a creature, they should still abstain from giving the appearance of that worship, because if someone who has turned away from the cult of gods notices the same custom among us, will that person not return to the old beliefs thinking that probably Christians and nonbelievers are doing the same thing?
>
> When the sun rises at daybreak, there are some people so foolish as to worship it from the highest elevations; even some Christians think they are

acting piously by following this practice, so that before entering the basilica of St Peter the apostle, dedicated to the only living and true God, when they have gone up the steps leading to the porch at the main entrance, they turn around to face the rising sun and, inclining the head, bow in honor of the brilliant disc.[29]

Leo objected to the gesture as problematic in itself, but there may have been a secondary issue at play as well – its private character.[30] Over the century up to the pontificate of Leo, there were tensions between papal insistence on public worship and deep-rooted traditions of private domestic devotions, particularly among aristocratic converts to Christianity. These devotions were Christian but celebrated in similar circumstances to earlier pagan rituals.[31] It is possible that papal reservations about private devotions worked against any traditions of domestic prayer facing east, a practice that would have had an inescapable solar dimension.

A fading interest in the cosmos

Leo differs from some earlier bishops in Italy, such as Zeno of Verona or Maximus of Turin, in giving less attention to the natural seasons, and to cosmic realities such as the solstice or the equinox. Leo's approach is moral and sacramental, and his approach to the mysteries of Christ's life more historical than cosmological.[32] He concentrated more on ethical notions of justice and mercy, replacing the rational cosmology of the influential Stoic philosophy with a system of discipline and clemency.[33] This fading interest in the cosmos inevitably impacted on the place of light and sun in Christian life.

Gregory the Great

Contemplation and the sun

Inheriting Augustine's emphasis on interiority, Gregory (pope 590–604) distinguished sharply between contemplation and action, marking decisively Western Christian spirituality.[34] For him, physical light is to be despised, and the faithful are to attend to the interior sun, running back to the splendour of interior clarity.[35] 'Contemplating the ray of the interior Sun the cloud of our corruption interposes itself and the unchangeable Light does not burst forth such as it is to the weak eyes of our mind.' We behold God as it were 'in a vision of the night', in what Gregory calls 'shadowy contemplation'.[36]

Chinks of light

For Gregory, without interiority people focus exclusively on external things and the eternal light goes unnoticed, but, with interiority, a person can benefit even from external physical light, catching brief glimpses of the divine. He describes the fleeting character of the act of contemplation in an image of the sun shining through 'oblique' windows where the light enters by a narrow slit in a thick wall and illuminates a wide space. Similarly, a person in prayer catches brief glimpses of the otherwise inaccessible light and the mind broadens out in love and fervour.[37] This is the same comparison we saw in Origen, and it recurs, too, in the twentieth century.

'A distant region of the world': Insular Christianity

'Insular Christianity' is the church in the British Isles ('a distant region of the world' according the Romano-Briton Gildas) from the fifth century into the Middle Ages. We can distinguish different cultures – Romano-British, Anglo-Saxon and Celtic – even if there was considerable interaction between them. We will look at two individuals, at some examples of material culture, and at samples of the poetry of this era.

Two Romano-Britons: Patrick and Gildas

Patrick was born somewhere in Western Britain, probably in the fifth century. He was from the Romano-British elite calling himself a Roman citizen. Although the son of a deacon and grandson of a priest, he describes himself as non-believing.[38] On his account, he spent six years as a slave to Ireland where he had a religious conversion that never ceased to surprise him. Escaping, he trained as a priest, and returned to the land of his captivity as a missionary. His *Confessions,* a brief text written in old age, displays a solar rhetoric he acquired in his Romano-British Christian milieu.[39]

The solar religiosity evident at the Neolithic site at Newgrange in the Boyne Valley in Ireland (*c.* 3300 BCE), where a shaft of sunlight fills a burial chamber for seventeen minutes at the winter solstice, is both intriguing and indecipherable. It is tempting to imagine points of continuity with the Ireland of Patrick's lifetime, but there is no evidence. Indeed, apart from Patrick's words, there is no evidence of solar worship in fifth-century Ireland.[40] He insists that 'all those who adore that sun will come to a bad, miserable penalty. We, however, believe in and adore the true sun, that is, Christ, who will never perish'.[41] As regards the future, 'there is no doubt whatever that we will rise on the appointed day in the brightness of the sun, that is, in the glory of Christ Jesus our redeemer'.[42] Patrick describes a solar experience when he was young:

> That same night while I was sleeping, Satan strongly put me to the test – I will remember it as long as I live! It was as if an enormous rock fell on me, and I lost all power in my limbs. Although I knew little about the life of the spirit at the time, how was it that I knew to call upon Helias? While these things were happening, I saw the sun rise in the sky, and while I was calling 'Helias! Helias!' with all my strength, the splendour of the sun fell on me; and immediately, all

that weight was lifted from me. I believe that I was helped by Christ the Lord, and that his spirit cried out for me.[43]

How to interpret this passage is a knotty problem.[44] Suggestions that Patrick remembered youthful pagan sun worship, or that he remembered himself invoking Elijah, as Christ did on the cross, seem implausible. He describes himself as calling on Christ as Sun and receiving divine help as his night-time ordeal evaporates with the rising of the sun. But given his juvenile ignorance of the faith, Patrick is puzzled where the words 'Helias! Helias!' came from, just as he was puzzled as to how his youthful former self found himself rising before dawn during his captivity to devote himself to prayer. For our purposes, we note the link he makes between the rising of the physical sun and a spiritual visitation of Christ, and the density of solar motifs in such a short text as the *Confession* that points to the importance of sun symbolism in Patrick's Romano-British Christian world.

Gildas, a Romano-British deacon who wrote probably in the early sixth century, has been described as the first medieval theologian.[45] He employs a solar rhetoric similar to Patrick's:

> Meanwhile these islands, stiff with cold and frost, and in a distant region of the world, remote from the visible sun, received the beams of light, that is, the holy precepts of Christ, the true Sun, showing to the whole world his splendour, not only from the temporal firmament, but from the height of heaven.[46]

High crosses

High crosses were an important element in the visual culture of Insular Christianity. Whatever their origin, these freestanding stone artefacts were pioneered in the ambience of the Abbey of Whitby in the North of England, and their spread was encouraged by the impact of the Synod of Whitby in 664.[47] Early versions were constructed in Anglo-Saxon England, with later Irish artists making their own distinctive contributions. Many more of them (around 300) survived in Ireland than in England, where most of the crosses were destroyed after the Reformation.

The circular pattern of high crosses is probably not a relic of earlier Celtic pagan solar beliefs, as is sometimes suggested, even if for instance bronze-age sun discs discovered at Coggalbeg, Co. Roscomon in 2009 have a strikingly similar form. The characteristic ring head may have been a technical development to reinforce the structure of the crosses.[48] Even more likely is that it is a variant of the cross-in-circle (itself a solar motif) from continental Christianity that we see in the mausoleum of Galla Placidia and the apse of Sant'Apollinare in Classe at Ravenna.[49] The solar cross illumines the cosmos, an idea expressed in verse by John Scotus Eriugena, the ninth-century Irish translator of Dionysius the Areopagite: 'Behold the orb that shines with the rays of the sun, / which the Cross of Salvation spreads from its height, / Embracing the earth, the sea, the winds and the sky / And everything else believed to exist far away.'[50]

Two high crosses from the eighth-century Anglo-Saxon kingdom of Northumbria, the Bewcastle Cross and the Ruthwell Cross, have clear solar motifs.[51] The panels of the Bewcastle Cross are to be read following the movement of the sun throughout the day and throughout the year. In the morning, the sun shines on the eastern side, in the afternoon on the western. This cross sports the earliest surviving sundial in the British Isles. The Ruthwell Cross was destroyed in 1642 but later reconstituted from surviving fragments.[52] There is no sundial, but it too is designed so that the sun shines progressively on a series of panels as the day progresses, and as the year moves through its equinoxes and solstices. Christ is shown in the guise of a Germanic warrior hero – an inscription quotes the Anglo-Saxon poem *The Dream of the Rood*: 'Then the young warrior, Almighty God, mounted the Cross, in the sight of many.' Such high crosses were a creative remake of pre-Christian standing stones of the local pagan cultures and have been described as 'triumphs of liturgical inculturation'.[53] When the *Benedictus* was recited at Lauds in Ruthwell, the sun would have risen behind the figure of John the Baptist whose right index finger points across his body to the local horizon.

In a recent study of Irish high crosses, Roger Stalley identifies an artistic genius from the early tenth century based at the monastery of Monasterboice in County Louth whom he dubs the Muiredach Master. Stalley emphasizes the originality of Irish artistic achievements within the broader context of Christian iconography. The crosses studied are oriented on an east/west axis and were originally in the open air. To protect them from the elements, they are increasingly located indoors, and much is lost:

> When crosses remain in the open the experience varies according to the time and season, the panels being lit in sparkling sequence as the rays of the sun pass from east to west. On summer evenings at Monasterboice it is hard not to experience a sense of wonder as the northern face of Muiredach's cross is suddenly bathed in sunlight, the whole event over in just a few minutes, an experience we can still share with those who gazed at the monument a thousand years ago.[54]

Irish light

In *That They May Face the Rising Sun,* John McGahern describes the sun shining in the morning and at noon on Easter Sunday:

> Easter morning came clear. There was no wind on the lake. There was also a great stillness. When the bells rang out for Mass, the strokes trembling on the water, they had the entire Easter world to themselves.
>
> On such an Easter morning, as we were setting out for Mass, we were always shown the sun; Look how the molten globe and all the glittering rays are dancing. The whole of heaven is dancing in its joy that Christ has risen.[55]
>
> The sun was now high above the lake. There wasn't a wisp of cloud. Everywhere the water sparkled. A child could easily believe that the whole of heaven was dancing.[56]

McGahern's fascination with sparkling sunlight is not peculiar to him. The poet Seamus Heaney recounts what he calls 'a kind of small epiphany' in the 1960s as he enters and then leaves the dark interior of a dry-stone oratory on the Dingle Peninsula in County Kerry:

> But coming out of the cold heart of the stone, into the sunlight and the dazzle of grass and sea, I felt a list in my heart, a surge towards happiness that must have been experienced over and over again by those monks as they crossed that same threshold centuries ago. This surge towards praise, this sudden apprehension of the world as light, as illumination, this is what remains central to our first nature poetry and makes it a unique inheritance.[57]

Early Irish monks wrote in broad daylight, while earlier pagan poets wrote in darkened interiors.[58] An eighth- or ninth-century scribe rejoices: 'The clear cuckoo sings to me, lovely discourse, / in its grey cloak from the crest of the bushes; / truly – may the Lord protect me! – / Well do I write under the forest wood.'[59] In the early medieval period, windows in Irish churches were often especially small. As one historian put it, 'in the case of Irish churches it is almost as if those commissioning them were aiming to create an atmosphere that was as different as possible from the outdoors'.[60]

An early medieval poet longs for heaven: 'It were my mind's desire to dwell in bright Paradise. It / were my mind's desire to shine as shines the sun.'[61] There is a recurring vocabulary of brightness and sunlight: 'Holy Jesus, / gentle friend, / star of the morning, / glorious sun of the noonday, / bright light of believers and of truth.'[62] Solar epithets for Christ like 'King of the bright sun' or 'King of the splendid sun' get their resonance from a close observation of natural light – a ninth-century scribe writes in the margin of his manuscript: 'Pleasant to me is the glittering of the sun today upon these margins, because it flickers so.'[63]

Conclusion

In the early Latin church, Christian solar symbolism begins to assume its characteristically Western form. While Ambrose's hymns exploit the spiritual potential of the physical phenomena of light, there is, in Augustine and Leo, a fading interest in the cosmos. Augustine's personal history played a role in this, as did fears of solar paganism among Christians in the post-Constantinian church. The inward turn in Augustine and Gregory involved giving less attention to sun and to light. At the same time, Insular Christianity provides graphic examples of how Christian solar symbolism can assume new forms as it enters new cultural spaces.

Notes

1 Ambrose *Hexameron*, 4.1.2. *CSEL* 32, Part 1, p. 111. ET Saint Ambrose, *Hexameron, Paradise, and Cain and Abel* (trans. John J. Savage; FC, 42; New York: Fathers of the Church, 1961), p. 127.
2 Brian P. Dunkle, SJ, *Enchantment and Creed in the Hymns of Ambrose of Milan* (Oxford: Oxford University Press, 2016), pp. 63–7.
3 Ibid., p. 222.
4 Jacques Fontaine, et al. (eds), *Ambroise de Milan: hymnes* (repr., Paris: Cerf, 2008), p. 40. ET Dunkle, *Enchantment and Creed*, p. 115.
5 Dunkle, *Enchantment and Creed*, p. 223.
6 Augustine, *Confessions* 10.34.52. *CSEL* 33, p. 266. ET Dunkle, *Enchantment and Creed*, p. 115.
7 Peter Brown, *Augustine of Hippo: A Biography* (Berkeley and Los Angeles: University of California Press, 2000), p. 23.
8 Augustine, *Enarrationes in Psalmos* 45.7. PL 36. 518. ET *Expositions of the Psalms 33–50 (III/6)* (ed. John E. Rotelle, OSA; trans. and notes Maria Boulding, OSB; Hyde Park, NY: New City Press, 2000), p. 315.
9 Lydia Schumacher, *Divine Illumination: The History and Future of Augustine's Theory of Knowledge* (Chichester: Wiley-Blackwell, 2011), pp. 60–2.
10 Augustine, *Soliloquium* 1.23. PL 32. 882.
11 Augustine, *Enarrationes in Psalmos* 41.9. PL 36. 470. ET 'Augustine of Hippo Sermon on Psalm 41(Vulgate)' (trans. Bernard McGinn), in *The Essential Writings of Christian Mysticism* (ed. Bernard McGinn; New York: Random House, 2006), pp. 21–34 (24).
12 Augustine, *Sermon* 4.5. CCL 41, p. 22. ET *Sermons 1 (1–19) on the Old Testament* (ed. John E. Rotelle, OSA; trans. and notes Edmund Hill, OP; Brooklyn, NY: New City Press, 1990), p. 187.
13 Robin Lane Fox, *Augustine: Conversions and Confessions* (London: Penguin, 2015), p. 128.
14 Augustine, *Contra Fortunatum Disputatio* 3. *CSEL* 25, p. 85.
15 Augustine, *Confessions* 7.10. *CSEL* 33, p. 157. ET Augustine, *Confessions* (ed. Michael P. Foley; trans. F. J. Sheed; introduction Peter Brown; repr., Indianapolis and Cambridge: Hackett Publishing Company, 2nd edn, 2006), pp. 128–9.
16 Augustine, *Ad Simplicianum de diversis quaestionibus*. 2.4. CCL 44, pp. 86–7. Andrew Louth, 'The Body in Western Catholic Christianity', in *Religion and the Body* (ed. Sarah Coakley; Cambridge: Cambridge University Press, 1997), pp. 111–30 (116–17).
17 Augustine, *De sermone Domini in monte* 5.18. PL 34.1277. ET 'The Lord's Sermon on the Mount'(trans. Michael G. Campbell, OSA; introduced and annotated by Boniface Ramsay), in *New Testament I and II* (ed. Boniface Ramsay; The Works of St Augustine, 15–16; Hyde Park, NY: New City Press, 2014), pp. 9–129 (77–8).
18 Augustine, *Enarrationes in Psalmos* 103.20. PL 37. 1373–4. ET *Expositions of the Psalms (Enarrationes in Psalmos) 99–120, III/19* (ed. Boniface Ramsay; trans. Maria Boulding, OSB; Hyde Park, NY: New City Press, 2003), pp. 160–1. Translation modified slightly.
19 Robert Dodaro, OSA, 'Light in the Thought of St Augustine', in *Light from Light: Scientists and Theologians in Dialogue* (eds Gerald O'Collins, SJ and Mary Ann Myers; Grand Rapids, MI and Cambridge, UK: Eerdmans, 2012), pp. 195–207.
20 Ibid., p. 207.

21 Eucherius of Lyons, *Formulae spiritalis intelligentiae*. CSEL 31, 3–62. ET *The Formulae of St Eucherius of Lyons* (trans. Karen Rae Keck; Grand Rapids, MI: Christian Classics Ethereal Library, 2000). Available online. http://www.ccel.org/ccel/eucherius/formulae.html (accessed 11 December 2020).
22 Eucherius, *Formulae*, Preface. J. F. Kelly, 'Eucherius of Lyons: Harbinger of the Middle Ages', *Studia Patristica* 23 (1989), pp. 138–42.
23 Eucherius, *Formulae* 2. ET p. 7.
24 Eucherius, *Formulae* 2. ET p. 6.
25 Eucherius, *Formulae* 3. ET p. 8.
26 'In a very different age his work played a crucial role in making us what we are.' Thomas O'Loughlin, 'The Symbol Gives Life: Eucherius of Lyons' Formula for Exegesis', in *Scriptural Interpretation in the Fathers: Letter and Spirit* (eds Thomas Finan and Vincent Twomey; Dublin: Four Courts Press, 1995), pp. 221–52 (252).
27 Leo the Great, *Sermo* 26.1. PL 54. 212. ET *St Leo the Great: Sermons* (trans. Jane Patricia Freeland, CSJB and Agnes Josephine Conway, SSJ; FC, 93; Washington, DC: Catholic University of America Press, 1996), p. 104.
28 Leo the Great, *Sermo* 34.4 PL 54. 247–8. ET *St Leo the Great: Sermons*, p. 147.
29 Leo the Great, *Sermo* 27.4. PL 54. 218–19. ET Susan K. Roll, *Towards the Origins of Christmas* (Kampen: Kok Pharos, 1995), p. 152. Leo had earlier condemned Christian sun worship in two versions of Sermon 22. PL 54. 218–19. Bronwen Neil, 'Pagan Ritual and Christian Liturgy: Leo the Great's Preaching on Sun-Worship', in *Liturgie und Ritual in der alten Kirche. Patristische Beiträge zum Studium der gottesdienstlichen Quellen in der alten Kirche* (eds Wolfram Kinzig, et al.; Leuven: Peeters, 2011), pp. 127–40 (134–40). Wallraff, *Christus Verus Sol*, pp. 187–9.
30 R. A. Markus, *The End of Ancient Christianity* (Cambridge: Cambridge University Press, 1998), pp. 129–30.
31 Kim Bowes, *Private Worship, Public Values, and Religious Change in Late Antiquity* (New York: Cambridge University Press, 2011), pp. 54, 78, 99–103.
32 Bernard Green, *The Soteriology of Leo the Great* (Oxford: Oxford University Press, 2008), pp. 96–7.
33 Susan Wessel, *Leo the Great and the Spiritual Rebuilding of a Universal Rome* (Leiden and Boston: Brill, 2008), p. 155.
34 G. R. Evans, *The Thought of Gregory the Great* (Cambridge: Cambridge University Press, 1986), pp. 105–11.
35 Carole Straw, *Gregory the Great: Perfection in Imperfection* (Berkeley, Los Angeles and London: University of California Press, 1988), pp. 226–7.
36 Gregory the Great, *Moralia in Job* 5.30.53. PL 75. 708. ET Bernard McGinn, *The Essential Writings of Christian Mysticism* (New York: Random House, 2006), p. 370.
37 Gregory the Great, *Homiliae in Ezechielem* 2.5.16–17. PL 76. 995. ET Bernard McGinn, 'Contemplation in Gregory the Great', in *Gregory the Great: A Symposium* (ed. John C. Cavadini; Notre Dame and London: University of Notre Dame Press, 1995), pp. 146–67 (154). See Dom Cuthbert Butler, *Western Mysticism: The Teaching of Augustine, Gregory and Bernard on Contemplation and the Contemplative Life* (London: Constable, 3rd edn, 1967), pp. 72–8.
38 Timothy E. Powell, 'Christianity or Solar Monotheism: The Early Religious Beliefs of St Patrick', *Journal of Ecclesiastical History* 43.4 (1992), pp. 531–40.
39 William Declan Swan, *The Experience of God in the Writings of Saint Patrick: Reworking a Faith Received* (Rome: Gregorian University, 2013), pp. 197–201.

40 Roy Flechner, *Saint Patrick Retold: The Legend and History of Ireland's Patron Saint* (Princeton and Oxford: Princeton University Press, 2019), pp. 142–3.
41 St Patrick, *Confessions* 60. ET *My Name is Patrick: St Patrick's Confessio* (trans. Pádraig McCarthy; Dublin: Royal Irish Academy, 2011), p. 31.
42 Ibid. 59, p. 31.
43 Ibid. 20, pp. 10–11.
44 Thomas O'Loughlin, *Discovering St Patrick* (London: Darton Longman and Todd, 2005), p. 152, n. 116. See also David Woods, 'St Patrick and the "Sun" (*Conf.* 20)', *Studia Hibernica* 34 (2006–7), pp. 9–16.
45 Thomas O'Loughlin, *Gildas and the Scriptures: Observing the World through a Biblical Lens* (Turnhout: Brepols, 2012), p. 25. François Kerlouégan, 'Gildas', in *Oxford Dictionary of National Biography, in Association with the British Academy: From the Earliest Times to the Year 2000, vol. 22* (eds H.C.G. Matthew and Brian Harrison; Oxford: Oxford University Press, 2004), pp. 223–4.
46 Gildas, *De Excidio Britanniae* 8. ET *The Works of Gildas Surnamed 'Sapiens', or The Wise* (trans. J.A. Giles; London: 1842). Available online: http://www.gutenberg.org/cache/epub/1949/pg1949-images.html (accessed 21 April 2020). Text adjusted slightly.
47 Janina Ramirez, *The Private Lives of the Saints: Power, Passion and Politics in Anglo-Saxon England* (London: W.H. Allen, 2016), pp. 191–2.
48 National Museum of Ireland, 'The Coggalbeg Hoard'. Available online: https://www.museum.ie/en-IE/Collections-Research/Collection/Resilience/Artefact/Test-7/3fa0198b-cee5-40dc-9649-76ef6725fa07 (accessed 23 March 2021). Ramirez, *Private Lives*, pp. 241–2.
49 Michael W. Herren and Shirley Ann Brown, *Christ in Celtic Christianity: Britain and Ireland from the Fifth to the Tenth Century* (Woodbridge: The Boydell Press, 2002), pp. 199–200.
50 John Scotus Eriugena, *Carmen* II. 1–4. *Iohannis Scotti Eriugenae Carmina* (trans. Michael W. Herren; Scriptores Latini Hiberniae, 12; Dublin: School of Celtic Studies, Dublin Institute for Advanced Studies, 1993), p. 65.
51 Éamonn Ó'Carragáin, 'Christian Inculturation in Eighth-Century Northumbria: The Bewcastle and Ruthwell Crosses', *Colloquium Journal* 4 (2007), n.p. Available online: https://ism.yale.edu/sites/default/files/files/Christian%20Inculturation%20in%20Eighth.pdf (accessed 21 April 2020).
52 Ramirez, *Private Lives*, p. 245.
53 Ó'Carragáin, 'Christian Inculturation in Eighth-Century Northumbria', n.p.
54 Roger Stalley, *Early Irish Sculpture and the Art of the High Crosses* (New Haven and London: Paul Mellon Centre for Studies in British Art, Yale University Press, 2020), p. 167. See also Éamonn Ó'Carragáin, 'High Crosses, the Sun's Course, and Local Theologies at Kells and Monasterboice', in *Insular and Anglo-Saxon Art and Thought in the Early Medieval Period* (ed. Colum Hourihane; Princeton, NJ: Princeton University Press, in association with Pennsylvania University Press, 2011), pp. 149–73.
55 John McGahern, *That They May Face the Rising Sun*, p. 251.
56 Ibid., p. 261.
57 Seamus Heaney, *Preoccupations: Selected Prose 1968–1978* (London: Faber and Faber, 1980), p. 189.
58 Patrick Crotty (ed.), *The Penguin Book of Irish Poetry* (London: Penguin, 2010), pp. lxiv–lxv. When a new secular poetic class developed later in the Middle Ages, with the

primary task of praising their patrons, the bards reverted to the custom of composing in darkened rooms (ibid., p. lxvii).
59 Kenneth Jackson, *Studies in Early Celtic Nature Poetry* (Cambridge: Cambridge University Press, 2011), p. 3.
60 Tomás Ó'Carragáin, *Churches in Early Medieval Ireland: Architecture, Ritual and Memory* (New Haven and London: Yale University Press, 2010), p. 177.
61 Gerald Murphy (ed. and trans.), *Early Irish Lyrics: Eighth to Twelfth Century* (Oxford: Clarendon Press, 1956), p. 61.
62 Pádraig Ó Fiannachta (ed.) and Desmond Forristal (trans.), *Saltair Urnaithe Dúchais: Prayers from the Irish Tradition* (Dublin: Columba, 1988), p. 80.
63 Kenneth Hurlstone Jackson, *A Celtic Miscellany: Translations from the Celtic Literatures* (Harmondsworth: Penguin, 1971), p. 177.

Chapter 4

THE MIDDLE AGES

We now turn to the Middle Ages, with an eye to the second of the three questions we raised in the Introduction: how did the purchase of Christian solar symbolism come to weaken? We see how light and sun continued as a staple of religious experience and were central to the conception of medieval churches but that confidence in the objective character of cosmic symbolism continued to decline. Turning to the writings of some particularly creative individuals from the Middle Ages, we find rich resources for the retrieval and revival of solar symbolism.

Light and its symbolism

Solar symbolism

The patristic link between scripture and cosmos continued into the early Middle Ages. For the Irish scholar John Scotus Eriugena (*c.* 800–*c.* 877), translator of Dionysius the Areopagite into Latin, the created world is a theophany, and symbolism is a key to understanding it. He saw theology as articulating meanings that are part of the objective physical reality of things, rather than what he calls mere allegory: 'So we did not use allegory when we said that Holy Scripture meant by the name of light the visible and intelligible form of things.'[1] Amalarius of Metz (*c.* 775–*c.* 850) shows how natural light was integrated into the celebration of the Sacred Triduum (the last three days of Holy Week beginning with Maundy Thursday). Each of the twenty-four lights used at *Tenebrae* (literally 'darkness', referring to lauds and readings during the Triduum) signified an hour of the day. Together the lights symbolize Christ who illuminates his church by day and by night. The True Sun rests in the tomb between Good Friday and Easter, mourned by his church and hidden from view – just as the sun is not visible during an eclipse – and, as a sign of sorrow, the lights are extinguished.[2] This exemplifies a symbolic mentality that continued into the twelfth century.[3] According to M.D. Chenu, it meant that fire, for instance, 'warms, casts light, purifies, burns, rejuvenates, consumes' and 'to constrict its meaning for the sake of conceptual clarity would have been to sterilize it, to kill its vitality'.[4]

Writing in a more theoretical vein, Anselm of Canterbury (1033/4–1109) could still sound like a church father from centuries earlier:

> Truly, Lord, this is the inaccessible light in which You dwell. For there is nothing else which can penetrate through so that it might discover You there. Truly I do not see this light since it is too much for me; and yet whatever I see I see through it, just as an eye that is weak sees what it sees by the light of the sun which it cannot look at in the sun itself.[5]

Similarly, Bernard of Clairvaux's Advent and Christmas sermons show how solar biblical texts used in third-century Alexandria figured in the devotional language of mediaeval France. In one sermon for Christmas Eve, we read: 'the Sun of Justice, like a huge and brilliant candle has enkindled and enlightened the prison of this world', and in another: 'for you who fear God, the Sun of Justice will arise'.[6] For the Epiphany, he writes, 'Today the Magi come from the East seeking the risen Sun of Justice, the one of whom we read, *Here is a man, the East is his name!*'[7]

Symbolic thinking did not, then, disappear in the Middle Ages, but it declined in influence from the thirteenth century. Henri de Lubac describes this process as moving from symbolism to dialectic.[8] Rather than letting natural symbols speak for themselves in a fresh and straightforward way, they were too often conceptualized or seen as a coded reference to be deciphered (as we saw with Eucherius of Lyons). Too many proposed interpretations of natural phenomena were far-fetched. The beryl, for instance, shining like sunlit water and warming the hand that holds it, was presented as an image of the Christian life warmed and illuminated by Christ the Sun.[9]

The study of physical light

The physical world was studied from another angle by scholars in universities and in monastic scriptoria using empirical observation and mathematical methods. Pioneers included Robert Grosseteste (1175–1253), Roger Bacon (1214–92) and Witelo, a Polish scholar at the papal court from 1270 to 1280. Nothing received more attention than astronomy and light (hence the title of a recent book, *The Light Ages*[10]). They were convinced that nature is a mirror reflecting divine order and giving access to the divine mind. This was the religious motivation for studying the movement of light rays, and phenomena such as crystals, dew drops or rainbows. Practical research into the use of lenses to correct myopia took off at the end of the thirteenth century (as we see in Umberto Eco's *The Name of the Rose*), and by the end of the fourteenth century, scholars were turning their attention to mirror arches and other illusions. They were on the threshold of optical physics and modern science.[11]

Medieval church light

Architecture and light

Physical light was pivotal in the conception of sacred spaces. The ninth-century chapel of St Zeno in the Roman basilica of Santa Prassede is a striking example. Images of the Virgin Mary and John the Baptist flank a space where there would usually be an image of Christ. Instead, there is a window facing east. Christ is represented by the light of the rising sun entering through the window. An inscription reads, *ego sum lux* – 'I am the Light'. In the Oratory of Santa Maria in Valle in Cividale, northeast Italy, on the western wall, six statues of women saints (probably from the mid-eighth century) flank a central window. The two figures on either side of the window gesture towards it in acclamation of Christ the Light.

Natural light was the primary source of illumination in churches, but the light of candles, or the gleaming of precious stones or stained-glass windows, had an ancillary role to the same end – symbolic access to divine light. The importance of light is clear from how much was spent on it. As well as candles on altars, from the thirteenth century onwards, sanctuary lamps marked the presence of the Blessed Sacrament, and increasingly tombs, shrines and statues were surrounded by votive lamps. The candles were made of beeswax which was more costly than oil or rushes. Chapels receiving the mortal remains of the deceased were generously illuminated. In 1422, 12,000 pounds of beeswax was burnt in the Cathedral of Notre Dame de Paris for the funeral rites of King Charles VI[12]. To this day, a chapel housing the body of a deceased person is termed in French *une chapelle ardente*. The cost of beeswax candles pales into insignificance, however, when compared with the investment in constructing cathedrals and churches. Church windows were the chief impetus behind the growth of the glass industry from the twelfth century, and mediaeval church architecture as a whole constitutes a colossal investment in the orchestration of light.

Ornate style

Suger (1081–1151), Abbot of Saint-Denis near Paris, gives the first sustained treatment of the use of light in worship in the tradition of Augustine.[13] The king gave gold and precious stones to Saint-Denis so that the church could be as radiant as the brightest ray of sunshine.[14] These stones were valued because they were transparent and light-bearing. The similar sound of 'Christ' and 'crystal' was thought to be providential,[15] and 'noble' substances such as gold or glass gave the divine light more effective expression than wood or stone, with different colours, for example, in stained glass windows, expressing different aspects of light.[16] Natural light directs attention to divine light[17] – verses inscribed at the main entrance to Saint-Denis urge the visitor:

> Marvel not at the gold and the expense but at the
> craftsmanship of the work.

> Bright is the noble work; but, being nobly bright, the work
> Should brighten the minds, so that they may travel,
> through the true lights,
> To the True Light where Christ is the true door.[18]

Ervin Panofsky and Otto von Simon credited Suger with a sophisticated Neoplatonist vision based on his study of Dionysius the Areopagite.[19] There is no evidence, however, that Suger read Dionysius, and his approach is more historical and liturgical than philosophical. Probably, he represents broad currents of mediaeval thought on light:

> In some form or other the great metaphor of light was built into the ordinary Christian perception of the world, and had become part of the stock in trade of everyone who ever preached a sermon. There is perhaps a sense in which anyone who, like Browning, greets the sun in the morning and feels that 'God's in his heaven, all's right with the world', may be called a Platonist. It could be argued that … Suger was a diluted Platonist of this kind.[20]

He seems to have drawn his inspiration from the texts of the liturgy and the Bible, and from Christian poetry, rather than from Neoplatonist theory or scholastic theology.[21] In this, he resembles his critic Bernard of Clairvaux, as well as Hildegard of Bingen and Francis of Assisi.

Saint-Denis was the first major Gothic church. Other celebrated examples include Notre Dame de Paris (second half of the twelfth century), Reims (c. 1240–50) and most particularly Sainte Chapelle in Paris (c. 1260) where everything is sacrificed to light. Gothic pointed arches and spires direct the viewer upwards. Exuberance and aspiration are everywhere, in what John McGahern termed 'an elevation and emancipation of the soul, of love and light, height and openness'.[22] This verticality remains a permanent feature of Christian experience, and one of the reasons why medieval cathedrals are a resource for the revival of solar symbolism today.

Plain style

Bernard of Clairvaux (1090–1153) reacted against the work of Suger and against what he saw as the excessive splendour of the celebrated Abbey of Cluny. The sparkling colours of stained-glass windows and precious stones were vain and decadent.[23] At the same time, Bernard's religious order, the Cistercians, developed their own aesthetic of clean, simple spaces of unadulterated sunlight and daylight. The geometry of light was important for the planning of early Cistercian churches, where the slow movement of the sun shining into the church as the day went by was integrated but not intrusive. Like other monks, Cistercians depended on the sun for the regulation of their ordered life. A breakthrough in the design of mechanical clocks came around 1300,[24] but before the widespread introduction of effective clocks and pendulums in the seventeenth century, the principal clock for monks continued to be the sun. For Cistercian monasteries, it was only in 1429 that a regime of equal hours was established.[25]

Despite their differences, the architectures of Suger and the Cistercians were both Christian architectures of light and sun.[26] They shared a philosophy diametrically opposed to the dualism of the Cathars, which saw matter as intrinsically evil.[27] For mainstream medieval Christian thought, wherever there is matter there is light, and the omnipresence of physical light[28] is a model for the omnipresence of creative intelligible light.[29] Light was also the physical basis of all beauty, enabling all movement and expansion. While such theoretical notions and sophisticated symbolic patterns expressed in art may well have escaped the great mass of the faithful, the light entering ordinary medieval parish churches through stained-glass windows conveyed a vivid sense of divine glory and majesty.[30]

Three German women

Hildegard of Bingen

Hildegard (1098–1179) was a polymath described as one of the most influential women in church history.[31] Today, she combines a significant presence, as herbalist, composer and artist, in New Age material with the title Saint and Doctor of the Universal Church conferred on her by Pope Benedict XVI on 7 October 2012. In 1146, Hildegard wrote out of the blue to the best-known churchman of her day, Bernard of Clairvaux, asking him to authenticate her visions. She takes the traditional image of the eagle, the only creature thought to be able to look directly at the sun:

> Father Bernard, I want you to reassure me, and then I will be certain! In a vision two years ago I saw you as a man able to stare at the sun without flinching, a courageous man … You are the eagle staring at the sun![32]

Hildegard's view of the world was shot through with light and solar symbolism. In her letters, she refers to Mal. 4.2 (the Sun of Justice will come with healing in his wings) more than to any other scriptural text except Heb. 12.12 (the heavenly Jerusalem, the city of the living God).[33] In meditations on the incarnation and the paschal mystery, Christ is a radiant dawn:

> And in the earth too appears a radiance like the dawn, into which the flame is miraculously absorbed, without being separated from the blazing fire.[34]
>
> And you see a serene Man coming forth from this radiant dawn, Who pours out His brightness into the darkness; and it drives Him back with great force, so that He pours out the redness of blood and the whiteness of pallor into it, and strikes the darkness such a strong blow that the person who is lying in it is touched by Him, takes on a shining appearance and walks out of it upright.[35]

Even brief excerpts from Hildegard's writings reveal an original voice. The Holy Spirit speaks to her:

> I am also the fiery life of the divine essence – I flame above the beauty of the fields; I shine in the waters; in the sun, the moon and the stars, I burn ... Even the sun is alive in its own light; and when the moon is on the point of disappearing, it is kindled by the sun, so that it lives, as it were, afresh.[36]

In the cosmos, 'all living creatures are, so to speak, sparks from the radiation of God's brilliance, and the sparks emerge from God like the rays of the sun'.[37] She gave the word *viriditas* (greenness) new meaning: 'O most noble greenness, / you are rooted in the sun,/ and you shine in bright serenity / in a sphere / no earthly eminence / attains. // You are enfolded / in the embraces of divine / ministries. You blush like the dawn / and burn like a flame of the sun.'[38]

The Living Light is described in terms of Transfiguration and personified wisdom:

> She is so bright and glorious that you cannot look at her or her garments for the splendor with which she shines. For she is terrible with the terror of the avenging lightning, and gentle with the goodness of the bright sun; ... she is with everyone and in everyone, and so beautiful is her secret that no person can know the sweetness with which she sustains people, and spares them in an inscrutable mercy.[39]

Mechthild of Magdeburg

Mechthild of Magdeburg (c. 1212–c. 1282) was a Beguine (a member of a community of devout lay women) in northern Germany. Her visionary teachings, written in Low German, provoked strong opposition. After a period of poverty and isolation, she ended her days in the Cistercian convent at Helfta. Her time there as an old and blind resident overlapped with the early life of Gertrude the Great in the same convent. Mechthild's texts are vivid and original. In the following two excerpts, the creature is a mirror image of God, and we have God addressing the creature in terms of sight, taste and smell. It was usual to describe God in solar terms, but in Mechthild's bold conception God returns the compliment and uses the same imagery to describe a human being. The visionary addresses God: 'Lord, you are my lover, / My desire, / My flowing fount, / My sun; / And I am your reflection.'[40] God addresses the human soul: 'You taste like a grape. / Your fragrance is like Balsam. / Your radiance is like the sun. / You are an enhancement of my most sublime love.'[41]

Gertrude the Great of Helfta

The *Spiritual Exercises* of Gertrude the Great (1256–1301/2) are, according to Pope Benedict XVI, 'a rare jewel of mystical spiritual literature'.[42] Written for her fellow sisters, they integrate personal prayer into a life that revolves around the church's liturgy.[43] Christ speaks: 'I am, indeed, from the land of angels, an exemplar of radiance. / I am myself the spendor of the divine sun. / I am the most fulgent spring day.'[44]

In Exercise Five, Gertrude offers a series of prose poems to nourish around three hours of prayer spread over a day. The exercise seems to combine two originally distinct works. The first part of the exercise divides the day into three periods: morning, midday and evening. The second part has seven periods corresponding to the seven canonical hours. The exercises are designed 'for the kindling of your senses by the true sun, who is God, so that your love may never be extinguished but may grow from day to day.'[45] In the morning, Gertrude meditates: 'O serenest light of my soul, very brightest morning, ah, break into day in me now and begin so to shine for me that by your light I may see light and that through you my night may be turned into day.'[46] Christ is the 'imperial morning star, fulgent with divine brightness'.[47] 'At noonday, approach the spouse blazing in love for you so that he, the sun of justice, may kindle your luke-warmness with the fervor of his cherishing-love.'[48] In the evening, Jesus declares: 'There you will find me, Jesus, the true *today* of divine brightness, who am the beginning and the end of all creation.'[49]

Francis of Assisi

The Canticle of Brother Sun

> Praised be to you, my Lord, with all your creatures,
> especially Sir Brother Sun,
> who is the day, and by him you give us light.
> And he is beautiful and shining with great splendour,
> of you, Most High, he bears the sign.[50]

Pope Francis took the opening words of Francis's canticle – *Laudato sì* – as the title of his encyclical on care of the planet and poverty. Viewed historically, Francis of Assisi (1181/2–1226) and his poem are, in several respects, very different from many of our stereotypes. His profession of fraternity comes from suffering, and the Canticle is primarily a cry.[51] He was not a nature lover in the contemporary sense. He never used the word 'nature' and could cast a cold, unromantic eye on what today we call scenery, finding no delight in the fields and vineyards of Umbria.[52]

Thirteenth-century accounts present different strands in the composition of the Canticle, one anguished, the other serene. The anguish is true to the process of composition, the peace to the final product.[53] Most of the poem was written when Francis was at San Damiano in 1225, the year after he received the stigmata on Mount La Verna. He was in a desperate state, mentally and physically. Sunlight was painful because of an eye infection exacerbated by botched treatments and his cell rat-infested. After a sleepless night of fear that he might die and go to hell, he composed the first nine strophes of the *Canticle*. In 1226, he added the stanza on 'Sister Death' and died on the evening of 3 October, to the strains of the Canticle sung for him by brothers Angelo and Leo. After his mental and physical trials, Francis came to see creation bathed in a soft light, pure like the first light of morning, reconciled with itself in a universal brotherhood of creatures. Death loses its sting, and the primal human fear becomes Sister Death.

Creator and creation

The sources of the poem are in the Bible (e.g. Ps. 148) and the liturgy. His interest is the Creator and his creation, and he talks about Brother Sun because, like him, the sun is a creature. He wrote the Canticle to make up for human ingratitude and sin. The first stanza says that God must be praised, but human beings are sinners and are not worthy to do it, and so he passes the baton on to inanimate creatures.[54] Ever since the thirteenth century, there have been questions: What does 'of' mean in the title? Is it by Brother Sun or through Brother Sun or for Brother Sun? Probably, as is frequent in poetry, the word has simultaneously a variety of meanings. Brother Sun is a creature who praises God, but he is also saluted. He is useful, giving us light, but in his splendour he points to another world – 'of you, Most High, he bears the sign'.

A call to conversion and praise

The poem is in equal measure fascinating and challenging. According to Francis, at dawn when the sun rises everyone should praise God the Creator, because it is by agency of the sun that our eyes are lit by daylight.[55] The *Canticle of Brother Sun* is a radically theocentric poem, above all an act of praise and gratitude. It is also for Francis a summons to conversion. He suggested that it could be sung to friars struggling to overcome some moral fault and had strophes 10 and 11 sung in front of the bishop's palace and the town hall in Assisi to effect a reconciliation between them.[56]

Thomas Aquinas

Transmitting solar tradition

Thomas Aquinas (1225–74) continued traditional solar themes. He viewed the Cathars as latter-day Manichees who saw God as infinite physical light and 'thought that the sun we see with our physical eyes was Christ the Lord'.[57] The sun expresses God's invisible perfections but is not to be worshipped. Just as the sun shines everywhere in the world without losing its identity, the Divine Goodness permeates the world in a non-dualistic way. The sun is always totally luminous, and it illuminates the whole world. When there is no sun, there is decay and ageing.[58] 'For Christ, the Sun of Justice, it is always day and the time for acting; but not with respect to us, because we are not always able to receive his grace due to some obstacle on our part.'[59]

Downgrading metaphor

At the same time, Aquinas contributed to a decline in the use of cosmic symbolism and metaphor in theology. According to M. D. Chenu, he tried to go beyond symbols and metaphors, which he saw as typical of an outmoded Platonic theology. Aquinas held that one cannot argue theologically using symbols – *theologia symbolica non est argumentativa*.[60] For the most part, he conceptualized metaphors and images when he applied them to God. The notion of intelligible light, for example, is entirely conceptualized. He favoured clear, precise, literal language and Chenu likens his clarity and precision to a cut diamond. But a price is paid as words are emptied of figurative power and images are divested of any reference to matter.[61] Aquinas saw the literal/metaphorical distinction as important, insisting that some terms, such as 'rock', can only be applied to God metaphorically.[62] For him, metaphorical statements come a poor second to literal assertions, expressing truth but in a deficient way.[63] A good example of Aquinas's approach is a comparison between human beings and bats and owls. Just as a bat cannot observe the sun because of its weak eyes, human beings cannot understand God because of the weakness of our intellect.[64] Any figurative power in the comparison has been drained off. The way he handles Malachi 4.2 is not entirely different: a sunray is created by the Divine Goodness and has some objective similarity to that Goodness; therefore, it is fitting that God be described, metaphorically, as sunlight.[65] Given the lowly status of metaphors, making 'symbol' and 'metaphor' equivalents (as in his expression *symbolice vel metaphorice*) means that to some degree cosmic symbols such as that of the sun are treated as simply human creations.[66] According to Cornelius Ernst, this approach 'suggests in germ the emergence of an acosmic humanism which is still with us'.[67] Natural objects in themselves have no symbolic meaning; at least, Aquinas nowhere said that they do. The symbolic cosmos of the early Middle Ages was giving way to something else.[68]

The language of light

Unlike Neoplatonists such as his contemporary Bonaventure or the earlier John Scotus Eriugena, Thomas Aquinas did not see physical light as a spiritual reality. He identified light with sunlight, asking how the physical light created on the first day of creation could come into existence before the sun.[69] For Bonaventure, by contrast, the primary literal meaning of 'light' is spiritual, and the word is used in a secondary, metaphorical sense when applied to daylight, sunlight or candlelight.[70] Aquinas's rival account is closer to how the language of light is actually used: the primary literal meaning of 'light' is physical light, and when the term is applied to spiritual realities such as human insight or the divine nature, it is given a stretched, 'analogical', meaning, or is used as a metaphor.

Illumination was an important notion in Aquinas's theology.[71] For him, 'intellectual light' is the power of the human mind to abstract from sensible data and grasp reality, and 'light' is used in a stretched, analogical but nevertheless literal, sense to describe the intellect – just as the word 'see' is used analogically when we say, 'See how it tastes.'[72] Similarly, talking about God, he gives 'light' a stretched, literal meaning. When he asserts that the divine essence, which is pure act, is light itself, he is speaking literally and not metaphorically.[73] In his theology, he puts a premium on precise argument couched in literal language. The sun and light language in scripture and in liturgy, however, is overwhelmingly metaphorical, and there is a twofold downside to Aquinas's approach: a lack of attention to the cosmos as a theological resource, and a neglect of the expressive power of metaphors. This downside is part of the background to the fact that, in modern Western theology and spirituality, the revealed symbols of light and sun have not received the attention called for by their place in scripture and tradition. There is nothing automatic about such a neglect of cosmic metaphors, however. In his *Divine Comedy*, Dante Alighieri (c. 1265–1321) expresses Christian faith in a poem integrating Aquinas's theology of intellectual light – 'light, pure light of intellect, all love'[74] – with finely observed descriptions of shades of sunlight[75] exploited to gesture towards the Love that moves the sun and the other stars.[76]

Conclusion

In the Middle Ages, traditional solar language continued and Hildegard of Bingen, Francis of Assisi and Dante, for instance, remain resources for a revival of Christian solar symbolism today. A Christian culture of light bore remarkable fruit in the cathedrals and churches of that epoch. These buildings and their artistic contents call out for a re-appropriation of their visual theology of light. Light was also the object of intense study in medieval universities and monasteries. At the same time, a tendency developed in the Middle Ages to invest natural phenomena with meanings that were sometimes unconvincing and artificial, rather than to let epiphanic cosmic symbols speak for themselves. Moreover, Aquinas's theological language tended to devalue symbols and metaphors. In Chapter 6, we will return to solar cosmic symbolism and its expression in metaphorical language with a view to recovering something that has been partially lost.

Notes

1 John Scotus Eriugena, *Periphyseon* 3.29.706C. *Iohannis Scotti Eriugenae Periphyseon (De Divisione Naturae), Liber Tertius* (ed. and trans. I.P. Sheldon-Williams, with the collaboration of Ludwig Bieler; Scriptores Latini Hiberniae, 11; Dublin: Dublin Institute for Advanced Studies, 1981), p. 225.
2 MacGregor, A. J., *Fire and Light in the Western Triduum: Their Use at Tenebrae and at the Paschal Vigil* (Collegeville, MN: The Liturgical Press, 1992), pp. 52–3.
3 M.-D. Chenu, *Nature, Man and Society in the Twelfth Century: Essays on New Theological Perspectives in the Latin West* (eds and trans. Jerome Taylor and Lester K. Little; Chicago and London: University of Chicago Press, 1968), pp. 99–145.
4 Chenu, *Nature, Man and Society*, p. 136.

5   Anselm, *Proslogion* 16. ET *St Anselm's* Proslogion *with A Reply on Behalf of the Fool by Gaunilo and* The Author's Reply to Gaunilo (trans. M. J. Charlesworth; Notre Dame, IN: University of Notre Dame Press, 1979), p. 137.
6   *Bernard of Clairvaux: Sermons for Advent and the Christmas Season* (ed. John Leinenweber; trans. Irene Edmonds, Wendy Mary Beckett and Conrad Greenia, OCSO; Cistercian Fathers, 51; Collegeville, MN: Liturgical Press, 2008), pp. 61, 93.
7   Ibid., p. 158. See Malachi 4.2; Zechariah 3.8, 6.12; Lk. 1.78.
8   Henri de Lubac, *Corpus Mysticum: The Eucharist and the Church in the Middle Ages* (eds Laurence Paul Hemming and Susan Frank Parsons; trans. Gemma Symmonds, CJ with Richard Price and Christopher Stephens; London: SCM, 2006), pp. 221–47.
9   Emile Mâle, *The Gothic Image: Religious Art in France of the Thirteenth Century* (trans. Dora Nussey; London: Collins, 1961), p. 30.
10 Seb Falk, *The Light Ages: A Medieval Journey of Discovery* (London: Allen Lane, 2020), pp. 112–16.
11 André Vauchez, 'Lumières au moyen âge', in *Séance de rentrée des cinq académies sur le thème: « la lumière » mardi 27 octobre 2009 sous la coupole* (Paris: Institut de France, 2009), p. 6. Available online: http://seance-cinq-academies-2010.institut-de-france.fr/discours/2009/vauchez.pdf (accessed 22 April 2020).
12 Ibid., p. 3.
13 *Abbot Suger on the Abbey Church of St.-Denis and Its Art Treasures* (ed. and trans. Erwin Panofsky; Princeton, NJ: Princeton University Press, 1979).
14 Joachim Gaus, 'Die Lichtsymbolik in der mittelalterlichen Kunst', *Symbolon: Jahrbuch für Symbolforschung*, Neue Folge 12 (1995), pp. 107–18 (109).
15 Ibid., p. 114.
16 Ibid., p. 108.
17 Ibid., p. 111. *Abbot Suger on the Abbey Church*, pp. 54–5.
18 *Abbot Suger on the Abbey Church,* pp. 47–9.
19 Otto Von Simon, *The Gothic Cathedral: Origins of Gothic Architecture and the Mediaeval Concept of Order* (Princeton, NJ: Princeton University Press, 1988), pp. 91–141.
20 Peter Kidson, 'Panofsky, Suger and St Denis', *Journal of the Warburg and Courtauld Institutes* 50 (1987), pp. 1–17 (7).
21 Andreas Speer, 'Is There a Theology of the Gothic Cathedral? A Re-reading of Abbot Suger's Writings on the Abbey Church of St.-Denis', in *The Mind's Eye: Art and Theological Argument in the Middle Ages* (eds Jeffrey F. Hamburger and Anne-Marie Bouché; Princeton, NJ: Princeton University Press, 2006), pp. 65–83.
22 John McGahern, 'The Church and Its Spire', in *Love of the World: Essays* (London: Faber and Faber, 2009), pp. 133–48 (145).
23 Bernard of Clairvaux, *Apologia ad Guillelmum* 12.28. *Cistercians and Cluniacs: St Bernard's* Apologia *to Abbot William* (trans. Michael Casey, OCSO and introduction by Jean Leclercq, OSB; Athens, OH: Cistercian Publications, 1970), pp. 63–6. Robin M. Jensen, *The Substance of Things Seen: Art, Faith, and the Christian Community* (Grand Rapids, MI and Cambridge, UK: Eerdmans, 2004), pp. 81–5.
24 Falk, *The Light Ages*, p. 55.
25 Manuela Incerti, *Il disegno della luce nell'architettura cistercense: allineamenti astronomici nelle abbazie di Chiaravalle della Colomba, Fontevivo e San Martino de' Bocci* (Florence: Certosa Cultura, 1999), p. 8.
26 Jensen, *The Substance of Things Seen,* p. 84

27 Edgar De Bruyne, *Études d'esthétique médiévale III. Le XIII siècle* (Bruges: De Tempel, 1946), p. 17.
28 *Lux* indicated the substance of light itself and *lumen* the splendour of light, but even in the early seventh century Isidore of Seville noted that authors mixed them up: *Etymologiae* 13.10.14. San Isidoro de Sevilla, *Etimologiás, edición Bilingüe* (eds and trans. José Oroz Reta and Manuel-A. Marcos Casquero; Madrid: Biblioteca de Autores Cristianos, 2004), p. 968.
29 De Bruyne, *Études d'esthétique médiévale*, p. 21; Gaus, 'Die Lichtsymbolik', p. 110.
30 Kevin Madigan, *Medieval Christianity: A New History* (New Haven and London: Yale University Press, 2015), p. 306.
31 Ibid., p. 419.
32 Hildegard of Bingen, 'Hildegard to Bernard of Clairvaux, 1146 [Letter 1]', in *Hildegard of Bingen: Selected Writings* (trans. with introduction and notes Mark Atherton; London: Penguin, 2001), p. 4.
33 Hildegard of Bingen, *The Letters of Hildegard of Bingen* (trans. Joseph L. Baird and Radd K. Ehrman, 3 vols; New York and Oxford: Oxford University Press, 1994, 1998, 2004).
34 Hildegard of Bingen, *Scivias* 2.1.1. ET Hildegard of Bingen, *Scivias* (trans. Mother Columba Hart and Jane Bishop; New York and Mahwah: Paulist Press, 1990), p. 154.
35 Ibid. 2.1.13. ET, p. 154.
36 Hildegard of Bingen, *The Book of Divine Works* 1.2, quoted in *Hildegard of Bingen: An Anthology* (eds Fiona Bowie and Oliver Davies; London: SPCK, 1990), pp. 91–2.
37 Ibid. 4.11, ET, p. 33.
38 Hildegard of Bingen, *Saint Hildegard of Bingen*, Symphonia: *A Critical Edition of the Symphonia armonie celestium revelationum [Symphony of the Harmony of Celestial Revelations]* (ed. and trans. Barbara Newman; Ithaca and London: Cornell University Press, 1998), p. 219.
39 Hildegard of Bingen, *Scivias* 3.4.15. ET, p. 364.
40 Mechthild of Magdeburg, *The Flowing Light of the Godhead* 4. ET Mechtild of Magdeburg, *The Flowing Light of the Godhead* (trans. and introduction Frank Tobin; preface Margot Schmidt; New York and Mahwah: Paulist Press, 1998), p. 44.
41 Ibid. 16. ET Mechtild, *Flowing Light*, p. 47.
42 Pope Benedict XVI, General Audience, 6 October 2010. Available online: http://w2.vatican.va/content/benedict-xvi/en/audiences/2010/documents/hf_ben-xvi_aud_20101006.html (accessed 23 April 2020).
43 Cyprian Vagaggini, OSB, *Theological Dimensions of the Liturgy: A General Treatise on the Theology of the Liturgy* (Collegeville, MN: The Liturgical Press, 1976), pp. 792–803.
44 Gertrude the Great of Helfta, *Spiritual Exercises* 3.7–9. ET *Gertrude the Great of Helfta, Spiritual Exercises* (trans. Gertrud Jaron Lewis and Jack Lewis; Cistercian Fathers Series, 49; Kalamazoo: Cistercian Publications, 1989), pp. 40–1.
45 Ibid. 5.464–6. ET, p. 90.
46 Ibid. 5.31–4. ET p. 74.
47 Ibid. 5.45–6. ET, p. 74.
48 Ibid. 5. 91–3. ET, p. 76.
49 Ibid. 5.526–7. ET, p. 92.
50 Francis of Assisi, 'Canticle of Brother Sun', in André Vauchez, *Francis of Assisi: The Life and Afterlife of a Mediaeval Saint* (trans. Michael F. Cusato; New Haven and London: Yale University Press, 2012), p. 277. Translation slightly modified.
51 Jacques Dalarun, *The Canticle of Brother Sun: Francis of Assisi Reconciled* (trans. Philippe Yates; New York: Franciscan Institute Publications, 2016), p. 1.

52 Ibid., p. 54.
53 Ibid., p. 100.
54 Ibid., p. 43.
55 Ibid., pp. 34–5.
56 Ibid., p. 34.
57 Thomas Aquinas, *Lectura super Evangelium S. Ioannis*. 8. 2. 1142. Saint Thomas Aquinas, *Commentary on the Gospel of John Chapters 1-8* (ed. The Aquinas Institute; trans. Fr. Fabian R. Larcher, O.P.; Latin/English Edition of the Works of St. Thomas Aquinas, 35; Lander, WY: The Aquinas Institute for the Study of Sacred Doctrine, 2013), p. 436.
58 Thomas Aquinas, *Super Librum Dionysii de Divinis Nominibus*. 4.3.306–12. S.Tommaso d'Aquino, *Commento ai nomi divini di Dionigi e testo integrale di Dionigi, vol. 1: capitoli 1–4* (trans. Battista Mondin; Bologna: Edizioni Studio Domenicano, 2004).
59 Thomas Aquinas, *Lectura super Evangelium S. Ioannis*. 9.1.1306. Saint Thomas Aquinas, *Commentary on the Gospel of John Chapters 9-21* (ed. The Aquinas Institute; trans. Fr. Fabian R. Larcher, O.P.; Latin/English Edition of the Works of St. Thomas Aquinas, 36; Lander, WY: The Aquinas Institute for the Study of Sacred Doctrine, 2013), p. 6.
60 Thomas Aquinas, *In 1 Sententiarum* Prol.1.5c. *S. Thomae Aquinatis Scriptum Super Libros Sententiarum Magistri Petri Lombardi Episcopi Parisiensis, vol. 1* (ed. P. Mandonnet; Paris: P. Lethielleux, 1929), p. 18.
61 M.D. Chenu, *Toward Understanding St Thomas* (eds and trans. A.-M. Landry and D. Hughes; Chicago: Henry Regnery Company, 1963), p. 172.
62 Thomas Aquinas, ST I, q.13, a.3 ad 1. Thomas Aquinas, *Summa Theologiae, vol. 3: (1a 12–13) Knowing and Naming God* (ed. Thomas Gilby, OP; trans. Herbert McCabe, OP; repr., Cambridge: Cambridge University Press, 2006), p. 59.
63 Paul Murray, OP, *Aquinas at Prayer: The Bible, Mysticism and Poetry* (London: Bloomsbury, 2013), pp. 177–85.
64 ST I. q.12. a.1.
65 Thomas Aquinas, *Super Librum Dionysii De Divinis Nominibus*. 4.3.306.
66 Thomas Aquinas, *In 1 Sententiarum* Dist.4, q.1, a. 1; *S. Thomae Aquinatis Scriptum Super Libros Sententiarum*, p. 131.
67 Cornelius Ernst, OP, *Multiple Echo: Explorations in Theology* (eds Fergus Kerr, OP and Timothy Radcliffe, OP; London: Darton, Longman and Todd, 1979), pp. 66, 73.
68 Umberto Eco, *Art and Beauty in the Middle Ages* (New Haven and London: Yale University Press, 2002), pp. 63–4.
69 Thomas Aquinas, ST I q.67 a.4. Aquinas, *Super Librum Dionysii De Divinis Nominibus*. 4.3.313.
70 De Bruyne, *Études d'esthétique médiévale*, p. 19.
71 Schumacher, *Divine Illumination*, pp. 173–8.
72 Thomas Aquinas, ST I, q.67, a.1. ET Thomas Aquinas, *Summa Theologiae, vol. 10: (1a 65–74) Cosmogony* (ed. Thomas Gilby, OP; trans. William A. Wallace; repr., Cambridge: Cambridge University Press, 2006), p. 55.
73 David L. Whidden III, *Christ the Light: The Theology of Light and Illumination in Thomas Aquinas* (Minneapolis: Fortress Press, 2014), p. 82.
74 Dante Alighieri, *The Divine Comedy*, Paradiso, 30.40. ET Dante Alighieri, *The Divine Comedy* (ed. and trans. Robin Kirkpatrick; repr., London: Penguin, 2012), p. 464.
75 Ibid., 5.133–7. ET p. 342–3; Ibid., 23.79–81. ET p. 430.
76 Ibid., 33.145. ET p. 482.

Chapter 5

INTO THE MODERN ERA

The birth of the modern era

Michelangelo's The Last Judgment

Ending a survey of world history, J. M. Roberts remarked that 'only two general truths emerge from the study of history. One is that things tend to change much more, and more quickly, than one might think. The other is that they tend to change much less, and much more slowly, than one might think'.[1] An era of rapid change, and equally of deep continuity with the past, was underway when Michelangelo started work on the fresco of *The Last Judgement* in the Sistine Chapel in 1536. When it was cleaned and restored in the 1990s, its original solar character became evident. The fresco is light and bright, and the young beardless figure of Christ at the centre of the fresco is clearly modelled on the classical sun god Apollo. The circular structure of the fresco gives it a cosmic character. Michelangelo scholar Charles de Tornay noted parallels with the heliocentric vision of Copernicus, only to discount any influence because Copernicus's pioneering work *Revolutions* was only published in 1543, two years after the unveiling of *The Last Judgement* on 31 October 1541.[2] Copernicus's ideas were, however, circulating for decades before *Revolutions* was published, and Michelangelo was familiar with them, having resided in Bologna and in Rome when Copernicus was active in those cities. Other influences on Michelangelo included traditional Christian sun symbolism that he was exposed to through his involvement with church reform movements in Italy. The cosmology of Dante was also an influence – Michelangelo was an enthusiastic reader of his works – as was Renaissance Neoplatonism, with its intense concentration on solar symbolism.

Renaissance and Reformation

Apollo, a sun god but also god of poetry and music, loomed large in Renaissance Rome. The idea that ancient Rome was a providential precursor of the papal city had a long lineage and St Peter was sometimes presented as being buried in the temple of Apollo. Renaissance popes were sometimes seen as ruling at the centre of the world, initiating a golden age of art and poetry. In 1517, Pope Leo X listened to a laudatory discourse in which he is depicted as Apollo or the sun, and the Vatican as Parnassus, the Hill of Apollo.³ The idea of a new era full of sunlight was, however, a wider European phenomenon. Rabelais asked:

> What is the cause, most learned Tiraqueau, that in our time, so full of light, in which we see all branches of learning restored to their former estate by some singular favor of the gods, we find men so constituted that they either will not or cannot break out of the thick, almost Cimmerian fog of Gothic times, or raise their eyes towards the dazzling torch of the sun?⁴

Florentine Neoplatonist Marsilio Ficino gives the sun a centrality unparalleled in the earlier tradition; it replaces Christ as a theological and spiritual focus:

> Perhaps light is itself the celestial spirit's sense of sight, or its act of seeing, operating from a distance, linking all things to heaven, yet never leaving heaven nor mixing with external things … Just look at the skies, I pray you, citizens of heavenly fatherland … The sun can signify God himself to you, and who shall dare to say the sun is false.⁵

While Christian in intention, Ficino's solar theology was essentially a naturalistic theology couched in Christian terminology⁶ and the long-term influence of Renaissance Neoplatonism was limited. As regards the Reformation, it is continuity rather than change that predominates. In later chapters, we will see examples of traditional Christian solar symbolism in Lutheranism, Anglicanism and the Church of Scotland.

Tommaso Campanella

Tommaso Campanella (1568–1639), an almost exact contemporary of Galileo, exemplifies solar interest in the intellectual world of the early modern era. He was a maverick Dominican thinker most celebrated as the author of *The City of the Sun*, a utopia written in a prison cell of the Inquisition in 1602 and published in 1637. He did not himself support Copernican heliocentrism but wrote an *Apology for Galileo* in 1616. He defended the 'Matematico Fiorentino', as he called Galileo, asserting the right to study the Book of Nature objectively. Campanella died at dawn on 31 May 1639, whilst practising natural magic (the distinctions between science and magic were not clear at that time) to prevent a forthcoming solar eclipse. In his utopia, the sun had a central place in the ideal religion:

> No creature but God do they deem worthy of *latria*, and Him they serve under the sign of the sun which is the symbol and visage of God from Whom comes light and warmth and every other thing. For this reason their altar is shaped like a sun, and their priests pray to God in the sun and in the stars as though these were His altars, and they pray to Him in the sky as though that were His temple.⁷

The rise of modern science

In the words of Herbert Butterfield, it is the scientific revolution that 'outshines everything since the rise of Christianity and reduces the Renaissance and Reformation to the rank of mere episodes, mere internal displacements, within the system of mediaeval Christendom'.[8] Science and technology have changed the experience of light and darkness more than the Renaissance or the Reformation. Columbus landed in the New World when Copernicus was nineteen, and navigation needed a more satisfactory astronomy than that of Ptolemy and an improvement on the Julian calendar. In the early 1500s, Copernicus was already working on a new calendar and in 1514 he circulated an outline of his heliocentric hypothesis. In 1609, Galileo (1564–1642) confirmed it empirically. By 1700, Galileo's view was generally accepted and cautiously taught even in church institutions, despite Pope Urban VIII's 1616 condemnation.[9] These developments made surprisingly little difference to Christian solar symbolism. Medieval astronomical research, at its best conducted with a rigour and openness that anticipated modern scientific research, often saw the earth as spherical, not flat, giving it a lowly location on maps of the cosmos.[10] In the long term, it is not at the level of a particular proposition, such as heliocentrism, that science has impacted on traditional solar symbolism, but in the effects of technology on daily life. Heliocentrism would, in fact, offer new devotional opportunities.

As the modern era developed, even when most scientists were theists, as Galileo and Newton were, God came to be seen as establishing and operating laws by his divine will, from outside creation, in such a way that nature itself does not mediate communion with anything higher, and transcendence, or even beauty, could come to be attributed solely to the subjective reactions of the human observer.[11] This philosophical approach hollows out cosmic symbolism, but is not itself a scientific proposition. To tell the time, medieval monks could easily use their own shadow or a stick. They constructed sundials to celebrate the regular pattern of their monastic life in a divinely ordered cosmos.[12] Symbolism and the objective study of the universe are not mutually exclusive.

Christian solar symbolism in a new era

New devotional possibilities

Astronomy revealed an immense universe that Blaise Pascal found overwhelming: 'In the end it is the greatest perceivable sign of God's overwhelming power that our imagination loses itself in this thought.'[13] In this new context, there is deep continuity with the solar symbolism of earlier eras, and in the architecture and church design of the seventeenth and eighteenth centuries, solar rays figure in the 'glories' of Baroque church interiors.[14] But there is also profound change. The interior of St Peter's Basilica in Rome is a good example of how, in the Baroque era, the theatre of the Christian life is no longer the medieval cosmos, but the church interior and the interior life of the soul. Light streams down through clear windows proclaiming the reality of sanctifying grace.[15]

Pierre de Bérulle

Pierre de Bérulle (1575–1629) was a pioneer in what has come to be called the French School of spirituality that centres on Christ and the mystery of the incarnation. Bérulle uses the traditional descriptions of Christ as the True Sun, Sun of Justice and even 'East', proposing 'to contemplate the true Sun of the world, the Sun of this sun that enlightens us, the Sun of justice who enlightens everyone coming into the world'.[16] Recounting the ancient custom of facing east during baptism, he concludes: 'As I say, we should adore him as an Orient, but an eternal Orient; an Orient that exists always at midday by the fullness of its light and always in its Orient by the state and perfection of its birth, which continues forever and never finishes, just as it never has a beginning.'[17] The physical sun is an image of Jesus: 'He is a sun who chose to depict and represent himself by the natural sun, which is only his shadow and symbol. For the sun is the image of God, the Father of nature, universal source of life. And Jesus is the true and living image of the eternal Father.'[18]

Bérulle was a contemporary of Galileo and embraced the devotional possibilities he saw opening with the Copernican revolution. Prudently, he declared that, even if the theory is not taken up in the science of astronomy, it 'is useful and should be followed in the science of salvation'.[19] A Christian life centres round the person of Christ, just as the planets circle round the sun: 'Jesus is the true centre of the world and the world should be in continuous movement towards him. Jesus is the Sun of our souls and from him we receive every grace, every light and every effect of his power.'[20]

The Society of Jesus and a modern solar emblem

When Ignatius of Loyola (1491–1556), founder of the Society of Jesus, went to his place of work, 'he would stand there and take off his hat; without stirring, he would fix his eyes on the heavens for a short while. Then, sinking to his knees, he would make a lowly gesture of reverence to God'.[21] In his *Spiritual Exercises*, justice, goodness, pity and mercy come from God like rays descending from the sun.[22] Ignatius says he saw Christ as a light emitting rays on many occasions. Once he saw something white emitting rays that he took to be God's creation of light. Another time, at the elevation of the host, he saw with interior eyes white rays coming down from above.[23] Again, in his *Diary* for 6 March 1544, he writes: 'I felt and saw, not obscurely but brightly, in full light, the very Being or Essence of God, appearing as a sphere, a little larger than the sun appears.'[24] Given the Inquisition's allergy to *alumbrados* and any claims to divine illumination, this light and sun language is remarkable. Ignatius's recurring imagery of descending sunrays expresses an invitation to active service in a world illumined by God's presence.[25]

The monogram IHS was used on the frontispiece of the first printed edition of Ignatius's *Spiritual Exercises* in 1549. When the seal of the Society of Jesus was being designed, under the personal supervision of Ignatius, it had the three letters plus sunrays indicating that Jesus was the Sun of Justice.[26] Alternating rectilinear and undulating rays give the image a vibrant feel, like a fiery sunburst. The primary focus is the name and person of Jesus, with a secondary solar motif – sometimes IHS has a solar surrounding, sometimes not. The monogram has been used widely in modern Catholicism, and Pope Francis, a Jesuit, has it in its solar form in his coat of arms.

The IHS Christogram, sometimes written as 'Ihesus', was pre-medieval. One inscription reads: 'I am IHS of Nazareth, King of the Jews.'[27] The Franciscan Bernardine of Siena (1380–1440) gave it a solar character. His distinctive contribution was a painted wooden tablet with the initials IHS surrounded by sunrays, against a blue background. 'This name, glorious above all others, must be set in the most glorious place in the world, namely in the sun.'[28] His tablet with sunrays was sometimes called his 'sun'[29] – and rival religious orders alleged superstition and even idolatry. Remarkably, anxieties about solar idolatry among Christians could still resurface. Bernardine was vindicated in ecclesiastical trials, and the devotion spread rapidly. While this modern solar emblem is analogous to the ancient winged solar disc, it has a more personal character.

Sun and eucharist

The monstrance, the ornate metal object used to display the sacred host, first appeared in the thirteenth century.[30] As early as 1405, we have a reference to a sun monstrance, and often it had twelve rays. The preaching of Bernardine of Siena, with his solar IHS tablet, and the developing feast of Corpus Christi favoured its use, and by 1486 it is referred to as 'a sun where you place the sacred host'.[31] During the Counter Reformation the sunburst monstrance, with a circular glass space surrounded by sun rays, became one of the standard designs, as the ceremony of Benediction grew in popularity along with devotions such as Perpetual Adoration and the Forty Hours. Another current linked with eucharistic piety in this era was devotion to the Sacred Heart of Jesus which was associated with Marguerite-Marie Alacoque (1647–90) who described the Heart of Christ as shining more brilliantly than the sun.[32] She was part of a wider current. Polish Jesuit Gasper Druzbicki (1589–1662) presents the Sacred Heart as 'the sun in the sky' to be contemplated with the boldness of young eagles, to prepare for Holy Communion.[33] Eucharistic devotions continued throughout the modern era. In nineteenth-century France, Pierre-Julien Eymard (1811–68) declares:

> It is not astonishing that the pagans should have adored it as the god of the world. In actual fact, the sun obeys a supreme Sun, the divine Word, Jesus Christ, who illumines everyone coming into this world and who, through the Eucharist, Sacrament of life, acts in person in the very depths of souls in order to form Christian families and peoples.[34]

Poets often articulate subliminal meaning and two twentieth-century poets reveal how solar eucharistic piety may have faded but it had not disappeared. Patrick Kavanagh describes Benediction during the pilgrimage at Lough Derg in Ireland: 'The Sacramental sun turns round and "Holy, Holy, Holy"'.[35] Seamus Heaney recalls the devotions of his youth: 'Altar-stone was dawn and monstrance noon.'[36]

Solar symbolism in the new world

An Aztec solar Christ

When Cortés started his conquest of Mexico in 1519 and Francisco Pizarro of Peru a little later, they encountered cultures with vigorous solar cults. At Chiapas, in southern Mexico, on 15 February 2016, Pope Francis quoted the *Popol Vuh*, a pre-Christian Maya text: 'The dawn rises on all of the tribes together. The face of the earth was immediately healed by the sun.'[37] The Nahua or Aztecs offered human hearts to the sun, to maintain the cosmic order, and many came to see Spaniards and Christianity as fulfilling ancient prophecies of a new solar epoch. As well as conquistadors, there arrived mendicant friars in possession of a Christian solar rhetoric. They had an outlook that was 'millennial, militant, and medieval'[38] and, like the Aztecs, they lived in a symbolically charged cosmos.[39] Solar symbolism took on new forms in the encounter with the cultures of the new world which began two generations before the Council of Trent.

Among the factors that contributed to the conversion of the Aztecs to Christianity was a successful process of inculturation through a marriage of Aztec and Christian symbolism. Translated into Nahuatl, Christian expressions picked up new symbolic associations and the meaning of Nahuatl terms was changed under Christian influence.[40] The Aztecs believed the souls of fallen warriors join the rising sun in heaven, where, taking the shape of brightly coloured birds, they suck the nectar of paradise. Christ as the Rising Sun became for the Aztecs a deity who has taken the place of the sun, presiding over a new age.[41] Mt. 17.2, where Jesus's face shines like the sun, was translated into Nahuatl as: 'Indeed, the face of our lord Jesus Christ, the way it greatly shone, the way it greatly shimmered, it was like the sun.'[42] A responsory 'From you has risen the Sun of Justice' becomes 'From you was born the possessor of proper living, the divine sun'.[43] Many saw the Christ-Sun as representing cosmic order, touching living people and their crops[44] – the Aztec worldview was monist, without rigid divisions between the material and the spiritual, the natural and the supernatural.

Just over thirty years after the arrival of the Spaniards, Aztec aristocrat Antonio Cortés Totoquihuatzin calls Emperor Charles V the one who leads pagans from darkness to the clear light possessed by Christians, to the Sun of Justice which is Christ.[45] Aztec converts worked with their European mentors, and, despite inevitable ambiguities and confusion, a new Christian aesthetic developed.[46] We can speak of a healthy syncretism where enactment and ritual were as important as belief and doctrine.[47] Sun and blood were primary images for the Aztecs, who used volcanic glass for dark mirrors in the cult of the sun god Hitziliopochtl and also to gouge out the hearts of sacrificial victims.[48] Missionaries placed obsidian mirrors on outdoor crosses, so that the physical sun could shine on the site of the True Sun's bloody sacrifice.

The 'Sacramented Sun'

Missionaries used the sunburst monstrance to link the sun and Christ present in the 'eucharistic tortilla'. He was the 'Sacramented Sun' (*sol sacramentado*) or the 'Divine Sun' (*sol divino*). In a papal brief of 1558, Pope Paul IV advises: 'The days which the Indians, according to their ancient rites, dedicate to the sun and their idols should be replaced with feasts in honour of the *true sun*, Jesus Christ.'[49] According to Bartolomé de Las Casas, 'one needs only to help them substitute the Creator, the Sun of Justice, for the sun, the material creature'.[50] The process of ritual substitution was successful. During a total eclipse of the sun in 1611, the terrified faithful ran into the churches to reverence the exposed Blessed Sacrament 'so that, it being the true Sun of Justice, they might obtain mercy from it'.[51]

The Virgin of Guadalupe

The image of the Virgin of Guadalupe, perhaps the most important item of Christian material culture in Latin America, helped create a new culture. In the *Nican Mopohua*, a seventeenth-century Nahuatl text that describes the apparition of the Virgin Mary to the Aztec Juan Diego as he ascends the hill of Tepeyac, near Mexico City, the imagery of luminosity and sun is striking:

> 7. And as he drew near the little hill called Tepeyac it was beginning to dawn.
> 11. He was looking up toward the top of the hill, towards the direction the sun rises from, toward where the precious heavenly song was coming from.
> 17. her clothing was shining like the sun, as if it was sending out waves of light,
> 18. And the stone, the crag on which she stood, seemed to be giving out rays;
> 20. The earth seemed to shine with the brilliance of a rainbow in the mist.[52]

The image, with its mandorla and sunrays, is evidently solar. Nahuatl pictographic codices explain other details: forty-two stars indicate the constellation of stars at the Mexican winter solstice, and a small jasmine flower symbolized the sun god. The imagery points to the dawn of a sacred revelation at midwinter, the Virgin bearing a Divine Son who brings light.[53] The light that surrounds the Virgin in the image is the light of the Sun of Justice shining from her womb: 'The Sun is born of this Lady, and in her it remains: the Sun is within this Lady, and its rays break forth to the outside.'[54]

Sor Juana Inés de la Cruz

Sor Juana Inés de la Cruz (1651–95), a Mexican prodigy and polymath called the 'Tenth Muse of Mexico' during her lifetime, and who figures on recent Mexican banknotes, understood Mexican Christianity as springing from an encounter between Spaniards and 'Noble Mexicans / whose ancient line / traces its origin / to the sun's clear rays'.[55] In a song accompanied by music for the feast of the conception of the Virgin Mary, 1698, Mary takes on the persona of a black slave. Her blackness is a symbol of beauty and purity that grow the more the divine sun shines on her. The refrain repeats: 'Black is the bride/The sun shines on her face.' She is not black because she is in darkness; rather 'her purity is fired/in the furnace of the sun.' When, as in the Magnificat, she humbles herself as the Lord's slave, she is freed from human slavery – 'the more she revealed the Master/who had purchased her freedom/and so was free of any other'. The more she embraces her identity as a creature, the darker she becomes, and the more beautiful: 'In the sun's divine light/all creatures are dark;/but their beauty grows/as they draw closer to him.'[56] In another work, a novena for the feast of the Annunciation, Juana has the Virgin Mary soar upwards as an eagle: 'Hail, Hail, Queen of birds … Teach us like the eagle who teaches her chicks by flying above them. Inspire the flight of our contemplation so that we may drink in the rays of the sun of justice.'[57]

John of the Cross and the discovery of night

A cultural shift

Back in Europe, in the latter part of the sixteenth century, a cultural shift occurred that has been spotted by art historians. Painters such as Caravaggio developed a new use of chiaroscuro where darkness takes on a new significance, so that areas of light in the picture – such as the figure of Christ in *The Call of St Matthew* – gain a new prominence.[58] This was part of a larger trend in religious culture, in which darkness and night took on a new positive significance. This cultural shift was not the result of technological progress. The most radical change in the experience of night would come some centuries later with electric light. In fact, the nocturnal culture of the early modern era resembled that of the Middle Ages more than it resembles ours. The night could be dangerous, but also a time of tranquility uniquely suited to prayer and study. Thomas More, for instance, rose habitually in the middle of the night for this purpose. The middle of the night was often valued as a special peaceful time in the daily rhythm. Only in the eighteenth century did people cease to speak habitually of the first and second sleep.

With his Dark Night of the Soul, John of the Cross (1542–91) gave a new impetus to the symbol of good darkness we saw in Origen and Dionysius the Areopagite. Anglican and Lutheran writers also expressed positive thoughts and feelings about night, in milieus outside the influence of the Spanish Carmelite. According to John Donne (1572–1631), 'churches are best for prayer, that have least light: / To see God only, I go out of sight, / And, to 'scape stormy days, I choos an Everlasting night'.[59] Welshman Henry Vaughan (1621–95) drew on Dionysius the Areopagite for 'The Night', a poetic meditation on Nicodemus's nocturnal encounter with Christ in John's Gospel: 'There is in God (some say) / A deep, but dazzling darkness.' The scene is night, at the sacred shrine of the Virgin, where believers receive doubly reflected light, like glow worms receiving sunlight from the moon. The night is not a time of separation from God, but paradoxically a privileged time to meet the Sun of Justice who comes with healing in his wings (Mal 4.2): 'Most blest believer he! / Who in that land of darkness and blind eyes / The long expected healing wings could see, / When thou didst rise, / And what can never more be done, / Did at mid-night speak with the Sun!'

A poet of the night

Writing on the same Dionysian trajectory as Vaughan, John of the Cross effected a shift in spiritual symbolism. He was a poet of genius. The first people to hear his *Canticle* recited, the Carmelite nuns in Beas, were enthralled and pleaded with him to write a commentary on the verses they found so captivating[60]:

> the tranquil night
> at the time of the rising dawn,
> silent music,
> sounding solitude,
> the supper that refreshes, and
> deepens love.[61]

In his poetry and prose, John gave a new version of the traditional symbol of divine darkness, his Dark Night of the Soul, which he presents as an exciting discovery like the new worlds opened by European adventurers. Nine months' incarceration in a small dark cell at the Carmelite monastery in Toledo in 1577–8 fed into the symbol of a Dark Night, as did the delights of the fresh Spanish night after the heat of the day. Night was not just a prelude to dawn, but a distinct reality, irreducible and positive, and he used the symbol of the Dark Night for all the stages of the spiritual life from initial ascetical effort to advanced mystical union. Nocturnal imagery came to occupy a central place in Catholic spiritual theology.

Night and sun

Far from having a nocturnal lifestyle, John would in fact walk up to thirty miles a day under a hot sun, and solar imagery reflects this experience. To those who find what he says incredible (about the Dark Night for example), he replies that the Father of lights (Jas 1.17) 'is not closefisted but diffuses himself abundantly as the sun does its rays … always showing himself gladly among the highways and byways'.[62] While sinfulness obstructs the divine light like a smudgy window cutting out daylight,[63] the more somebody grows in holiness, the more they are exposed to actual sunlight, and 'The sun so obscures all other lights that they do not seem to be lights at all when it is shining, and instead of affording vision to the eyes, it overwhelms, blinds, and deprives them of vision since its light is excessive and unproportioned to the visual faculty'.[64] For John, this blinding effect of the direct sun is the 'ray of darkness' of Dionysius that renders human beings sightless like an owl or a bat in broad daylight.[65]

What he terms 'dark contemplation' is a painful purification sometimes experienced as a loving illumination. 'Then the soul, like one who has been unshackled and released from the dungeon and who can enjoy the benefit of spaciousness and freedom, experiences great sweetness of peace and loving friendship with God in a ready abundance of spiritual communication.'[66] While Irish monastic poets left their dark cells to write in broad daylight, and Francis of Assisi wrote his Canticle after emerging into the light of morning at San Damiano, when John of the Cross was 'unshackled and released from the dungeon' in Toledo, it was at night and he went out into a night 'more lovely than the dawn'. John insists that the imagery of darkness is at the service of light: 'Even though this happy night darkens the spirit, it does so only to impart light concerning all things.'[67] The night, however, has more symbolic weight than the sun. If the sun shines, it is to reveal treasures that have been gained in nocturnal darkness – when it shines on the surface of the sea revealing pearls and other treasures in the depths, 'in spite of the excellence of this illumination, it gives no increase to the soul; it only brings to light what was previously possessed so she may have enjoyment of it'.[68]

As we enter the modern era, solar imagery, vibrant in the new world, has not disappeared in the old world, but it is weakened. A Catholic terminological guide to mysticism written in 1640 has entries for 'night', 'dusk' and 'midnight', but none for 'dawn', 'day' or 'sun'.[69] The fourteenth-century Middle English work *The Cloud of Unknowing*, a treatise on mysticism in the tradition of Dionysius the Areopagite, would enjoy a far wider diffusion in the twentieth century than it did in the Middle Ages. A list of keywords to characterize the tenor of Catholic thought on mysticism in the late twentieth and early twenty-first centuries would certainly include 'cloud', 'darkness' and 'night'. 'Light' would probably be included, but not 'day' or 'sun'.

Thomas Traherne

A theological aesthetic

Thomas Traherne (1636–74) was a seventeenth-century Anglican clergyman whose book of meditations, *Centuries,* was described by C. S. Lewis as one of the most beautiful prose works in the English language.[70] He died while still in his thirties, leaving behind a body of work which, except for one polemical tract, was only published in the early twentieth century. He is often seen as a nature mystic, but as more of his unpublished works come to light, it becomes clear that his primary identity is that of a mainstream Christian spiritual writer, and more particularly an Anglican theologian in the Calvinist tradition, influenced by the Renaissance Neoplatonists.[71] The world is God's metaphorical body: 'The world is that body, which the Deity hath assumed to manifest His Beauty and by which he maketh Himself as visible, as it is possible He should.'[72] Creation spoke to Traherne: 'The world resembled his eternity, / In which my soul did walk; / And ev'ry thing that I did see / Did with me talk.'[73] He was following John Calvin's teaching on how creation makes the invisible God visible: 'In respect of his essence, God undoubtedly dwells in light that is inaccessible; but as he irradiates the whole world by his splendour, this is the garment in which He, who is hidden in himself, appears in a manner visible to us.'[74]

'Things strange yet common'

Traherne's theology of nature speaks to us today. His voice is a distinctive one: 'The *Centuries* are ecstatic, autobiographical, repetitive and rich.'[75] As he began to write *Centuries*, he wanted to communicate a sense of wonder at the marvels that are everywhere in daily life: 'An empty book is like an Infant's Soul, in which anything may be written. It is capable of all things, but containeth nothing. I have a mind to fill this with profitable wonders.'[76] He invites us to attend to 'things strange yet common, incredible, yet known; most high, yet plain; infinitely profitable, but not esteemed'.[77] He had a natural feel for nature – he recounts how, when he was a child, 'It was a difficult matter to persuade me that the tinseled ware upon a hobbyhorse was a fine thing.'[78] But his vision is essentially theological, and not exclusively rural. Urban scenes, too, had their visionary gleam: 'Eternity was manifest in the Light of the Day, and something infinite behind everything appeared: which talked with my expectation and moved my desire. The city seemed to stand in Eden, or to be built in Heaven.'[79]

As Traherne looked at the world, the sun had a special place: 'The sun must burn and cannot choose but shine; / Remove its rays, / Remove its all. It doth itself refine, / Promote, delight, exalt, and clothe with praise, / It crowns itself by shedding forth its rays.'[80] Daylight was a particular source of joy:

> The riches of the Light of the Works of God which are the portion and inheritance of His sons ... the Light and the Day, great and fathomless in use and excellency, true, necessary, freely given, proceeding wholly from His infinite love. As worthy as they are easy to be enjoyed: obliging us to love Him and to delight in Him, filling us with gratitude, and making us to overflow with praises and thanksgivings.[81]

Solar practices

Traherne's appreciation of nature was not just a personal inclination. It was nourished with disciplined, systematic meditation and, like Gertrude the Great of Helfta in the Middle Ages, he proposed practices: 'Place yourself therefore in the midst of the world, as if you were alone, and meditate upon all the services which it doth unto you. Suppose the Sun were absent; and conceive the world to be a dungeon of darkness and death about you: you will then find his beams more delightful than the approach of Angels.'[82] He advises his readers: 'Having once studied these principles you are eternally to practise them. You are to warm yourselves at these fires, and have recourse to them every day. When you think not of these things you are in the dark. And if you would walk in the light of them, you must frequently meditate.'[83]

Focusing on the sun shining directly on to blades of grass, he noticed how each one was 'wholly illuminated' by the sun, 'as if it did entirely shine upon that alone'.[84] This insight is original but, at the same time, profoundly traditional. We can associate it with a traditional analogy identified by Katheryn Tanner: 'Like the light of the sun, God's light remains just as it is, undiminished and undivided no matter how many partake of it.'[85] There is a family resemblance, for instance, between Traherne and the fourth-century Basil of Caesarea, who insists:

> He [God] is present to each in his fullness, and in his fullness is present everywhere. He is divided, but does not suffer by the division; all share in him, but he remains whole, like a sunbeam whose kindly influence benefits each creature as though it were present to that creature alone, and shines over land and sea and dissolves in the air.[86]

For Traherne, in reading the Book of Nature, the response of the reader is part of the meaning of the text. According to poet Elizabeth Jennings, the key to the *Centuries* is the statement, 'For God hath made you able to create worlds in your own mind which are more precious unto him than those which He created.'[87] The work of meditative imagination, with its resulting patterns of thought and feeling, is rooted in the real. These are not vain musings that have no real contact with the universe as it is. Words, images, metaphors and feelings track reality and are not stepping-stones or stages, something to be rejected one by one for a loftier vision. His writing is an exercise in the art of accumulation, not of relegation or disposal. In Traherne's view, the whole universe is permeated by God and so all things are sacred. 'It was His wisdom made you need the Sun. It was His goodness made you the sea. Be sensible of what you need, or enjoy neither. Consider how much you need them, for thence they derive their value.'[88]

Conclusion

In the modern era, it was above all science-based technology rather than the Renaissance or the Reformation, or indeed heliocentrism as such, that would later change the experience of sun and its light. Traditional solar rhetoric continued, and sun-symbolism found new visual expressions in paraliturgical contexts such as Benediction of the Blessed Sacrament. Pierre de Bérulle re-expressed solar images in a post-Copernican world, while the inculturation of Christianity in the world of the Aztecs shows how a creative re-moulding of solar motifs is both necessary and possible in new contexts. With John of the Cross, a new expression of Dionysian good darkness would come to mark Western Catholicism. Although John continued traditional sun imagery, his Dark Night lodged in the Western spiritual imagination, but without a corresponding attention to light and sun. Thomas Traherne's closely observed account of a Christian experience of sunlight is a precious resource for re-balancing the symbolism of light and darkness.

Notes

1. J. M. Roberts, *The Penguin History of the World* (London: Penguin, 1997), p. 1109.
2. Valerie Shrimplin, *Michelangelo, Copernicus and the Sistine Chapel: The Last Judgement Decoded* (Saarbrücken: Lap Lambert Academic Publishing, 2013), pp. 42–3.
3. Elisabeth Schröter, 'Der Vatikan als Hügel Apollons und der Musen. Kunst und Panegyrik von Nikolaus V. bis Julius II.', *Römische Quartalschrift für christliche Altertumskunde und Kirchengeschichte* 74 (1979), pp. 208-40 (234-40). Over a century later, Urban VIII (pope 1623-44) had a fresco of the morning sun, a family emblem, painted in the papal apartments. See Stella P. Revard, 'Christ and Apollo in the Seventeenth-Century Religious Lyric', in *New Perspectives on the Seventeenth-Century English Religious Lyric* (ed. John R. Roberts; Colombia and London: University of Missouri Press, 1994), pp. 143-67 (147).
4. François Rabelais, *The Complete Works of François Rabelais* (trans. Donald M. Frame; Oakland: University of California Press, 1992), p. 741.
5. Marsilio Ficino, *Liber de Sole*, in *Opera, vol. 1* (Basel: Henric Petrina, 1576), p. 966. ET Thomas S. Kuhn, *The Copernican Revolution: Planetary Astronomy in the Development of Western Thought* (Cambridge, MA: Harvard University Press, 1996), p. 129.
6. Louis Dupré, *Passage to Modernity: An Essay in the Hermeneutics of Nature and Culture* (New Haven and London: Yale University Press, 1993), p. 202.
7. Tommaso Campanella, *La città del sole: dialogo poetico = The City of the Sun: A Poetical Dialogue* (trans. Daniel J. Donno; Berkeley, Los Angeles and London: University of California Press, 1981), pp. 108-11.
8. Herbert Butterfield, *The Origins of Modern Science: 1300-1800* (London: Bell and Hyman, 1957), p. vii.
9. J. L. Heilbron, *The Sun in the Church: Cathedrals as Solar Observatories* (Cambridge, MA and London: Harvard University Press, 1999), p. 22.
10. Seb Falk, *The Light Ages: A Journey of Discovery* (London: Allen Lane, 2020), pp. 90, 293.
11. Terence L. Nicholls, *The Sacred Cosmos: Christian Faith and the Challenge of Naturalism* (Eugene, OR: Wipf and Stock, 2009), pp. 42–3.
12. Falk, *The Light Ages*, p. 23.
13. Pascal, *Pensées*, no. 230. Blaise Pascal, *Pensées and Other Writings* (trans. Honor Levi; Oxford: Oxford University Press, 2008), p. 66.
14. Frédéric Tixier, *La monstrance eucharistique: genèse, typologie et fonctions d'un objet d'orfèvrerie (xiii–xvi siècle)* (Rennes: Presses Universitaires de Renne, 2014), p. 155, n. 346.
15. Thomas F. O'Meara, OP, *Theology of Ministry* (Mahwah, NJ: Paulist Press, 1999), p. 116.
16. Pierre de Bérulle, 'Discourse on the State and Grandeurs of Jesus' 2.1. ET *Pierre de Bérulle and the French School: Selected Writings* (ed. William M. Thompson; trans. Lowell L. Glendon, SS; New York and Mahwah: Paulist, 1989), p. 115.

17 Ibid. 10.1. ET p. 152.
18 Ibid. 2.2. ET p. 115.
19 Ibid. 2.2. ET p. 116.
20 Ibid. 2.2. ET p. 117.
21 Charles E. O'Neill, SJ, '*Acatamiento*: Ignatian Reverence in History and Contemporary Culture', *Studies in the Spirituality of Jesuits* 8.1 (1976), pp. 2–41 (7).
22 *Spiritual Exercises* 237. Saint Ignatius of Loyola, *Personal Writings: Reminiscences, Spiritual Diary, Select Letters, including the texts of The Spiritual Exercises* (trans. with introductions and notes Joseph A. Munitiz and Philip Endean; London: Penguin, 1996), p. 330.
23 Ignatius of Loyola, 'Reminiscences/Autobiography' 29. *Personal Writings*, p. 26.
24 *Personal Writings*, p. 93.
25 Sylvie Robert, *Les chemins de Dieu avec Ignace de Loyola* (Paris: Editions Facultés Jésuites de Paris, 2009), p. 72.
26 H. Pfeifer, 'Iconografia', in *Ignazio e l'arte dei gesuiti* (ed. Giovanni Sale, SJ; Rome: La Civiltà Cattolica, 2003), pp. 171–206 (171).
27 Maurizio Gronchi, *La cristologia di S. Bernardino da Siena: l'imago Christi nella predicazione in volgare* (Bologna: Marietti, 1992), p. 194.
28 Iris Origo, *The World of San Bernardino* (London: Jonathan Cape, 1963), p. 118.
29 Ibid., p. 119.
30 Tixier, *La monstrance eucharistique*, p. 25.
31 Ibid., p. 137.
32 John M. McDermott, 'Soleil', in *Dictionnaire de spiritualité ascétique et mystique, doctrine et histoire, vol.14* (eds M. Viller et al.; Paris: Beauchesne, 1990), pp. 981–99 (996).
33 Gaspar Druzbicki, SJ, *Meta Cordium Cor Jesu* (repr., Lviv: Ludova, 1875), pp. 57–8.
34 Pierre-Julien Eymard, *La sainte eucharistie: la présence réelle, vol. 1* (Paris: Librarie Eucharistique, 1950), pp. 270–1. ET 'Eucharist: sacrament of life'. Available online: http://www.ssscongregatio.org/index.php/en/about-us/the-founder/feast-day-liturgy (accessed 22 December 2020).
35 Patrick Kavanagh, 'Lough Derg', in *Collected Poems* (ed. Antoinette Quinn; London: Penguin, 2005), p. 91.
36 Seamus Heaney, 'In Illo Tempore', in *New Selected Poems 1966-1987* (London: Faber and Faber, 1990), p. 206.
37 Pope Francis, Homily Chiapas, Mexico, 15 February 2016. Available online: https://w2.vatican.va/content/francesco/en/homilies/2016/documents/papa-francesco_20160215_omelia-messico-chiapas.html (accessed 23 April 2020).
38 Mark R. Francis, CSV, *Local Worship, Global Church: Popular Religion and the Liturgy* (Collegeville, MN: Liturgical Press, 2014), p. 106. Fernando Cervantes, *Conquistadores: A New History* (London: Allen Lane, 2020), pp. 200–24.
39 This symbolic realism has continued in contemporary US Latino religious culture: Roberto S. Goizueta, 'The Symbolic Realism of U.S. Latino/a Popular Catholicism', *Theological Studies* 65.2 (2004), pp. 255–74.
40 Louise M. Burkhart, 'The Solar Christ in Nahuatl Doctrinal Texts of Early Colonial Mexico', *Ethnohistory* 35.3 (1998), pp. 234–56 (235).
41 Ibid., pp. 239, 249.
42 Ibid., pp. 250.
43 Ibid., pp. 245.
44 Ibid., p. 252.

45 Andrew Laird, 'Nahua Humanism and Political Identity in Sixteenth-century Mexico: A Latin Letter from Antonio Cortés Totoquihuatzin, Native Ruler of Tlacopan, to Emperor Charles V (1552)', *Renaissance Forum* 10 (2016), pp. 127–72 (158). Available online: http://www.renaessanceforum.dk/10_2016/06_laird_nahua_humanism.pdf (accessed 23 April 2020).

46 In Latin America, we see 'the emergence of religious cultures that were neither a covert survival of pre-Hispanic religions nor a pessimistic surrender to conquest. They were Christian cultures fed by the vibrant liturgical imagination of people who used indigenous metaphors, symbols and values to encourage a rich transfusion of Christian message into the very essence of each local culture.' Cervantes, *Conquistadores*, pp. 351–2.

47 'Anthropologically, syncretism is a quality of cultural change that is largely inevitable. At no point in time is there ever a pure Christianity. It has never existed and never will.' Gerald A. Arbuckle, *Culture, Inculturation, and Theologians: A Post-modern Critique* (Collegeville, MN: Liturgical Press, 2010), p. 184. Cervantes, *Conquistadores*, p. 223.

48 Jaime Lara, 'A Meaty Incarnation: Making Sense of Divine Flesh for Aztec Christians', in *Image and Incarnation: The Early Modern Doctrine of the Pictorial Image* (eds Walter S. Melion and Lee Palmer Wandel; Leiden: Brill, 2015), pp. 109–36 (132).

49 Jaime Lara, *Christian Texts for Aztecs: Art and Liturgy in Colonial Mexico* (Notre Dame, IN: University of Notre Dame Press, 2008), p. 197. Missionaries invoked similar counsels given by Gregory the Great to Augustine of Canterbury: Cervantes, *Conquistadores*, pp. 209–10.

50 Lara, *Christian Texts for Aztecs*, p. 197.

51 Ibid., p. 198.

52 D.K. Jordan (trans.), *Readings in Classical Nahuatl: Nican Mopohua: Here It Is Told* (University of California San Diego, n.d.), n.p. Available online: https://pages.ucsd.edu/~dkjordan/nahuatl/nican/NicanMopohua.html (accessed 24 April 2020).

53 Henry Shea, SJ, 'Inculturation and the Guadalupana', *Lumen et Vita* 6.1 (2015), n.p. Available online: https://doi.org/10.6017/lv.v6i1.9146 (accessed 24 April 2020).

54 Luis de Santa Theresa, sermon published in 1683: Francisco Raymund Schulte, OSB, *A Mexican Spirituality of Divine Election for a Mission: Its Sources in Published Guadalupan Sermons, 1661–1821* (Rome: Gregorian University, 1994), p. 100.

55 Sor Juana Inés de la Cruz, 'Loa to Divine Narcissus: An Allegory', Sc. 1, lines 1–9. ET *Sor Juana Inés de la Cruz, Selected Writings* (trans. and introduction by Pamela Kirk Rappaport; Mahwah, NJ: Paulist Press, 2005), p. 69.

56 Sor Juana Inés de la Cruz, '*Villancico* VII for the Feast of the Conception of Mary, 1689', in ibid., pp. 47–8.

57 Sor Juana Inés de la Cruz, 'Devotional Exercises for the Nine Days before the Feast of the Most Pure Incarnation of the Son of God, Christ Our Lord', in ibid., p. 186.

58 Craig Koslofsky, *Evening's Empire: A History of the Night in Early Modern Europe* (Cambridge: Cambridge University Press, 2011), p. 46.

59 John Donne, 'A Hymn to Christ, At the Author's Last Going into Germany'.

60 John of the Cross, *The Collected Works of Saint John of the Cross* (trans. Kieran Kavanagh, OCD and Ottilio Rodriguez, OCD; Washington, DC: ICS Publications, 1991), p. 465.

61 *The Spiritual Canticle* 14. *Collected Works*, p. 46.

62 *The Living Flame of Love*, 'Stanza1' 15. *Collected Works*, p. 646; see also 'Stanza3' 47. *Collected Works*, p. 692.

63 *The Ascent of Mount Carmel* 2.5.6. *Collected Works*, p. 164.

64 Ibid. 2.3.1. *Collected Works*, p. 157.

65 *The Dark Night* 2.5.3. *Collected Works*, pp. 401–2.
66 Ibid. 2.7.4. *Collected Works*, p. 408.
67 Ibid. 2.9.1. *Collected Works*, p. 412.
68 *The Spiritual Canticle*, 'Stanzas 20 & 21' 14. *Collected Works*, p. 557.
69 Maximilian van der Sandt, SJ, *Pro Theologia Mystica Clavis Elucidarium, Onomasticon Vocabulorum et Loquutionum Obscurarum* (repr., Heverlee-Louvain: Éditions de la Bibliothèque SJ, 1963).
70 'I'm re-reading Traherne's *Centuries of Meditations* which I think almost the most beautiful book (in prose, I mean, excluding poets) in English.' *They Stand Together: The Letters of C.S. Lewis to Arthur Greeves (1914–1963)* (ed. Walter Hooper; London: Collins, 1979), p. 492.
71 He refers, for example, to Pico Mirandola: Thomas Traherne, *Centuries* (London and Oxford: Mowbray, 1960), 4.74 and 4.78, pp. 204, 206.
72 Ibid., 2.20, p. 65.
73 Thomas Traherne, 'Wonder', lines 5–8. Available online: https://www.poetryfoundation.org/poems/45418/wonder-56d22507c0b42 (accessed 24 April 2020).
74 John Calvin, *Commentary on the Book of Psalms, vol. 6* (trans. James Anderson; repr., Grand Rapids, MI: Baker Book House, 1989), p. 145, quoted Belden C. Lane, 'Thomas Traherne and the Awakening of Want', *Anglican Theological Review* 81.4 (1975), pp. 651–64 (661, n. 31).
75 Denise Inge (ed.), *Happiness and Holiness: Thomas Traherne and His Writings* (Norwich: Canterbury Press, 2008), p. 24.
76 Traherne, *Centuries*, 1.1, p. 3.
77 Ibid., 1.3, p. 3.
78 Ibid., 3.9, p. 114.
79 Ibid., 3.3, p. 110.
80 Thomas Traherne, 'Activity 1', in *Commentaries of Heaven: The Poems* (ed. D. C. C. Chambers; Salzburg: Institut für Anglistik und Amerikanistik, 1989), p. 15. English modernized.
81 Traherne, *Centuries*, 1.35, p. 17.
82 Ibid., 2.7, p. 59.
83 Ibid., 3.94, p. 216.
84 Thomas Traherne, *Christian Ethicks* (ed. George Robert Guffrey and general introduction and commentary by Carol L. Marks; Ithaca, NY: Cornell University Press, 1968), p. 40.
85 Katheryn E. Tanner, 'The Use of Perceived Properties of Light as a Theological Analogy', in *Light from Light: Scientists and Theologians in Dialogue* (eds Gerald O'Collins, SJ and Mary Ann Myers; Grand Rapids, MI and Cambridge, UK: Eerdmans, 2012), pp. 122–30 (129).
86 Basil of Caesarea, *De Spiritu Sancto* 9.22. PG 32. 109. ET *Divine Office*, vol. 2, p. 671.
87 Elizabeth Jennings, *Every Changing Shape: Mystical Experience and the Making of Poems* (Manchester: Carcanet, 1996), p. 86.
88 Traherne, *Centuries*, 1.46, p. 22.

Part II

REVIVAL

Chapter 6

REVIVING SOLAR SYMBOLISM

In Part II we explore how to recapture and re-express light and sun symbolism. Because there are no general studies to guide us, this task is exploratory. In this chapter we look first at the theological and spiritual symbolism of natural sun and light, and what can be learnt from the more balanced symbolism of light and darkness in the Eastern churches. Then we turn to the expression of solar symbolism in metaphors.

Towards a natural theology of sunlight

Reading the Book of Nature

At the end of his *Paradiso,* Dante gazes into the divine light and sees the multiple leaves that make up the universe: 'bound up and gathered in a single book'.[1] His metaphor of a single-volume Book of Nature is all the more telling given the difficulty and cost of medieval bookbinding – he never saw the whole of his *Divine Comedy* bound together. Pope Francis urges us to re-open this Book of Nature traditionally read alongside the Book of Scripture.[2] It is a metaphor with a long history. Evagrius of Pontus (345–99) has Anthony the Great assert: 'My book is the nature of creatures, and this book is always in front of me when I want to read the words of God.'[3] For Hugh of St Victor (1096–1141), the universe is an illuminated manuscript written by the finger of God. With the Fall, however, human beings could no longer read it and healing is needed.[4] Alan of Lille (*c.* 1128–1202/3) added other metaphors: every creature of the world is a book or picture for us, and a mirror.[5] In the modern era, Galileo reserved reading the world to the highly numerate: the world is written in the language of geometry and without this a person is lost in a dark labyrinth.[6] This contrasts with Augustine's contention that the world is a book that even the illiterate can read, a perspective that did not die out in the Middle Ages: Sir Walter Raleigh (1552–1618) in his *History of the World* conceives the world as God's language, 'whose Hieroglyphical Characters are the unnumbered stars, the sun and moon written on those larger volumes of the firmament',[7] and for Sir Thomas Browne (1605–82), it is a 'universal and public Manuscript'.[8]

Natural theology

Hans Urs von Balthasar and Henri de Lubac thought that theological symbols prominent in the early church should be revived.[9] Light and sun are such symbols. Alister McGrath suggests a renewed 'natural theology'. This is not an attempt to prove the existence of God, but to be open to the world as it is – as well as asking what scripture and tradition warrant and enable, it is a matter of seeing and noticing, of asking what phenomena 'signify, intimate, or disclose'.[10] If we want to follow these paths indicated by Balthasar, de Lubac and McGrath, we can aspire to a 'second naivety' and let sun and light speak for themselves. As the poet Wallace Stevens put it: 'You must become an ignorant man again / And see the sun again with an ignorant eye.'[11]

A natural theology of sunlight involves attending to art and architecture as well as discourse. The cathedral of Sagrada Familia in Barcelona provides a fine example. On Sunday 7 November 2010, Pope Benedict celebrated a Mass of dedication. In his homily, he says of the cathedral, 'it stands as a visible sign of the invisible God, to whose glory these spires rise like arrows pointing towards absolute light and to the One who is Light, Height and Beauty itself'.[12] Travel writer John Giuffo recounts his reactions to the cathedral:

> Light pours in from windows and electric lights positioned at the top, giving the impression of the sun's rays poking through a forest canopy ... And oh, those windows! Climbing two stories high, they punctuate the walls on both sides, and let in splashes of color that seem to dye the white walls around them. There are other windows, high above the main altar, that let in rich white sunlight, and climb to the top of the altar space to a summit that pours a bath of light down onto the proceedings below. In short, the church uses light in one of the most impressive displays I've ever seen.[13]

East and West

A church breathing with two lungs

The church needs to breathe with both lungs, drawing on both its Eastern and Western traditions.[14] It is no accident that, In *Laudato si*, his encyclical on the care of the planet, Pope Francis acknowledges his debt to Patriarch Bartholomew of Constantinople.[15] Eastern churches have continued cosmic emphases of the patristic era, maintaining the biblical symbolic balance of light and darkness more closely than the modern West with its keen interest in the secondary imagery of darkness and cloud. All the same, there is no dichotomy between an Eastern theology of light and a Western theology of darkness – it is rather a question of striving for an optimal balance.[16] Orthodox theologian Olivier Clément has some simple advice for Western Christians: 'The "contemplation of nature" can give spiritual flavour to our lives even if we lay no claim to be in any way "mystics" in the rather particular sense that this word has acquired in the West.' This is the opposite of the esotericism we will examine later in this chapter. As Clément puts it, 'A little loving attention and the light of the Risen Christ is enough.'[17]

A recent work in the Western tradition

In *The Joy of God*, Sister Mary David Totah draws on Eastern traditions. She has two chapters entitled 'Darkness' and 'Light'.[18] Light and darkness are complementary:

> Clouds and rain go to the making of a rainbow, as well as sunlight ... We may be under a cloud, but if we turn our gaze on the Sun of Justice we shall see his arc against the dark background of our sorrow, and the more we turn to him the greater shall our comfort be.[19]

Classic sun symbolism retains its place, with light the predominant symbol and sun imagery secondary. She takes up John of the Cross's metaphor of sinfulness as a dirty window excluding the sunlight, as well as Thérèse of Lisieux's image of a weak bird looking in the direction of the divine Sun it no longer sees,[20] while adding a touch from a world marked by Edison's light bulbs: 'Only when all our lights are off can we grasp the divine light in all its purity.'[21]

Eastern influence is clear in her treatment of deification and the light of the Transfiguration. She quotes Bernard of Clairvaux to the effect that the brightness of a person's heart can be manifest in their appearance. For Sister Mary David, 'the glory he describes is not just metaphorical. The faces and bodies of holy people shine visibly with divine light'.[22] Bernard lists actions, words, looks, movements, gestures, habits and even laughter as manifesting the inner self,[23] but laughter and words are not, in fact, literally luminous. The distinction Sister Mary David is working with is not between a metaphor and a literal statement, but between a metaphor and a true statement: 'The light of the age to come is an existent reality, not a mere metaphor.'[24] We can, indeed, talk about somebody being radiantly healthy or happy. Equally, spiritual dispositions can manifest themselves in a person's appearance. But that is not to say that healthy or holy people are literally luminous.

Sister Mary David gives Valentine Zander's account of the Russian Seraphim of Sarov (1754–1833) shining like the sun: 'Then I looked at the Staretz and was panic-stricken. Picture, in the sun's orb, in the most dazzling brightness of its noon-day shining, the face of a man who is talking to you.'[25] This is a putative paranormal light phenomenon analogous, for example, to the stigmata of Pio of Pietrelcina (1887–1968) in the Western tradition. Such rare phenomena are in principle empirically verifiable and descriptions of them are literal, not metaphorical. For Valentine Zander, as the snow fell on the two of them, Seraphim literally shone with the light of the sun. This is untypical of solar epithets applied to people, which are almost universally metaphorical – as when, for example, Thomas Merton described citizens of Louisville, Kentucky as shining like the sun.[26] To revive solar symbolism, giving more attention to physical light and sun is a more promising way forward than looking at other people or (as we will see later in this chapter) looking within ourselves. We will return to the distinction between literal and metaphorical discourse in Eastern and Western spiritual theology in Chapter 8.

Sense experience and spiritual perception

'Spiritual senses'

A tradition of talking in terms of 'spiritual senses' goes back to Origen.[27] There is, however, no single, evolving doctrine of spiritual senses down the centuries, but rather a wide variety of descriptions of interaction with God in terms of metaphors drawn from the senses of sight, smell, hearing, taste and touch. For Aquinas, there are no spiritual senses distinct from the operations of intellect and will.[28] This seems convincing – examples of putative spiritual senses turn out to be metaphorical descriptions of varieties of knowing and willing. When reading Jn 4.14, for instance, referring to an inner spring of water 'gushing up to eternal life', we are not tempted to imagine a literal inner dampness or wetness. By contrast, we can easily imagine that descriptions of an inner light are literal. In fact, they too are metaphorical.[29] On the account I am offering, seeing an interior light, and experiencing an impulse to compassion or forgiveness, could be two descriptions, one metaphorical and the other literal, referring to the same experience.

Hans Urs von Balthasar

Hans Urs von Balthasar (1905–88) uses the vocabulary of 'spiritual senses' to articulate a fresh account of spiritual perception. First, he resists a dualistic account of Christian experience where the bodily and the sensate have little place.[30] Secondly, he rejects an elitist view of spiritual perception that would make it the preserve of 'mystics'. Encountering God in the concrete experiences of everyday life is not something left behind as one advances spiritually.[31] Thirdly, he rejects 'a parallel set of spiritual sense faculties'.[32] I suggest that, in this, he is rejecting the sort of faculties described by Rudolf Steiner that feature in some New Age thinking, as we shall see later in this chapter. Finally, Christian experience, described in perceptual terms, is always oriented out of the self towards the other.[33] In a nutshell, Balthasar proposes a framework that is non-dualist, non-elitist, non-esoteric and non-solipsistic that can help us see how for a believer perceiving physical light can be a real experience of God.

This approach is illuminating but Balthasar couches it in terms of an inadequate distinction between the metaphorical and the literal. He postulates five distinct senses that are not 'merely metaphorical'[34]; they are, in Mark McInroy's terms, transformed versions of the ordinary perceptions of the body. We must ask what a transformed physical perception can amount to if not a variety of physical perception. I suggest that Balthasar's account suffers from a blurred distinction between the literal and the metaphorical. He is proposing that metaphors of perceiving God in sensate terms are, in effect, a subset of literal statements. An ordinary perception of light, however, even in some transformed version, cannot be a literal perception of God who is invisible. When poet Patrick Kavanagh writes of farmers seeing God the Father when sun shines between the branches of a tree,[35] what is seen literally is sunlight.

Balthasar's general approach to metaphor is problematic. He tries to invest literal statements like 'God changes' with features proper to metaphorical statements, insisting that there can be change in God, a non-creaturely change, and that we can say this because this literal statement is quasi-metaphorical.[36] This ends up reducing God to the status of a creature. By the same token, investing metaphorical statements about sensate perception of God with features proper to literal statements – they are not 'merely metaphorical' – ends up elevating the object of perception, the sun in our example, to the status of the divine. This is, of course, the last thing Balthasar would want to do. He wants to say that sense experience can be a real experience of God, but at the same time he holds that to be cognitively respectable statements must be more than 'merely metaphorical'. Fortunately, this arguably defective approach to metaphor can be jettisoned and his basic account of meeting God in concrete perception (of sunlight for instance) remains intact.

Idolatry and the esoteric

A short story by John McGahern concretizes a discussion often couched in abstract terms. In 'The Wine Breath', he describes how for a priest a particular quality of evening light evokes a memory from thirty years earlier when 'never before or since had he experienced the Mystery in such awesomeness'.[37] And yet 'all that was there was the white light of the lamp on the open book, on the white marble; the brief sun of God on beechwood, and the sudden light of that glistening snow, and the timeless mourners moving towards the yews on Killeelan Hill almost thirty years ago'.[38] This is a description of a religious experience of light. The perceived light is numinous but there is nothing esoteric about it. There is no need to invoke a distinct 'spiritual sense' to explain how the light visible to everyone can be described as 'the brief sun of God on beechwood'.

Some currents of New Age or esoteric thought provide a helpful contrast with the position I am developing. Rudolf Steiner (1861–1925) continues to have a wide influence, especially in circles espousing 'theosophy' or 'anthroposophy'. For him, under Constantine 'Christianity assumed the form which denies the sun', and Julian the 'Apostate' was a martyr to the ancient Mystery of the Sun.[39] Steiner rejected spiritualism and psychic research as a mistaken materialism of the spirit. He favoured instead developing organs of cognition that permit a distinct spiritual perception. 'The purest appearance of the outer physical body of the Logos is the light of the Sun. Sunlight is not only material light. To spiritual perception it is also the garment of the Logos.'[40] In this view, meditation techniques or esoteric practices can induce new perceptive faculties. To hold that to look at sunlight is to look at something that is literally the Logos is, however, to fall into the idolatrous sun worship condemned in the Bible and so troubling to Augustine and Leo. Distinct spiritual sense faculties are not necessary to give an account of the process of spiritual conversion: 'It is neither the case that the perfect have distinct and different sense-faculties from the rest, nor that the objects which come before them are somehow different.'[41] The light of the sun accessible to everyone can be for the believer a revealed symbol of the divine, and a rich source of metaphors for the person and saving activity of Christ.

Metaphors of light and sun

Light and darkness

Part of the task of theology is to distinguish between what is metaphorical and what is literal.[42] Most solar and light language about God or Christ is metaphorical. God and Christ are not literally solar, and light is predicated of God metaphorically. The Russian theologian Vladimir Lossky took a different view: the language of darkness is metaphorical, but the language of light is not: 'The theology of darkness – which was but a metaphor of a dogmatic truth – will give way to a theology of the uncreated light, a real element in mystical experience.'[43] This view does not stand up to scrutiny. Like darkness, light is metaphorical when applied to God. John Chrysostom, for instance, interprets light in the biblical statement 'You are the light of the world' as an intelligible light, superior to the rays of the sun, just as spiritual salt is superior to ordinary salt. He is not postulating a special variety of light, any more than he is saying that some sort of celestial or spiritual salt exists. Both light and salt are being used metaphorically.[44]

An interior sun

The language of introspection, for example, of perceiving an inner light, is metaphorical. Teresa of Avila's principal metaphor is a castle, with a variety of rooms. At the centre is His Majesty the Sun. His light penetrates all the rooms. The sun at the centre of the person is seen indirectly through its effects in the growth of virtues: 'A quantity of water could not fall on us unless it came from some source – so the soul feels certain ... that there is a sun whence this brilliant light streams forth from the interior of the spirit to its faculties.'[45] In this account, the metaphor of a sudden drenching is used to explain how virtues are, metaphorically, the rays of an unseen sun. The interior sun is not, for Teresa, an object of literal, physical vision. Similarly, with inverted commas around 'within', Elizabeth of the Trinity indicates that the solar image she uses and her introspection, are metaphorical: 'It is this intimacy with Him [the divine Three] "within" that has been the beautiful sun illuminating my life, making it already an anticipated Heaven.'[46]

How metaphor works

An illuminating fiction

By metaphor we mean 'the use of language to refer to something other than what it was originally applied to, or what it "literally" means, in order to suggest some resemblance or make a connection between the two things'.[47] A metaphor is an illuminating fiction, and for it to work it must be literally false. The metaphor 'The Lord is my rock' would disintegrate if there was an attendant claim that God's geology is unusual and 'God dwells in unapproachable light' would lose its force if it referred to a puzzle in physics. Aquinas gives examples of terms that can only be applied metaphorically to God, such as star, fire or sun. In his view, scripture uses base phenomena frequently to refer to God because there is no danger at all that they could be taken literally. A more 'noble' phenomenon such as the sun is used less frequently because it is just possible that simple people might think that the sun is literally God.[48]

Meaning and truth

We have no evidence of an Arian preacher comparing Christ to the sun.[49] Arians understood that to describe Christ as metaphorically the sun would count against their view of him as simply a high-level creature. Metaphors are used to make assertions – 'When I called you a rat I was speaking metaphorically, I didn't mean that you are a long-tailed rodent' is not much of an apology. Metaphors have cognitive content, but they cannot be translated into literal paraphrase without remainder. The metaphor of Christ the Rising Sun, for instance, is freighted with multiple connotations and with subliminal associations impossible to articulate fully in literal statements – metaphors can have an expressive power that literal utterances lack. The following text from a sixteenth-century Mexican polyphonic motet combines the imagery of sun and good darkness, in a dense expression of eucharistic faith: 'In that bread which hides Him / I saw my hidden Sun / … Seeing Him clearly does not take place in the heights / where one may ascend/but rather within the dark cloud / which embraces the brightest sun.'[50] At the same time, metaphor can be used to make a precise statement, as in Herbert McCabe's assertion: 'The sense in which I hold that the consecrated elements at the eucharist are *really* the body and blood of Christ is that they are not, except metaphorically, bread and wine anymore.'[51]

A different logic

According to Janet Martin Soskice, a study of a metaphor in Christian tradition 'would, in a great part, be a study of gloss upon gloss, use and re-use of the figures which comprise an interweaving of meaning so complex that the possible readings are never exhausted'.[52] We can think of the image of the eagle used by the Alexandrian *Physiologus,* by Hildegard of Bingen, Sor Juana Inés de la Cruz and Thérèse of Lisieux. Metaphors are freestanding and can be combined in a way that literal statements cannot. We can say that the Lord is a dark cloud and a shining sun, without any contradiction. In the same hymn, 'Splendor paternae gloriae', Ambrose refers to Christ as the sun itself and as a separate ray of sunshine. In literal discourse, this would be incoherent. Christ can be an amazing sun, a heavenly *sol mirabilis*, without contradicting the assertion that in the heavenly world the sun no longer shines.[53] Again, solar imagery used for Christ is applied to the Virgin Mary: when she was born the world was filled with light; she is a dawn; the Immaculate Conception is described with Transfiguration imagery – 'your garments are white as snow, your face shines like the sun'; her assumption into heaven is the sun rising at dawn, the *anatole*.[54] And yet at the same time, as part of the church, she has no light that is not a received, lunar light.[55] Without contradiction, then, metaphorically she shines with sunlight and she also shines with no light that is not just moonlight.

Plasticity and discipline

Sun and light are such basic features of the world that they mark just about every area of human life and culture.[56] When Shakespeare writes 'Juliet is the sun' and 'Anthony is the sun', he is highlighting quite different personal characteristics.[57] Even a single motif like the sun as all-seeing can receive quite different tonalities, as we can see in the following two snippets from works of fiction. 'At that exact moment, 6-0-0 the sun climbed over the skyline of oaks, revealing its full summer angry-God self. Its reflection flared across the river towards our house, a long, blaring finger aimed at me through our frail bedroom curtains. Accusing: *You have been seen. You will be seen.*' On the other hand, a young woman is working at the harvest: 'The scythe rises, falls, rises, falls, catches the sun across its blade and flicks the light back into my eye – a bright wink of God. I watch you, the scythe says, rippling through the green sea, catching the sun, casting it back to me.'[58]

Given this plasticity of solar symbolism, a critical awareness is called for. When solar imagery, even with a Christian colouring, is used outside Bible-based guidelines, the fluidity of meaning can increase exponentially, as we can see in William Blake: '"*You* never saw the spiritual Sun. I have. I saw him on Primrose Hill." He said, "Do you take me for the Greek Apollo?" "No!" I said. "*That* (pointing to the sky) that is the Greek Apollo, He is Satan."'[59] When, at a pageant in London in 1501 to welcome Katharine of Aragon for her marriage to Prince Arthur, one of the floats featured the Prince as the *Sol Justitiae*, we sense that something is awry.[60] For Don Cupitt, the symbol of the rising sun, the *anatole*, takes on quite a different significance from that given to it by Luke's Gospel – for Cupitt, the original, historical Jesus was a 'solar Jesus' as distinct the 'Catholic Jesus', the rigorous and otherworldly teacher he sees as superimposed in the Gospels. For the original Jesus, his followers 'should make themselves conspicuous: they should shine, they should let it all hang out, they should *radiate*'.[61] Solarity, in this view, describes joyous self-expression, a 'cosmic happiness' that is the equivalent of eternal life, the supreme good in Catholic Christianity.[62] For Cupitt, the New Testament symbol of a rising light, the *anatole*, represents an '*aporia*', as it is used both for Christ and for Satan, also known as Lucifer.⁶³

Fortunately, solar metaphors do not have to run out of control like this. Whereas for instance in the cult of Mithras there was such fluidity that it is difficult to speak about a single deity,⁶⁴ a framework of Bible-based doctrine and church institution favours rule-based creativity in the history of Christian sun metaphors. The Anglican priest and poet George Herbert (1593–1633) combines literary creativity and theological discipline. He continues traditional symbolism: in 'The Sacrifice', Christ in the Garden of Gethsemane exclaims: 'How with their lanterns do they seek the sun!/Was ever grief like mine?' The warmth and joy of the True Sun contrast with the physical sun: 'a willing shiner, that shall shine as gladly,/As frost-nipt sunnes look sadly'.⁶⁵ Reflecting on how to write good religious poetry, however, he admits that at times he found himself piling up metaphors for effect: 'My thoughts began to burnish, sprout, and swell.' In his flights of fancy, 'Nothing could seem too rich to clothe the sun,/Much less those joys which trample on his head.'⁶⁶ He felt the need for self-censorship.

Conclusion

Light and sun are revealed cosmic symbols of God and Christ that are prominent in the tradition of the Eastern church but have often been neglected in recent spiritual theology in the West. The resulting imbalance can be rectified by opening again the 'Book of Nature', letting the concrete realities of sun and daylight speak for themselves, in a renewed 'natural theology'. When solar symbolism is expressed in language, we must let metaphors be metaphors, giving full scope to their expressive power and their truth-bearing character.

Notes

1. Dante Alighieri, *The Divine Comedy*, Paradiso, 33. 86. ET Dante Alighieri, *The Divine Comedy*, p. 480. Prue Shaw, *Reading Dante: From Here to Eternity* (New York and London: Liveright, W.W. Norton & Company, 2015), p. 480.
2. Pope Francis, Encyclical Letter *Laudato sì* On Care for Our Common Home 84, 225. Available online: http://w2.vatican.va/content/francesco/en/encyclicals/documents/papa-francesco_20150524_enciclica-si.html (accessed 25 April 2020). See Denis Edwards, '"Sublime Communion": The Theology of the Natural World in Laudato sì, *Theological Studies* 77.2 (2016), pp. 377–91 (383–4). Giuseppe Tanzella-Nitti, 'The Two Books Prior to the Scientific Revolution', *Annales Theologici* 18 (2004), pp. 51–83.
3. Evagrius of Pontus, *Practicus* 92. Évagre le Pontique, *Traité pratique ou le moine* (trad., commentary and tables by Antoine Guillaumont and Claire Guillaumont; SC, 171; Paris: Cerf, 1971), p. 694. ET Olivier Clément, *The Roots of Christian Mysticism: Text and Commentary* (Welwyn Garden City: New City, 2015), p. 215.

4   Boyd Taylor Coolman, *The Theology of Hugh of St Victor: An Interpretation* (Cambridge: Cambridge University Press, 2010), pp. 86, 172–3.
5   Alan of Lille, *Rhythmus de Incarnatione Christi*. PL 210. 579.
6   Tanzella-Nitti, 'The Two Books Prior to the Scientific Revolution', p. 75.
7   Sir Walter Raleigh, *The History of the World*. Quoted Denise Inge (ed.), *Happiness and Wholeness*, p. 70.
8   Sir Thomas Browne, *Religio Medici* (1643). Quoted in Tanzella-Nitti, 'The Two Books Prior to the Scientific Revolution', p. 77, n. 57.
9   Kevin Mongrain, *The Systematic Thought of Hans Urs von Balthasar: An Irenaean Retrieval* (New York: Crossroad, 2002), pp. 5–6.
10 Allister E. McGrath, *Re-imagining Nature: The Promise of a Christian Natural Theology* (Oxford: Wiley Blackwell, 2017), pp. 7–8, 48.
11 Wallace Stevens, 'Notes Towards a Supreme Fiction', in *Selected Poems* (repr., London: Faber and Faber, 2010), p. 85.
12 Pope Benedict XVI, Homily of His Holiness Benedict XVI, Barcelona, Sunday, 7 November 2010. Available online: http://w2.vatican.va/content/benedict-xvi/en/homilies/2010/documents/hf_ben-xvi_hom_20101107_barcelona.html (accessed 22 April 2020).
13 John Giuffo, 'The Power of Light in La Sagrada Familia', in *Forbes*, 13 May 2011. Available online: https://www.forbes.com/sites/johngiuffo/2011/05/13/the-power-of-light-in-la-sagrada-familia/#774b356f603d (accessed 22 April 2020).
14 The image originated with Russian scholar Vjaceslav Ivanov (1866–1949). It was taken up by Pope John-Paul II in his encyclical *Ut unum sint* 54. Pope St John-Paul II, Encyclical Letter *Ut unum sint*. Available online: http://www.vatican.va/content/john-paul-ii/en/encyclicals/documents/hf_jp-ii_enc_25051995_ut-unum-sint.html (accessed 29 August 2020).
15 Pope Francis, *Laudato sì* 7–9.
16 See John Chryssavgis, *Light through Darkness: The Orthodox Tradition* (London: Darton, Longman and Todd, 2004).
17 Clément, *The Roots of Christian Mysticism*, p. 227.
18 Sister Mary David, *The Joy of God: Collected Writings* (London: Bloomsbury Continuum, 2019), pp. 118–34, 135–52.
19 Mother Janet Erskine Stuart, *Prayer in Faith: Thoughts for Liturgical Seasons and Feasts*, vol. 2 (ed. L. Kepple; London: Longmans, Green and Co., 1936), pp. 19–20. Quoted Sister Mary David, *The Joy of God*, p. 118.
20 Sister Mary David, *The Joy of God*, pp. 115, 135–6. For Thérèse's image, see below, p. 128. For John of the Cross, see above, p. 66.
21 Ibid., p. 128.
22 Ibid., p. 149.
23 Bernard of Clairvaux, *Sermons on the Song of Songs*, vol. 4 (trans. Irene M. Edmonds; Cistercian Fathers, 40; Collegeville, MN: Liturgical Press, 1980), p. 207. Cited *The Joy of God*, pp. 148–9.
24 Sister Mary David, *The Joy of God*, p. 149.
25 Valentine Zander, *St Seraphim of Sarov* (trans. Sister Gabriel Anne SSC; London: SPCK, 1975), pp. 90–1. Quoted Sister Mary David, *The Joy of God*, p. 149.
26 See below, p. 98.
27 Paul L. Gavrilyuk and Sarah Coakley (eds), *The Spiritual Senses: Perceiving God in Western Christianity* (Cambridge and New York: Cambridge University Press, 2012).

28 Richard Cross, 'Thomas Aquinas', in Gavrilyuk and Coakley, *The Spiritual Senses*, pp. 174–89.
29 Alleged preternatural phenomena such as apparitions or bilocation are interesting precisely because descriptions of them are literal.
30 Mark McInroy, *Balthasar on the Spiritual Senses: Perceiving Splendour* (Oxford: Oxford University Press, 2014), pp. 12, 121, 187.
31 Ibid., pp. 172–3.
32 Ibid., pp. 125.
33 Ibid., pp. 123–4.
34 Ibid., pp. 3–4, 20. He was probably influenced by Augustin Poulain's and Karl Rahner's view that spiritual senses are not metaphor but 'analogical'.
35 Patrick Kavanagh, 'The Great Hunger', in *Collected Poems* (ed. Antoinette Quinn; London: Penguin, 2005), p. 68.
36 Kevin Duffy, 'Change, Suffering and Surprise in God: Von Balthasar's Use of Metaphor', *Irish Theological Quarterly* 76.4 (2011), pp. 370–87.
37 John McGahern, 'The Wine Breath', in *Collected Stories* (London: Faber and Faber, 2014), pp. 178–87 (179).
38 Ibid., p. 187.
39 Rudolf Steiner, *The Sun-Mystery in the Course of Human History: The Palladium, A Lecture by Rudolf Steiner, Dornach*, 6 November 1921, *GA 20* (trans. D. S. Osmund; London: Rudolf Steiner Publishing Co., 1955). Available online: https://wn.rsarchive.org/GA/GA0208/19211106p01.html (accessed 25 April 2020).
40 Rudolf Steiner, *The Gospel of John* (Hudson, NY: Anthroposophic Press, 1984), n.p. Quoted in Arthur Zajonc, *Catching the Light: The Entwined History of Light and Mind* (New York and Oxford: Oxford University Press, 1995), p. 220.
41 Philip Endean, 'The Ignatian Prayer of the Senses', *Heythrop Journal* 31.4 (1990), pp. 391–418 (412).
42 N. T. Wright and Michael F. Bird, *The New Testament and Its World: An Introduction to the History, Literature and Theology of the First Christians* (London: SPCK, 2019), p. 174.
43 Vladimir Lossky, *In the Image and Likeness of God* (Crestwood, NY: St Vladimir's Seminary Press, 1974), p. 43.
44 John Chrysostom, *Homilia* 15.7. PG 57. 232. ET *Divine Office*, vol. 3, pp. 429–31.
45 Teresa of Avila, *The Interior Castle* 7.2.8. ET Teresa of Avila, 'The Interior Castle 7.1–2', in *The Essential Writings of Christian Mysticism* (ed. Bernard McGinn; New York: Random House, 2006), pp. 451–9 (457).
46 Elizabeth of the Trinity, *I Have Found God: The Complete Works, vol. 2: Letters from Carmel* (trans. Anne Englund Nash; Washington, DC: ISC Publications, 1995), p. 358.
47 Murray Knowles and Rosamund Moon, *Introducing Metaphor* (London: Routledge, 2006), p. 3.
48 Thomas Aquinas, *In 1 Sententiarum* 34.3.2; *S. Thomae Aquinatis Scriptum super Libros Sententiarum*, p. 500.
49 Andreas Merkt, *Maximus I. von Turin: Die Verkündigung eines Bischofs der frühen Reichskirche im zeitgeschichtlichen, gesellschaftlichen und liturgischen Kontext* (Leiden, New York and Cologne: Brill, 1997), p. 180.
50 *En aquel pan miré mi Sol* by Juan de Padilla (1605–73). ET Jaime Lara, *Christian Texts for Aztecs*, p. 199.
51 Herbert McCabe, *God Matters* (London: Chapman, 1987), p. 72.
52 Janet Martin Soskice, *Metaphor and Religious Language* (Oxford: Clarendon Press, 1987), p. 158.

53 'They will enter into glory / Where shines the true light of peace / Christ, the Amazing Sun.' *introibunt ad gloriam / ubi fulget vera pacis / lux christus, sol mirabilis.* Rabanus Maurus, *Carmina* 1.31. PL 112. 1619. Author's translation.
54 Birthday of the Virgin Mary, 8 September, morning prayer, antiphon 2, *Divine Office*, vol. 3, p. 238*; Our Lady of Lourdes, 11 February, morning prayer, Benedictus antiphon, *Divine Office*, vol. 1, p. 153*; Immaculate Conception, 8 December, evening prayer, antiphon 3, *Divine Office*, vol. 1, p. 30*; Assumption, 15 August, morning prayer, Benedictus antiphon, *Divine Office*, vol. 3, p. 195*.
55 Origen, *Homilia in Genesim* 1.5. PG 12. 150. From an early German miniature: 'The moon fosters the Sun, from whom she derives her light.' Hugo Rahner, *Greek Myths and Christian Mystery*, p. 167.
56 See Richard Cohen, *Chasing the Sun: The Epic Story of the Star That Gives Us Life* (London: Simon and Schuster, 2011).
57 Roger M. White, *The Structure of Metaphor: The Way the Language of Metaphor Works* (Oxford: Blackwell, 1996), pp. 192–3.
58 Gillian Flynn, *Gone Girl* (London: Phoenix, 2013), pp. 3–4; Hannah Kent, *Burial Rites* (Sydney: Picador Pan Macmillan, 2013), p. 104.
59 Bentley, G. E., Jr. (ed.), *Blake Records: Documents (1741–1841) Concerning the Life of William Blake and His Family* (New Haven and London: Yale University Press, 2nd edn, 2004), p. 698.
60 Sydney Anglo, 'The London Pageants for the Reception of Katharine of Aragon: November 1501', *Journal of the Warburg and Courtauld Institutes* 26.1/2 (1963), pp. 53-89. Hendrik Ziegler 'Sonne', in *Handbuch der politischen Ikonographie, vol. 2: Imperator bis Zwerg* (eds Martin Warnke et al.; Munich: C. H. Beck, 2011), pp. 358–65. Ernst H. Kantorowicz, 'Oriens Augusti – Lever du Roi', *Dumbarton Oak Papers* 17 (1963), pp. 117–77.
61 Don Cupitt, *The Last Testament* (London: SCM, 2012), p. 27, emphasis original.
62 Ibid., p. 132.
63 Ibid., p. 70.
64 Philippa Adrych et al., *Images of Mithra* (Oxford: Oxford University Press, 2017), p. 171; Claudia Brittenham, 'Quetzalcoatl and Mithra', in ibid., pp. 173–82.
65 George Herbert, 'Christmas'.
66 George Herbert, 'Jordan (2)'.

Chapter 7

RESOURCES FOR RECASTING

In this chapter we sample some resources for reviving solar symbolism. We ask what does contemporary astronomy reveal about the place of the earth and its sun in an unimaginably immense universe? From the earliest days of the church, Christians have prayed in accordance with diurnal rhythms. What does science teach us about these rhythms? We then turn to some complementary teachings of Popes Benedict and Francis before sampling a selection of monks and poets.

Science and technology: Challenges and opportunities

Astronomy

For the dramatist Luigi Pirandello (1867–1936), Copernicus rendered the universe meaningless: 'I can only repeat my usual motto: A curse on Copernicus.' In the play *The Late Mattia Pascal* (1904), Mattia finds himself 'on a little maddened grain of sand, which spins and spins and spins, without knowing why'.[1] By contrast, Pierre de Bérulle saw Copernicus as an opportunity. Can we say the same for the results of more recent research? Contemporary astronomy reveals a universe made up of unimaginable expanses of time and space. Our sun is around 4.6 billion years old and is one of 400 billion stars in the Milky Way Galaxy, which in turn is one of around 350 billion galaxies that we can presently detect. If our solar system were twenty-four hours old, *Homo sapiens* would have arrived six seconds ago.[2] While it is true that the sun is 'a star of typical mass, typical colour and luminosity, a middle-aged star',[3] the findings of astrophysics make our anthropic home on our blue planet even more remarkable. Mathematics is proving a means to re-enchant the world. 'The trick as an educated citizen of the twenty-first century is to realize that nature is far stranger and more wonderful than human imagination.'[4] Our planetary ecosystem, miniscule in cosmic terms, is what Pope Francis terms our common home. For astrophysicist Brian Cox, nothing is more remarkable than the fact that, as far as we know, this is the only place anywhere in any universe where love exists.[5] While cosmic light is stimulating for theologians as well as scientists,[6] our sun emerges as a very local and time-limited phenomenon fuelling all the processes of life on earth. As Richard Dawkins puts it, 'perhaps those ancient peoples would have worshipped the sun even more devotedly if they had realized just how much all life depends on it'.[7] It is this sun and our experience of its light on its third planet that furnishes the metaphors for God and Christ that are the subject of the present work.

Chronobiology

It is technology, however, that impacts most forcefully on how we live. In 1880, the Edison Electric Light Company in New York began marketing electric light bulbs.[8] The benefits of Thomas Edison's innovation have been incalculable, but there are downsides to our technological advances. Many city dwellers can no longer see the stars at night. In 2007, the UNESCO La Palma Declaration presented an unpolluted night sky as an inalienable human right.[9] Access to the light of the sun is an even more fundamental right. More than anything, it is electric light that has revolutionized our way of living the cycle of night and day.

In 2017, the Nobel Prize for Physiology and Medicine was given to three American scientists for their research on circadian rhythms synchronized with twenty-four-hour light–dark cycles. Reinforcing light–dark patterns is beneficial to health – natural daylight and sunshine during the day, and a night as dark as possible.[10] As the author of a survey of scientific research on circadian rhythms put it, 'we evolved on a rotating planet, when day was day and night was night: it's time to reconnect with those extremes'.[11] From a Christian perspective, such a reconnection can also give renewed access to the God-given symbolism of night and day.

Ray Bradbury, Fahrenheit 451

The science fiction writer Ray Bradbury describes a dystopia of slavery to visual displays in his 1953 novel *Fahrenheit 451*. It is a futuristic nightmare world where the main character is a fireman, Guy Montag, whose task is not to extinguish fires but to burn books and any houses that contain them. Suicide and murder are common. People are entertained and distracted by huge screens on their living room walls projecting endless soap operas. One night, Montag meets a mysterious young woman, Clarisse McClennan. She does things that are considered subversive and insane, such as delighting in nature. Montag asks her how old she is. 'Well', she said, 'I'm seventeen and I'm crazy … Isn't this a nice time of night to walk? I like to smell things and look at things, and sometimes stay up all night, walking, and watch the sun rise'.[12] Bradbury's nightmare world seems more menacing now than when he imagined it in the middle of the twentieth century. Perhaps he was also prescient in his instinct that at least a partial antidote for the cultural terrors he pictures can be found in simple contemplative practices. Clarisse walks at night, observes the night sky and waits for the coming of dawn.[13]

Dietrich Bonhoeffer

Science and electric light have made the night less threatening. In the short-lived (1935–7) illegal seminary of the Confessing Church at Finkenwalde, the

Lutheran theologian Dietrich Bonhoeffer (1906–45) meditated on the beginning of the Christian day: 'Christ is the "Sun of righteousness" who has risen upon the expectant congregation (Mal. 4.2).' For Bonhoeffer, 'the early morning belongs to the church of the risen Christ'.[14] He asks how can we recapture the morning feelings of our Christian forebears given that we no longer have their fear of the darkness and the night. With his insistence on prayer in the morning, Bonhoeffer gives a very traditional answer to his modern question:

> For Christians the beginning of the day should not be burdened and haunted by the various kinds of concerns they face during the working day. The Lord stands above the new day, for God has made it. All the darkness and confusion of the night with its dreams gives way to the clear light of Jesus Christ and his awakening Word. All restlessness, all impurity, all worry and anxiety flee before him. Therefore, in the early morning hours of the day may our many thoughts and our many idle words be silent, and may the first thought and the first word belong to the one to whom our whole life belongs. 'Sleeper, awake! Rise from the dead, and Christ will shine on you (Eph. 5.14).'[15]

Pope Benedict XVI

Theology of light: Joseph Ratzinger

In the early sixties, Joseph Ratzinger analysed Christian light symbolism.[16] Light captures aspects of the dialogue between God and human beings – in the Bible, light is linked with word, the latter having the priority.[17] Light and darkness are not ultimate cosmic principles, as in Zoroastrianism or the Manicheism of the early Augustine, but rather historical and moral categories. Symbolically, darkness comes when parts of creation turn in on themselves, and away from God. This is negative darkness. Christian experience of God involves a tension between the symbolism of God as light in whom there is no darkness (1 Jn 1.5) and the (good) darkness of the divine cloud. Early Christianity took over symbols from the pagan world, such as the journey of the sun from west to east during the night which was demythologized and used to symbolize Christ's journey into Hades.

Ratzinger repeatedly emphasized cosmic aspects of the liturgy.[18] For Augustine, darkness is turning away from God (*aversio a Deo*). We have here some roots of Ratzinger's emphasis on direction in liturgy which expresses, for him, the link between the personal and the cosmic. As to liturgical direction, 'there is only one inner direction of the Eucharist, namely, from Christ in the Holy Spirit to the Father. The only question is how this can be best expressed in liturgical form.'[19] Continuing research on east-facing direction as a liturgical form reveals less clarity over a longer period in the Western church than Ratzinger envisaged when he said that awareness of orientation was lost from at least the nineteenth century.[20] We will return to this question in the next two chapters.

Pope Benedict

On 21 December 2008, the winter solstice, Pope Benedict addressed the crowd in St Peter's Square, reflecting on solar aspects of the Piazza.[21] It was his predecessor Gregory XIII who introduced the modern 'Gregorian' calendar, and astronomy and prayer were linked in tradition, he said, with the time of the midday Angelus determined by the shadow of the obelisk functioning as a meridian. The following year, 2009, would be the Year of Astronomy, four centuries after Galileo used his telescope in 1609. On 6 January 2009, the pope continued his reflections.[22] In the Middle Ages, the cosmos was read as a book in the light of the Reality Dante called the love that moves the sun and other stars. Today, he continued, if faith and reason work together, astrophysics can lead to a renewed grasp of the significance of the universe.

In his seven Easter Vigil homilies from 2006 to 2012, Benedict presents themes we have seen in the Bible and in patristic tradition. In 2007, he meditates on the descent of Christ among the dead, when the Lord brings light to the gloom of Hades. As the icons of the Eastern church show, Christ enters the world of the dead, clothed with light. For Benedict, Christ descends into the abyss of our modern age, and 'by his death he now clasped the hand of Adam, of every man and woman who awaits him, and brings them to the light'.[23]

Benedict wrote most of Pope Francis's first encyclical *Lumen Fidei*. In its first paragraph, Christ is presented as the True Sun, with quotations from Justin Martyr and Clement of Alexandria:

> The pagan world, which hungered for light, had seen the growth of the cult of the sun god, *Sol Invictus*, invoked each day at sunrise. Yet though the sun was born anew each morning, it was clearly incapable of casting its light in all of human existence. The sun does not illumine all reality; its rays cannot penetrate to the shadow of death, the place where men's eyes are closed to its light. 'No one – Saint Justin Martyr writes – has ever been ready to die for his faith in the sun'. Conscious of the immense horizon which their faith opened before them, Christians invoked Jesus as the true sun 'whose rays bestow life'.[24]

Benedict suggests that unless we constantly turn to the true light, life loses its shape and direction, and breaks down into disconnected desires. 'Idolatry, then, is always polytheism, and aimless passing from one lord to another.'[25] This rings true. In the fifth century, Pope Leo saw turning to the sun as a danger for Christian faith. At the beginning of the twenty-first century, when idolatry and polytheism are lived out on the technological treadmill of screens and mobile devices, giving renewed attention to the sun could be a partial antidote.

Pope Francis

Laudato sì: *Sir Brother Sun*

'Beyond the sun' is the title of the final, eschatological section of Pope Francis's encyclical *Laudato sì*, named after Francis of Assisi's *Canticle of Brother Sun*.[26]

In eternity, there will be no need of the sun (Rev. 21.23). The 'infinite light' of the risen Christ will illumine all things and the present role of the sun will have ended.[27] In the present dispensation, the risen Christ penetrates the world as light (as in the solar IHS on Francis's escutcheon). To perceive the presence of Christ, the spiritual sun, in our present world, we need to cultivate a new way of seeing, without our constructions and projections.[28] The physical sun, Sir Brother Sun, is just there; it is given to us; we do not control it.[29]

The Book of Nature

Creation is a book, according to Francis, and nature is filled with words of love. To learn to read this Book of Nature, a childlike sense of wonder is called for. 'The ideal is not only to pass from the exterior to the interior to discover the action of God in the soul, but also to discover God in all things.'[30] Francis is re-balancing a spirituality that can be self-preoccupied and inward-looking. St Bonaventure insists that contemplation favours meeting God in other creatures, and, in the words of Sufi mystic Ali al-Khawwas, 'there is a mystical meaning to be found in a leaf, in a mountain trail, in a dew drop, in a poor person's face'.[31] People need access to beauty, and real contact with people and nature as distinct from virtual reality. To live properly, we must respect the rhythms inscribed in our nature by the hand of the Creator.[32] These aspirations expressed by the pope are widely shared by believers and non-believers. For D. H. Lawrence, they are attainable: 'The machine has no windows. But even the most mechanised human being has only got his windows nailed up, or bricked in.'[33]

The sun shines in the city: Carlos María Galli

In his Apostolic Letter *Evangelii Gaudium*, Francis claims that a new urban culture is developing. 'We need to look at our cities with a contemplative gaze', discerning the presence of God.[34] If we follow the pope's suggestion, we witness increasing global urbanization and, in the words of Mircea Eliade, for many people in the modern city, 'the cosmos has become opaque, inert, mute; it transmits no message, it holds no cipher' and even for believing Christians, it is no longer felt as the work of God.[35]

For Carlos María Galli, Argentinian theologian and long-time collaborator of Pope Francis, to appreciate Francis's concerns, we need to look not only to Assisi but also to Buenos Aires, the metropolis where he was archbishop for fifteen years. God and Christ are present in a variety of analogous ways: in human faces and in nature (city parks have a special significance), and in the often negative realities of city life.[36] The divine 'Sun' is always shining, even if so many forms of dying block the view.[37] Even when the sky is clouded over, or the sun is obscured by buildings towering above, it is there, shining.[38] God allows himself to be seen in the deep shadows of urban violence, poverty and individualism.

For Galli, the 'Sun' shines in a special way precisely when his light is absent.[39] This is a common theme in Christian solar symbolism. John McGahern recounts how at Easter my mother always showed us the sun. "Look how the molten globe and all the glittering rays are dancing! The whole of heaven is dancing in its joy that Christ is risen." When Easter arrived with overcast skies and we asked for the sun, she assured us it was dancing behind the clouds. Blessed are those who have not seen but have believed.[40]

For Sister Mary David Totah, 'the sun is there even on a cloudy day; we may not see the light at a certain moment but we know we *have* seen it. We have known it once, and at times that will have to satisfy'.[41]

Francis's Argentinian theological advisor quotes Pope John XXIII opening the Second Vatican Council: 'Dawn has hardly broken, and already the first rays of the rising sun are warming your hearts.' For Pope Francis, the church is the *mysterium lunae*, the mystery of the moon reflecting the light of the sun. According to Galli, if the church can focus on the 'Sun of Christ', the conciliar dawn that Pope John spoke about will give way to the splendour of noonday, and the light of Christ will transform the church and the world.[42]

A selection of hymns

Ancient and Modern

Ancient and Modern is a standard collection of current English hymnody, with many hymns dating from the centuries following the Reformation. Traditional light and solar symbolism continues, with for instance three English versions of the ancient evening light hymn the *Phos Hilaron*.[43] Overall, as is to be expected, it is light language that is most prevalent, with solar symbolism appearing intermittently throughout the volume, for example, in 'Sun of my soul, thou Saviour dear' and the popular contemporary hymn 'Colours of day dawn into my mind', where solar motifs occur in each of the three strophes.[44]

The first two lines of the first hymn in the collection evoke the natural phenomenon of the sun – 'Awake, my soul, and with the sun / thy daily stage of duty run'. (Thomas Ken [1637–1711])[45] – while the first strophe of the second hymn in the anthology rehearses the ancient themes of Christ the Sun of Justice and the *Anatole*, the dawn sun who rises from on high:

> Christ, whose glory fills the skies,
>   Christ, the true, the only light,
> Sun of Righteousness, arise,
>   triumph o'er the shades of night;
> Dayspring from on high, be near;
> Day-star, in my heart appear. (Charles Wesley [1707–88])[46]

Charles Wesley, the brother of John Wesley, the founder of Methodism, can be confidently called the most significant hymn-writer in the modern English-speaking world. His 'Hark the Herald Angels Sing', which first appeared in 1739, remains one of the most loved Christmas carols:

> Hail the heav'n born Prince of Peace!
> Hail the Sun of Righteousness!
> Light and life to all He brings,
> Ris'n with healing in His wings.[47]

Mal 4.2, the Old Testament verse taken up with such enthusiasm by the Christians of Alexandria as expressing solar messianism, was clearly not forgotten in eighteenth-century England. Neither was the patristic appropriation of pagan imagery to articulate Christian faith – in his hymn 'God of unexampled grace', written in 1745 (it does not appear in *Ancient and Modern*), Wesley describes Christ on the cross:

> Dies the glorious Cause of all,
>   The true eternal Pan,
> Falls to raise us from our fall,
>   To ransom sinful man:
> Well may *Sol* withdraw his light,
>   With the Sufferer sympathize,
> Leave the world in sudden night,
>   While his Creator dies.[48]

George Matheson

George Matheson (1842–1906) was the author of 'O love that wilt not let me go'.[49] His personal history is important for the hymn's solar imagery. A minister in the Presbyterian Church of Scotland, he was a preacher of renown and prolific writer of theological and devotional books, including a volume of religious verse *Sacred Songs* (1904). While still a student, he became virtually blind. When he shared the fact that he was losing his sight with his fiancée, she replied that she could not spend her life married to a blind man. Matheson never married. His public prayers and sermons had wide appeal and, in a tradition where the term was not used frequently, a (laudatory) biographer described him as a 'mystic'.[50]

George Matheson was a virtually blind man whose first public sermon was on the significance of natural light.[51] In one of his devotional writings, he meditates on Mt 4.16 ('And for those who sat in the region and the shadow of death light has dawned'):

> What I want is light. It may be that when the light comes, I shall find that death needs no transforming. It may be, the sunshine will reveal it to be already a form of life. I want the sunshine; I want something to see by, something to judge by, something to read by. I do not ask that the valley should be made a mountain; I want light in the valley.[52]

In 'O love that wilt not let me go' Matheson presents a mysticism of darkness, light and sun:

> O light that followest all my way,
> I yield my flickering torch to thee;
> My heart restores its borrowed ray,
> That in thy sunshine's blaze its day
> May brighter, fairer be. ...
> I trace the rainbow through the rain,
> And feel the promise is not vain,
> That morn shall tearless be.

In John Bunyan's *The Pilgrim's Progress*, a significant influence on Matheson's biblical spirituality, Faithful has sunshine throughout his journey through the Valley of the Shadow of Death.[53] For Matheson sunshine in the valley is refracted in a rainbow of tears: 'And all its tears are rainbow bright/When Calvary crowns the way.'[54] He only changed one word in 'O love that wilt not let me go', at the insistence of the editors. Originally, 'I trace the rainbow through the rain' read 'I climb the rainbow through the rain'. The place of journey is the valley of Psalm 23, and for Matheson it is, at the same time, a cloud-covered Mount Sinai – 'Thy valley is our mountain height;/Within Thy cloud we see.'[55] Writing in a very different milieu from John of the Cross, Matheson arrives at a place not far from John's Dark Night and his Ascent of Mount Carmel.

He wrote his famous hymn in his manse at Innelan on the evening of 6 June 1882, when he was forty years old. His sister who had been his assistant throughout his adult life had married that day, and he was alone. He says simply that the hymn was the fruit of intense mental suffering known only to him. Matheson was no poet of the calibre of John of the Cross or George Herbert and he readily acknowledged that he had no natural gift of rhythm. However, this hymn was written in a few minutes. 'It was the quickest bit of work I ever did in my life,' he says. 'All the other verses I have ever written are manufactured articles; this came like a dayspring from on high. [see Lk 1.78]'[56]

'Dayspring of Eternity'

Lutheran hymns frequently invoke the Sun of Justice/Righteousness (*Sonne der Gerechtigkeit*), and the motif of the morning light appears frequently.[57] The hymn 'Morgenglanz der Ewigkeit', written by Christian Knorr von Rosenroth (1636–89), integrates traditional solar motifs and natural symbolism. This seventeenth-century composition became a favourite in the German Protestant hymnal, with different versions of the hymn appearing, and from the 1930s it was taken up by German Catholics. There are various translations into English such as 'Dayspring of Eternity, Brightness of the Father's glory' by John Henry Hopkins which has appeared widely in US hymnals. This is a translation of one contemporary German version:

Bright Dawn of Eternity
light from uncreated light,
Send your sunrays on our morning faces
With your might, drive out our night.
Let your dew fall, and our conscience stir.
Console us in the hardships of this life,
Make us, your people, truly alive.
Kill off our deeds of coldness with your lovely warmth.
May your dawn bring courage and new heart.
May we be truly risen before we depart at dusk.
O Sun that rises from on high,
Transfigure our bodies on the Last Day.
May our bodies, free from all ills,
Exult on that joyous path.
Shine on us in the next world,
O glorious Sun of grace.
Lead us through this valley of tears
To pastures green and joy eternal.[58]

Catholics and pagans

Carthusian monks

The Carthusians were founded in the eleventh century. Even though contemporary Carthusians can refer to yoga or psychoanalysis, their style has a certain timelessness, and they can describe their experience in terms of natural symbolism that is fresh and immediate. Distinctions between post-conciliar and pre-conciliar, or even between mediaeval and post-medieval, seem secondary. 'The cross stands still while the world turns' has been commonly used as a Carthusian motto since the nineteenth century.[59] Paradoxically, a relatively timeless way of life has as its de facto motto an expression that would have been inconceivable before the Copernican revolution.

Guigo de Ponte (died 1297) was a monk of the Grande Chartreuse. In Book Two of his *De Contemplatione*, he employs traditional symbolism enriched by a close observation of natural light and sun.[60] Sinners 'cannot see or sense the Sun of righteousness'. A second group can sense God's reality but cannot see the sun because their vision is obstructed by an opaque cloud. The ascetical path is one of clearing away the clouds of sin. The more the cloud covering thins out, 'the closer to the sun one's line of sight is'. A third group can make out the sun shining brightly but they cannot look at it directly because it is blinding. As the person approaches the Sun of Righteousness, the process of conversion touches deeper levels of the person, 'not only the flowers but also the roots of virtues'. Every now and then, the clouds divide for an instant, and they can glimpse 'the Sun of Righteousness, the true light who illumines every light in heaven and on earth'. Guigo is confident that one day he will be able to stare at God directly. It will be like viewing the rising sun in the morning: 'One can indeed see the sun clearly without being blinded by its brilliance – if one is in the open country early in the morning. That is how God is seen in heaven.'

Six hundred years after Giuigo de Ponte wrote his meditation on dawn, a modern Carthusian monk meditates on the same phenomenon:

> Such is truly the dawn of day; the rising of the Sun of Justice within the soul. As nature awakens and appears to come to life again with each dawn; as the truths of the spirit become luminous in the measure in which one discovers them, so the soul, enlightened by God, sees herself and all things in a new radiance.[61]

In another Carthusian work from the late twentieth century, a series of talks given to trainee monks, a novice master integrates the Dark Night of the Soul of John of the Cross into a wider pattern of light symbolism. He asks himself, 'How to pray? I no longer know how to pray. Why light a candle in broad daylight?'[62] There are two chapters on the Dark Night of the Spirit, the first of which ends with these words: 'Essential Love is not subject to observation. Its most beautiful triumphs are disguised beneath the thickest veil of mysterious and often painful darkness. This is how the love of Christ triumphed, and how the light of the resurrection appeared shining through the morning mist.'[63]

Thomas Merton (1915–68)

The Cistercian monk and writer Thomas Merton's best-known utterance on solar matters is marked by a monument in the centre of Louisville, Kentucky. The inscription recounts how, in 1958 at the corner of Fourth and Walnut, when he was on a shopping errand, he was at a loss how to communicate to his fellow human beings that they were 'walking around shining like the sun'.

In *The Seven Storey Mountain*, he recounts his unconverted experience of dawn as a young man in New York when he would find himself waiting at the Flushing bus station, returning home after an evening in a night club and a few hours on somebody's couch:

> The thing that depressed me most of all was the shame and despair that invaded my whole nature when the sun came up, and all the laborers were going to work: men healthy and awake and quiet, with their eyes clear, and some rational purpose before them. This humiliation and sense of my own misery and of the fruitless waste of what I had done was the nearest I could get to contrition. It was the reaction of nature.[64]

Some decades later, now a Trappist in the monastery of Gethsemane, he recounts experiences of the same time of day:

A spring morning alone in the woods. Sunrise: the enormous yoke of energy spreading and spreading as if to take over the entire sky. After that: the ceremonies of the birds feeding in the wet grass. The meadowlark, feeding and singing. Then the quiet, totally silent, dry, sun-drenched midmorning of spring, under the climbing sun … How absolutely central is the truth that we are first of all *part of nature*, though we are a very special part, that which is conscious of God.[65]

Sunrise is an event that calls for solemn music in the very depths of man's nature, as if one's whole being had to attune itself to the cosmos and praise God for the new day, praise Him in the name of all the creatures that ever were or ever will be. I look at the rising sun and feel that now upon me falls the responsibility of seeing what all my ancestors have seen, in the Stone Age and even before it, praising God before me. Whether or not they praised Him then, for themselves, they must praise Him now in me. When the sun rises each one of us is summoned by the living and the dead to praise God.[66]

Paul Murray (1947–)

We find the same morning impulse to praise shared with 'pagans' in Dominican poet Paul Murray:

This morning,
on entering the cold chapel,
   I looked first
to the sun, as the pagan does,
not by strict custom
nor by constraint, but because
   I too, as creature,
sense man's primitive emotion:
his need to praise
And so, like priest or pagan,
   according
as the sun moves, I perform
this ancient ritual.[67]

Conclusion

From the disparate resources we have sampled, new perspectives emerge on human life on planet earth. Science offers new possibilities for theology and spirituality. Recent studies in astronomy and chronobiology show that we are finely tuned to live in harmony with rhythms of light and darkness intimately linked with our sun, which is a miniscule, fleeting phenomenon in a universe of unimaginable expanses of time and space. In a perspective of faith, articulated in the Book of Genesis, the sun is there for us and the remarkable convergence of factors that make our human existence possible is part of God's plan. Popes Benedict and Francis present complementary resources for re-expressing traditional solar symbolism in this new context. Benedict brings traditional light and solar symbolism to bear on our present reality. In an increasingly urban and environmentally threatened world, Francis retrieves the symbol of the Book of Nature, urging the church to look outwards at other human beings and other creatures, with a call to conversion expressed in terms drawn from Francis of Assisi's *Canticle of Brother Sun*. We have also seen how traditional solar symbolism is given continued expression in the hymnody of different Christian confessions and how contemporary Christians sometimes register affinities with 'pagans' of the past as they find themselves in awe before 'Sir Brother Sun'.

Notes

1. Luigi Pirandello, *The Late Mattia Pascal* (trans. William Weaver; New York: The New York Review of Books, 2005), pp. 2–3.
2. Philip Judge, *The Sun: A Very Short Introduction* (Oxford: Oxford University Press), p. 141.
3. Ibid., p. 3.
4. Brian Cox and Andrew Cohen, *Human Universe* (London: William Collins, 2015), p. 31.
5. Cox and Cohen, *Human Universe*, pp. 3, 241.
6. O'Collins and Meyers, *Light from Light*, pp. 17–100.
7. Richard Dawkins, *The Magic of Reality: How We Know What's Really True* (London: Black Swan, 2012), p. 143.
8. Steven W. Lockley and Russell G. Foster, *Sleep: A Very Short Introduction* (Oxford: Oxford University Press, 2012), p. 120.
9. Unesco, et al., *Starlight: Declaration in Defence of the Night Sky and the Right to Starlight* (La Palma: Starlight Institute, 2007). Available online: http://www.archeoastronomy.org/downloads/starlightdeclarationc.pdf (accessed 26 April 2020).
10. Lockley and Foster, *Sleep*, pp. 132–3.
11. Linda Geddes, *Chasing the Sun: The New Science of Sunlight and How It Shapes Our Bodies and Minds* (London: Profile Books, 2019), p. 14.
12. Ray Bradbury, *Fahrenheit 451* (repr., New York: Simon and Schuster, 2012), p. 5.
13. See also de Certeau's treatment of 'walking in the city' as an act of cultural resistance: Michel de Certeau, *The Practice of Everyday Life* (Berkeley and Los Angeles: University of California Press, 1984), pp. 91–110.
14. Dietrich Bonhoeffer, *Works, vol. 5: Life Together: Prayerbook of the Bible* (ed. Geffrey B. Kelly; trans. Daniel W. Bloesch and James H. Burtness; Minneapolis: Fortress Press, 1996), pp. 48–9.
15. Ibid., pp. 51–2.
16. Joseph Ratzinger, 'Licht', pp. 44–54.
17. Pope Francis, Encyclical Letter *Lumen Fidei* 29. Available online: http://w2.vatican.va/content/francesco/en/encyclicals/documents/papa-francesco_20130629_enciclica-

lumen-fidei.html (accessed 26 April 2020). The encyclical was largely the work of Pope Benedict.
18 Joseph Ratzinger, *The Feast of Faith: Approaches to a Theology of the Liturgy* (trans. Graham Harrison; San Francisco: Ignatius Press, 1986); *The Spirit of the Liturgy* (San Francisco: Ignatius Press, 2000). Uwe Michael Lang, 'Benedict XVI and the Theological Foundations of Church Architecture', in *Benedict XVI and Beauty in Sacred Art and Architecture* (ed. D. Vincent Twomey, SVD and Janet E. Rutherford; Dublin: Four Courts Press, 2011), pp. 112–21.
19 Ratzinger, *The Feast of Faith*, p. 140.
20 Ibid., p. 142.
21 Pope Benedict XVI, Angelus 21 December 2008. Available online: http://www.vatican.va/content/benedict-xvi/en/angelus/2008/documents/hf_ben-xvi_ang_20081221.html (accessed 11 December 2020).
22 Pope Benedict XVI, Homily Epiphany 2009. Available online: 6 January 2009: Solemnity of the Epiphany of the Lord | BENEDICT XVI (vatican.va) (accessed 10 December 2020).
23 Pope Benedict XVI, Homily Easter Vigil 2007. Accessible online: 7 April 2007: Easter Vigil | BENEDICT XVI (vatican.va) (accessed 11 December 2020).
24 Pope Francis, *Lumen Fidei* 1.
25 Pope Francis, *Lumen Fidei* 13.
26 Pope Francis, *Laudato sì* 243.
27 Ibid. 83.
28 Ibid. 225.
29 Ibid. 228.
30 Ibid. 233. See Denis Edwards, '"Sublime Communion": The Theology of the Natural World in *Laudato sì*', pp. 383–4.
31 Ibid., Eva de Vitray-Meyerovitch (ed.), *Anthologie du soufisme* (Paris: Sindbad, 1978), p. 200.
32 Pope Francis, *Laudato sì* 43–7.
33 D. H. Lawrence, 'Pan in America', in *Phoenix: The Posthumous Papers of D. H. Lawrence* (ed. Edward D. McDonald; London: William Heineman, 1936). Quoted in *The Green Studies Reader: From Romanticism to Ecocriticism* (ed. Lawrence Coupe; London and New York: Routledge, 2000), p. 72.
34 Pope Francis, Apostolic Letter *Evangelii Gaudium* 71–3. Available online: http://w2.vatican.va/content/francesco/en/apost_exhortations/documents/papa-francesco_esortazione-ap_20131124_evangelii-gaudium.html (accessed 26 April 2020).
35 Mircea Eliade, *The Sacred and the Profane: The Nature of Religion* (New York: Harper & Row, 1961), pp. 178–9.
36 Carlos María Galli, *Dio vive in città: verso una nuova pastorale urbana* (Vatican City: Libreria Editrice Vaticana, 2014), pp. 19, 142, 165.
37 Ibid., p. 186.
38 Ibid., p. 176.
39 Ibid., p. 305.
40 John McGahern, *Memoir* (London: Faber and Faber, 2005), p. 11.
41 Sister Mary David, *The Joy of God*, p. 9.
42 Galli, *Dio vive in città*, p. 348.
43 Tim Ruffer, et al. (eds), *Ancient and Modern: Hymns and Songs for Refreshing Worship* (London: Hymns Ancient and Modern, 2013), nos. 17, 18, 20.

44 Ibid., nos. 23, 27.
45 Ibid., no. 1.
46 Ibid., no. 2.
47 Ibid., no. 66.
48 John and Charles Wesley, *Selected Prayers, Hymns, Journal Notes, Sermons, Letters and Treatises* (ed. Frank Whaling; London: SPCK, 1981), p. 253.
49 *Ancient and Modern*, no. 752.
50 D. Macmillan, *The Life of George Matheson* (London: Hodder and Stoughton, 1910), pp. 12, 186, 260.
51 Ibid., pp. 81–3.
52 George Matheson, *Searchings in the Silence: A Series of Devotional Meditations* (London: Cassell, 1895), p. 4.
53 John Bunyan, *The Pilgrim's Progress* (ed. N. H. Keeble; Oxford: Oxford University Press, 1998), p. 61.
54 George Matheson, 'The Solace of the Valley', in George Matheson, *Sacred Songs* (Edinburgh and London: William Blackwood and Sons, 1904), p. 86.
55 'The Christian Burden', in ibid., p. 38.
56 Comments originally published in the Church of Scotland magazine *Life and Work*, January 1883. Kenneth W. Osbeck, *101 Hymn Stories* (Grand Rapids, MI: Kregel Publications, 1982), p. 190.
57 Hans-Bernhard Schönborn, '*Die Morgenröte*: Eine Naturerscheinung in Literatur und Kirchenlied', *Jahrbuch für Liturgik und Hymnologie* 23 (1979), pp. 145–57.
58 Author's translation. The German text is available online: http://www.liederdatenbank.de/song/1671 (accessed 3 January 2020).
59 '*Stat Crux*'. See http://www.cartusiana.org/node/4943 (accessed 26 April 2020).
60 *Carthusian Spirituality: The Writings of Hugh of Balma and Guigo de Ponte* (trans. Dennis D. Martin; New York and Mahwah: Paulist Press, 1997), pp. 206–7.
61 *Where Silence Is Praise: From the Writings of a Carthusian* (trans. A Monk of Parkminster; London: Darton, Longman and Todd, 1997), pp. 59–60.
62 A Carthusian, *Interior Prayer: Carthusian Novice Conferences* (trans. Sister Maureen Scrine; Leominster: Gracewing, 2006), p. 11.
63 Ibid., p. 155.
64 Thomas Merton, *The Seven Storey Mountain* (London: Sheldon Press, 1975), p. 158.
65 Thomas Merton, *Conjectures of a Guilty Bystander* (London: Burns and Oates, 1968), p. 268.
66 Ibid., p. 256.
67 Paul Murray, 'Introibit', in Paul Murray, *Rites and Meditations* (Dublin: The Dolmen Press, 1982), p. 10.

Chapter 8

SACRED DIRECTION: ARE CHRISTIANS TO PRAY TOWARDS THE SUN?

Varieties of sacred direction

Muslims praying towards Mecca, Jews praying towards Jerusalem or Christians facing east for prayer are all examples of horizontal sacred direction. Direction can also be vertical, as when prayer is directed upwards or 'heavenwards', or inwards, for example, when rituals are performed with eyes closed and hands joined. When we use the expressions 'oriented' or 'orientation' in this chapter, we mean an eastward sacred direction, that is, facing the rising sun.

Ad orientem

The expression *ad orientem* (to the rising sun, dawn or east) represents a rare occurrence of solar vocabulary in contemporary theological discourse. It is used as a catchphrase for an arrangement of liturgical space where the celebrant of the eucharist faces the near side of the altar, in the same direction as the faithful. The Muslims in Abidjan airport mentioned in the Introduction took pains to direct their prayer geographically towards Mecca. Is orientation important for Christian private and liturgical prayer? In other words, is the east the Christian Mecca? Since Christian prayer is addressed to God, it is in a broad sense directional, in a way that Buddhist meditation for instance generally is not. In this chapter, we ask whether solar symbolism determines the posture adopted for personal prayer. The eucharist, the source and summit of Christian worship, has an intrinsically trinitarian direction: to the Father, through the Son, in the Holy Spirit. We ask whether solar symbolism figures in giving this fundamental direction concrete liturgical form.[1]

The direction of graves

Returning to the graveyard scene in John McGahern's novel *That They May Face the Rising Sun* that we saw in the Introduction, the body is mistakenly buried with the head in the east. For the body to face east, the head must in fact be buried in the west. You cannot help wondering whether McGahern had a Shakespearean scene in mind where there is the same confusion:

GUIDERIUS
Nay, Cadwal, we must lay his head to th' east;
My father hath a reason for't.
ARVIRAGUS
'Tis true.
GUIDERIUS
Come on then, and remove him.
    Cymbeline (act 4, scene 2).

Archaeological evidence from the pre-Constantinian era is scarce, and there is no evidence of the orientation of Christian graves in the Roman catacombs. Burying the deceased facing east developed in the fourth century.[2] A link was made between death and orientation – for instance, Gregory of Nyssa recounts that his sister Macrina's bed was turned to face east as she was dying[3] – and the fact that the cave where Christ was buried was thought to have been oriented may have been a factor.[4] Orientation seems to have become frequent for Christian burials without ever becoming an absolute requirement. As we will see with the orientation of churches and altars, the picture is mixed. In a seventh- or eighth-century Christian cemetery at Hartlepool, in North-East England, for instance, burial slabs with crosses and Christian inscriptions are all on a north/south axis rather than east/west.[5] The orientation of Christian graves became standard in the Middle Ages and continued, but sporadically.[6] In the sixteenth century, a certain Marco da Lisbona claimed to have found the body of St Francis of Assisi. To make his deception more credible, he had Francis seated in a chair facing east.[7] During the French Revolution, in 1794 Bishop Étienne-Charles de Loménie de Brienne died suddenly after being maltreated by revolutionaries. He was buried with little ceremony, but on an east/west axis. When his skeleton was discovered in 1943, the feet were in the west and the head in the east.[8] This could be the same confusion as in *Cymbeline* and in McGahern's burial scene. John McGahern witnesses to a practice never wholly forgotten but maintained with a persistently uncertain grasp of the symbolism involved. In this, it is typical of orientation in general. The symbolism of praying upwards, in contrast, is more straightforward.

Praying upwards

For the first Christians, and for contemporary Jews or 'pagans', the most natural position for prayer was out of doors, looking upwards or looking out through a door or window.[9] The prophet Daniel prays through an upper story window towards Jerusalem (Dan 6.10). In John's gospel, at the tomb of Lazarus and in his priestly prayer, Jesus looks upwards to the Father (Jn 11.41; 17.1), and in the Gospel of Mark he also looks up to heaven when healing a deaf and dumb man (Mk. 7.34). We find the same vertical prayer in the synoptic accounts of the miracle of the loaves and fishes described in strikingly eucharistic terms (Mt. 14.19; Mk 6.41; Lk. 9.16). Peter prays at noon on the roof of the house by the sea in Joppa, where he is lodging (Acts 10.9), while at Philippi a habitual place of prayer is by the side of a river (Acts 16.13). This practice of praying upwards continued in the early church. The Roman catacombs show Christians praying in the *orans* position, standing with arms outstretched, looking upwards. In the sixth-century apse mosaic of the Basilica of Sant'Apollinare in Classe, in Ravenna, St Apollinaris, bishop and martyr, prays with his hands raised vertically towards the heavenly cross above him.[10]

Oriented prayer

The early church

Like praying upwards, prayer facing the rising sun goes back to the earliest days of the church. The written evidence from around the beginning of the third century shows that it was widespread, with testimonies from Alexandria, Latin-speaking Africa and Asia Minor. The practice did not spring up suddenly in the final decades of the second century but neither did it have its origins in the Bible. It came from the general religious culture of the ancient world. Probably, early Christians took over a custom without much reflection and it was not mentioned before the beginning of the third century because it was not controversial.[11] Initially, it did not distinguish Christians from Jews. There is evidence of Jewish oriented prayer in the Book of Wisdom, written in Alexandria in the first century BCE (Wisd. 16.28). Jews may have come to focus on Jerusalem partly to distinguish themselves from the Christians[12] for whom orientation became a general practice. Origen insisted that oriented personal prayer 'in symbolic fashion as though the soul beheld the rising of the true light', even if facing a blank wall, is preferable to praying in another direction, even with a view upwards to the sky.[13] Christian orientation for private prayer seems to have been generally recognized without, however, becoming a strict universal obligation.

Accusations of sun-worship levelled against Christians because of oriented prayer, as Tertullian recounts at the end of the second century,[14] and remnants of idolatry among the Christian population, may account for the fact that, in the early centuries, a solar text such as Zech. 6.12 where East is a proper name did not figure in Christian justifications for praying to the east. It was one thing to use the metaphor of the True Sun or the Sun of Justice, and another to encourage bodily adoration of a man whose name was East.[15]

Christians often followed the traditional practice without knowing why. Origen says it would be difficult for people to say why they pray facing east just as they could not say why they genuflect.[16] According to Basil of Caesarea, 'thus we all look to the East at our prayers, but few of us know that we are seeking our own old country, Paradise, which God planted in Eden in the East'.[17] The practice was given various meanings, solar and non-solar (such as turning to the location of Eden), which came to form a loose symbolic cluster later summarized by John Damascene (676–749): orientation is an unwritten apostolic tradition, with a biblical warrant in the terms 'Sun of Justice' and *anatole*, and in Psalm 68, which (in the Greek version he used) has v. 34 referring to God riding in the heavens in the 'east'. In the book of Genesis, Eden our homeland is in the east, while in the Gospel of Matthew, Christ's second coming will be like lightning from the east.[18]

The Western church

Personal prayer facing east continued in the Middle Ages in the Latin church as well as in the East. An Arab chronicler of the Crusades recounts how a Muslim was saying his prayers when a crusader picked him up and unceremoniously dropped him down facing east, exclaiming: 'That is the way to pray!' Some other Templars apologized: 'He is a foreigner who has just arrived today from his homeland in the North, and he has never seen anyone pray facing any other direction than east.'[19] In the Middle Ages, orientation for prayer was maintained as a general principle in the Latin church and Aquinas lists four reasons why it is fitting to adore facing east: the daily movement of the heavens manifesting divine majesty is from that direction; it is the location of paradise; Jesus is called 'East'; and it is from there that he will return.[20] As we have seen, however, during the Middle Ages cosmic symbolism gradually weakened, with symbols interpreted in a forced or arbitrary way. The thirteenth-century liturgical codifier Durandus (*c.* 1237–96) argued, for instance, that orientation should be to the rising sun, not at the solstice as some argued, but at the equinox, because the church militant must conduct itself with equanimity, in bad and good times alike.[21] Even if it is difficult to say how widely personal orientation was practised in the Western Middle Ages, with time the practice declined.

At the same time, in his poem 'Good Friday 1613. Riding Westward' John Donne (1572–1631) is riding westwards from Warwickshire to Wales on Good Friday, but spiritually his direction is east: 'my soul's form bends towards the East'. On Good Friday, Christ's death caused earthquake and eclipse – 'It made His footstool crack, and the sun wink.' Donne knows he should be meditating on the death of Christ: 'There I should see a Sun by rising set, / And by that setting endless day beget.' Evidently, in the West a link between orientation and personal devotion had not disappeared without trace. But it did not survive the Middle Ages as a general practice – in Kashmir in India, a few years before Donne wrote his poem, Bento de Goes, a Portuguese Jesuit, had a quite different exchange with Muslims from that of the medieval crusader we saw earlier. When interrogated by the Sultan Mohammed, a descendant of Genghis Khan, who demanded what direction he faced when at prayer, he replied that he did not care about the direction as God is everywhere.[22]

Orientation in liturgy and church buildings

The early church

In the early church, it seems that the celebrant prayed facing east during the eucharist.[23] According to a third-century liturgical text from Syria, oriented prayer is 'required'.[24] Evidence about church buildings in the pre-Constantinian period is sparse. They were probably set up for prayer to the east, as we can see at Dura Europos in Syria, the site of the earliest extant Christian church building, but it is difficult to know how significant orientation was. Standard principles of building design, such as those given by Vitruvius (first century BCE), influenced the construction of synagogues and churches alike. In his *On Architecture*, Vitruvius had pagan temples constructed so that statues of the gods faced west with worshippers praying towards the east.[25] Greek temples, however, were frequently built with the façade in the east. Probably there was little of principle involved.[26] Christian church builders seem to have adopted the same approach. According to Sible De Blaauw, whether the apse was in the east or in the west was not significant.[27] Tertullian, at the beginning of the third century, compares a church directed to the rising sun (*ad lucem*) to a dovecote facing east, but he seems to have been talking about the eastern entrance of the church: 'Of our dove, however, how simple is the very home! – always in high and open places, and facing the light! As the symbol of the Holy Spirit, it loves the (radiant) East, that figure of Christ.'[28]

After Constantine, churches were generally constructed on an east/west axis.[29] Paulinus of Nola describes a church built on a north/south axis to face the graves of the martyrs, but he emphasizes that this is an exception to the normal practice. All the same, there were more departures from the norm in the Western church than in the Greek East. Churches in Rome itself have always had a variety of alignments, with the apse in the west predominating. In the century after Constantine, most basilicas constructed in the Latin church had the apse in the west and the façade in the east, as was the case at St Peter's and the Lateran Basilica in Rome, and the Holy Sepulchre in Jerusalem.[30]

It is often difficult to know what physical arrangements prevailed for worship in these buildings. When, in the Coptic rite, the deacon cried out at the beginning of the eucharistic rite proper, 'Look to the east!', we do not know whether the faithful moved physically or not. Equally, when Augustine ends sermons urging the faithful to pray having turned to the Lord – *conversi ad dominum* – this may have involved them physically changing direction.[31] It seems unlikely, however, that the faithful would have been required to turn their backs on the focal point of the altar at the most solemn moments in the liturgy. Again, we have seen how Pope Leo the Great criticized Christians for turning to reverence the rising sun before entering the Basilica of St Peter. It is unlikely that Roman Christians then turned their backs to the altar during the liturgy to face in the direction forbidden to them before they entered.

The Middle Ages and beyond

Orientation of churches continued into the Western Middle Ages. Churches in early medieval Ireland were oriented.[32] The only Parisian church in the early Middle Ages without the apse in the east was called *Benedictus male versus* – 'Benedict in the wrong direction'.[33] At the Catholic Shrine of Our Lady in Walsingham, in North Norfolk, England, the fourteenth-century Slipper Chapel is precisely oriented to the point on the horizon where the sun rises on the feast of St Catherine of Alexandria, the patron saint of the church, according to the Julian calendar.[34] This illustrates the pains sometimes taken in medieval Western Europe to orient churches precisely. In one and the same church building, however, Mass was often celebrated at different altars facing in different directions. As early as the sixth century, Gregory the Great notes without protest that the Bishop of Saintes in Gaul constructed a church with thirteen altars.[35] Walafrid Strabo, in the ninth century, pointed out that altars in St Peter's in Rome and in the Christianized Pantheon faced in many different directions, and argued that orientation was not therefore strictly obligatory.[36] Private masses became more common, celebrated on side altars, and high altars came to be modelled on the design of side altars. Altarpieces were often constructed behind the altar, thereby becoming a focus of attention. Apse windows in the east were sometimes filled in so that devotional frescos could be painted, such as those of Filippo Lippi in the cathedral of Spoleto in 1446.

In Italy, the east/west axis for church construction held until the end of the thirteenth century. From then on, urban churches of the mendicant orders were aligned without any reference to orientation. The early-fifteenth-century church of San Francesco in Arezzo was so constructed that the priest could only celebrate Mass with his back to the east. In Siena the cathedral has the altar in the east, but a fourteenth-century plan for a new cathedral has the cathedral on a north/south axis, which would have made the present cathedral into a transept. Overall, the direction of the altar was probably not important.[37] When, from the late fifteenth century, the pope celebrated Mass in the Sistine Chapel with its apse in the west, he did so facing west, with his back to the people. No solar symbolism was involved.

The sixteenth-century architectural authority Palladius taught that Christians were free as regards the alignment of churches and did not have to follow pagan ideas of orientation, and the ritual for the consecration of a church in the *Pontificale Romanum* of 1596 had no reference to orientation.[38] When Mass was celebrated in the modern era prior to the Second Vatican Council, usually immediately in front of a tabernacle, there was no sense of direction to the east. The proposal that the Mass be celebrated *ad orientem*, that is that the celebrant face in the same direction as the faithful, towards an altar usually aligned without any reference to orientation, has little to commend it in terms of solar symbolism.

An unstable symbolism

Orientation for burials, or in private or liturgical prayer, has not been a living solar symbol in common possession in the West since the late Middle Ages at the latest.

The Christian symbolic cluster around orientation inherited from late antiquity did not secure a permanent place there. To use a comparison from schoolboy chemistry, the cluster seems to have been more a mixture like sand and water than a unified chemical compound like copper sulphate. It had disintegrated by the sixteenth century, possibly because it was always a mixture of heterogeneous elements – Eden, the rising sun, the Second Coming and a venerable but little-understood custom. According to Robert Taft, even the Eastern churches never attached great significance to orientation as such. He never met a representative of Eastern Christianity who saw it as essential either for liturgy or for personal devotion. It was just taken for granted as an established practice. What Christians in the West can learn from the East, in his view, is to re-appropriate their own Western Christian identity that has been so eroded by secularization.[39]

Solar metaphors and interiority

The Western church

The Augustinian metaphor of looking inwards, developed by Gregory the Great, has shaped Western spirituality. The common custom of placing the apse in the west may have contributed, indirectly, to this inward turn and to a diminished reference to the cosmos, because an external physical reference point in the east was eliminated.[40] We have seen how Clement of Alexandria, for example, and more recently Teresa of Avila and Elizabeth of the Trinity speak in terms of a sun within the soul, and that the perception of an inner light or sun is metaphorical. Metaphorical descriptions have, however, sometimes been interpreted as if they were literal, in both Western and Eastern spiritual theology.

Modern Catholic spirituality frequently emphasizes darkness and inwardness, and it has often taken on a markedly psychological character. Sixteenth- and seventeenth-century spiritual writers focused increasingly on the psychology of religious experience. Taking over vocabulary from the Rhineland mystics, Francis de Sales (1567–1622) used the expression 'the fine point of the soul' to refer to a place in his psychological geography, whereas Eckhart had used it not to refer to an experience but to make an ontological statement.[41] For Francis, the fine point of the soul is something beyond the ordinary faculties of thinking and willing but involving some sort of interior perception. He compares it to the Holy of Holies in the Temple which the High Priest enters leaving behind the light of day. Francis almost finds himself in absolute darkness, but he does not close his eyes completely – there is some residual light.[42] This is a metaphor, but the detail given – eyes slightly ajar – invites the reader to see it as a literal description. Using similar terms, Jane Frances de Chantal (1572–1641) recounts how, after a spiritual experience of night and darkness, 'at dawn God made me taste, but almost imperceptibly, a small light at the fine point of my soul; the rest of my soul and the faculties did not experience it; but it only lasted about half the time of a Hail Mary.'[43] Again, a metaphor is presented as non-metaphorical. The precise timing given here – half the length of a Hail Mary – leaves the reader in no doubt that it is a literal account.

We saw in Chapter 5 how the emphasis on night in John of the Cross was part of wider cultural developments. Similarly, this emphasis on the inner self is of a piece with developments in philosophical thought in an era when René Descartes (1596–1650) would define the self as a *res cogitans*, a thinking thing, wholly distinct from the exterior material world of physical extension. Despite Francis de Sales's use of examples from nature in his *Introduction to the Devout Life*, there is a withdrawal from the world, and devotional language became more disincarnated and self-absorbed. There is movement in the direction of an 'acosmic piety'.[44] This movement inwards is taken a step further in the eighteenth-century work known as *Self-Abandonment to Divine Providence* first published in 1861. Formerly attributed to Jean-Pierre de Caussade, SJ, it is in the tradition of Francis de Sales and was clearly influenced by John of the Cross.[45] Traditional solar imagery continues in this work but metaphors of darkness and inwardness prevail over those of light and sun. Turning outwards to God's works in the cosmos and looking at the physical sun and sunlight is dismissed metaphorically as viewing the dim light of a watery sun. The introspection of Francis de Sales's image of half-closed eyes is taken further, the exterior world recedes, and eyes are now totally sightless:

> God is the fount of faith, a dark abyss from whose depths faith flows. All his words, all his works are, so to speak, only dim rays of that even more remote sun. We open our bodily eyes to see the sun and its rays, but the eyes of the soul, through which we see God and his works, are sightless. For here darkness takes the place of light, knowledge is ignorance, and not seeing we see.[46]

The Eastern church

We turn now to the metaphors of light and inward direction in some recent spiritual theology of the Eastern Orthodox churches. From the fourteenth century, theologians have spoken about seeing the uncreated divine light, especially in relation to the Transfiguration (where, in Matthew's account, Christ's face shines like the sun).[47] For Gregory Palamas (1296–1359), the light of Christ is not a divine attribute, not a phenomenal form through which God reveals himself, but is the 'unmediated presence of God himself'.[48] This unmediated presence is described in terms of a distinction between the uncreated essence of God and the uncreated energies by which he makes himself known. According to Kallistos Ware, 'light' is used literally (analogously) and not metaphorically, to refer to uncreated light in visions of the 'light of Tabor'.[49] This light was the subject of often polemical confrontation between East and West.

The Latin Catholic Church recognizes the richness of the Eastern traditions but has no official stance on Greek Orthodox teachings about the light of the Transfiguration. Catholic monastics and theologians do not question the claim to a real communion with the uncreated light. They tend to think that the experiences of prayer are fundamentally the same in East and West but that they are articulated in different symbolic and conceptual frameworks. 'The two mystic traditions – of darkness and of light – merely express in antithetical terms a spiritual experience that is fundamentally the same.'[50] Still, the conceptual frameworks cannot necessarily be mixed without misunderstanding. The distinction between the divine essence and divine energies has presented conceptual difficulties for several Western theologians.[51] As we look for resources for a creative retrieval of light and sun symbolism in the West, the aspiration sometimes expressed in Eastern writing to look inwards and see – literally and not metaphorically – the uncreated light of the Transfiguration is perhaps not to be imitated.

Another thread in the web of ideas in the Byzantine theology of divine light is the psycho-physical meditation techniques employed by Orthodox monks, particularly in the monastic settlements on Mount Athos. Theologians in the Byzantine tradition insist that no knowledge of God is attainable without divine grace or guaranteed by techniques of meditation, but they sometimes seem to have higher expectations of ascetical practices than their Western counterparts. While a contemporary Orthodox theologian refers to 'the Thaboric uncreated light that may be experienced by anyone who follows the ascetic way',[52] Catholic teaching authorities urge caution about phenomena of light.[53] We saw earlier in this chapter how metaphorical descriptions of inner light seem sometimes to be taken literally in the West. Perhaps something similar is happening with Eastern accounts of seeing the light of Thabor. In the words of Tom Wright, 'Our own metaphors seem so natural that we forget they are metaphors. Other people's metaphors, alien to our way of speaking, are often misinterpreted as though they are not metaphors at all.'[54] In any case, the search for phenomena of light by introspection is not a strategy that recommends itself for a 'natural theology' of light and sun. By contrast, Western Christians can learn from the more cosmic spirituality of the East, by looking outwards at the reality of the cosmos, and particularly at the phenomenon of sunlight.

Conclusion

The answer to the question in the title of this chapter is, in a nutshell, that Christians do not pray as a matter of principle towards the sun, and the east is not a Christian Mecca. When light streamed into the cathedral of Hagia Sophia in Constantinople or into a Western basilica, or sunlight shone through the side-windows of a medieval perpendicular church, it is more a matter of light shining into a sacred space than of worshippers directing their attention sunwards. Whether the light came in through an apse or through the entrance to the church was a secondary matter, and whether the celebrant faced the faithful or not was not a question at all. Despite the recent use of the expression *ad orientem*, the direction the celebrant faces at the eucharist is not an established vehicle for solar symbolism in the Roman Rite.

The deepest level of traditional symbolism of prayer in the eucharist is vertical, upwards towards the Father who dwells in inaccessible light. Any horizontal direction is towards the altar.⁵⁵ In neither case is the symbolism solar as such. Vertical prayer at the eucharist has biblical credentials (e.g. the synoptic accounts of the miracle of the loaves and fishes) that orientation lacks, and, as we will see in the next chapter, this is reflected in the texts of the current Roman Missal. Perhaps the clearest expression of traditional sacred direction is the ancient *orans* posture depicted in the Roman catacombs and enjoined for the celebrant in the Roman Rite. At the altar, prayer is directed not sunwards but upwards to the heavenly realm of light beyond the sun. The best route to re-appropriating the Christian symbolism of sun and light is not praying towards the sun in liturgical or personal orientation or looking inwards. It is in literally looking outwards at sunshine and daylight, not to pray to it but to relish it as symbol of the divine. Scriptural and liturgical language of light then takes on new meaning.

Notes

1 Ratzinger, *The Feast of Faith*, p. 140.
2 Wallraff, *Christus Verus Sol*, pp. 78–9.
3 Gregory of Nyssa, *De Vita S. Macrinae*. PG 46. 984.
4 Wallraff, *Christus Verus Sol*, p. 78.
5 T. D. Atkinson, 'Points of the Compass', in *Encyclopaedia of Religion and Ethics*, vol. 10 (ed. James Hastings; Edinburgh: Clark, 1908–26), pp. 73–88 (87).
6 'These general tendencies are interfered with by the survival or overlap of more ancient customs, by indifference and ignorance, and by local conditions such as a steep slope on the ground.' Ibid., p. 88.
7 Vauchez, *Francis of Assisi*, p. 154.
8 Marie-Christine Pénin, *Tombes et sepultures dans les cimitières et autres lieux. Loménie de Brienne Etienne Charles de (1727–16 février 1794) Eglise Saint-Savinien de Sens (Yonne)*. Available online: https://www.tombes-sepultures.com/crbst_1064.html (accessed 27 April 2020).
9 Martin Wallraff, 'Die Ursprünge der christlichen Gebetsostung', *Zeitschrift für Kirchengeschichte* 111 (2000), pp. 169–84 (178–9). Uwe Michael Lang, *Turning Towards the Lord: Orientation in Liturgical Prayer* (San Francisco: Ignatius Press, 2009), pp. 87–8.
10 Stefan Heid, 'Gebetshaltung und Ostung in frühchristlicher Zeit', *Rivista di Archeologia Cristiana* 82 (2006), pp. 347–404 (372–3).
11 Wallraff, 'Die Ursprünge der christlichen Gebetsostung', p. 181.
12 Martin Wallraff, 'Premesse', in *Spazio liturgico e orientamento: atti del IV convegno liturgico internazionale Bose, 1–3 giugno 2006* (ed. Goffredo Boselli; Magnano: Edizioni Qiqajon, 2007), pp. 155–65 (157).
13 Origen, *De Oratione* 32. PG 11. 556–7. ET *Origen's Treatise on Prayer, Translation and Notes with an Account of the Practice and Doctrine of Prayer from the New Testament Times to Origen* (ed. and trans. Eric George Jay; London: SPCK, 1954), pp. 215–16.
14 Tertullian, *Apologeticus* 16. PL 1. 371.
15 Henri Savon, 'Zacharie, 6, 12, et les justifications patristiques de la prière vers l'orient', *Augustinianum* 20 (1980), pp. 319–33 (332–3).
16 Origen, *Homily on Numbers* 5.1.4. Origène, *Homélies sur les Nombres I, homélies I–X* (ed. Louis Doutreleau; SC, 415; Paris: Cerf, 1996), pp. 122–5.

17 Basil of Caesarea, *De Spiritu Sancto* 27.66. PG 32. 189–92. ET *NPNF*, Second Series, vol. 8, p. 42.
18 John Damascene, *On the Orthodox Faith* 85.4.12. Bonifatius Kotter (ed.), *Die Schriften des Johannes von Damaskos, vol. 2* (Berlin and New York: Walter De Gruyter, 1973), pp. 190–1. ET Lang, *Turning towards the Lord*, pp. 59–60.
19 Francesco Gabrieli (ed.) and E. J. Costello (trans.), *Arab Historians of the Crusades* (London: Routledge, 2010), pp. 79–80.
20 Thomas Aquinas, ST 2.2. q.84, a.3, ad 3.
21 Guillelmus Durandus, *Rationale Divinorum Officiorum* 1.1.8. Guillelmi Duranti, *Rationale Divinorum Officiorum, vol. 1* (eds A. Davril, OSB and T. M. Thibodeau; Corpus Christianorum Continuatio Mediaevalis, 140; Turnhout: Brepols, 1995), p. 15.
22 Philip Caraman, *Tibet: The Jesuit Century* (Tiverton: Halsgrove, 1998), p. 22.
23 For the view that liturgical orientation was theologically important from the earliest days of the church: Joseph Ratzinger, *The Spirit of the Liturgy* (trans. John Saward; San Francisco: Ignatius Press, 2000), pp. 74–84.
24 *Didascalia Apostolorum* 12. ET *The Didascalia Apostolorum in English* (ed. and trans. Margaret Dunlop Gibson; repr., Cambridge: Cambridge University Press, 2011), p. 65.
25 Vitruvius, *De Architectura* 4.5.1. ET Vitruvius Pollo, *The Ten Books on Architecture* (trans. Morris Hickey Morgan; Cambridge, MA: Harvard University Press and London: Humphrey Milford, Oxford University Press, 1926), p. 116.
26 Wallraff, 'Die Ursprünge der christlichen Gebetsostung', pp. 181–3.
27 Sible De Blaauw, 'In vista della luce: un principio dimenticato nell'orientamento dell'edificio di culto paleocristiano', in *Arte medievale: le vie dello spazio liturgico* (ed. Paolo Piva; Milan: Jaca Book, 2012), pp. 19–48 (26–8).
28 Tertullian, *Adversus Valentinianos* 3. PL 2. 545. ET *ANF* 3, p. 504.
29 Wallraff, *Christus Verus Sol*, pp. 71–8.
30 From a total of fifty-three basilicas prior to around 420 studied by Vogel, thirty-seven have the apse in the west and eleven in the east; two are aligned north/south; three have no clearly defined alignment. Cyrille Vogel, 'Sol aequinoctialis: problèmes et technique de l'orientation dans le culte chrétien', *Revue des Sciences Religieuses* 36.3 (1962), pp. 175–211 (187).
31 Robin M. Jensen, 'Recovering Ancient Ecclesiology: The Place of the Altar and the Orientation of Prayer in the Early Latin Church', *Worship* 89.2 (2015), pp. 99–124 (117).
32 Tomás Ó'Carragáin, *Churches in Early Medieval Ireland: Architecture, Ritual and Memory* (New Haven and London: Yale University Press, 2010), pp. 174–5.
33 De Blaauw, 'In vista della luce', p. 28.
34 Peter G. Hoare and Hans Ketel, 'English Medieval Churches, "Festival Orientation" and William Wordsworth, SEAC 2011 Stars and Stones: Voyages in Archaeoastronomy and Cultural Astronomy, Proceedings of a conference held 19–22 September 2011', in *Archaeopress/British Archaeological Reports (2015)*, pp. 286–92. Available online: http://adsabs.harvard.edu/abs/2015ssva.conf.286H (accessed 27 April 2020).
35 Cyrille Vogel, 'Versus ad Orientem: l'orientation dans les *Ordines Romani* du haut moyen âge', *Studi Medievali* 3.1 (1960), pp. 447–69 (461).
36 Sible De Blaauw, 'Innovazioni nello spazio di culto fra basso medioevo e cinquecento: la perdita dell'orientamento liturgico e la liberazione della navata', in *Lo spazio e il culto: relazioni tra edificio ecclesiale e uso liturgico dal xv al xvi secolo* (ed. Jörg Strabenow; Venice: Marsilio, 2006), pp. 25–51 (32).
37 T. D. Atkinson, 'Points of the Compass', p. 83. Lang, *Turning towards the Lord*, p. 101.

38 De Blaauw, 'In vista della luce', p. 40
39 Robert Taft, 'Spazio e orientamento nelle liturgie dell'oriente e dell'occidente: convergenze e divergenze', in *Spazio liturgico e orientamento: atti del IV convegno liturgico internazionale Bose, 1–3 giugno 2006* (ed. Goffredo Boselli; Magnano: Edizioni Qiqajon, 2007), pp. 217–39 (231–3).
40 Wallraff, 'Premesse', p. 162.
41 Dominique Salin, *L'expérience spirituelle et son langage: leçons sur la tradition mystique chrétienne* (Paris: Editions Facultés Jésuites de Paris, 2015), p. 72.
42 Ibid., pp. 78–81.
43 Jeanne-Françoise Frémyot de Chantal, *Sa vie et ses œuvres, vol. 4: lettres* (Paris: E. Plon, 1877), pp. 20–1. Author's translation.
44 Louis Dupré, *Passage to Modernity: An Essay in the Hermeneutics of Nature and Culture* (New Haven and London: Yale University Press, 1993), p. 230.
45 Dominique Salin, 'The Treatise on Abandonment to Divine Providence', *The Way* 46.2 (2007), pp. 21–36.
46 Jean-Pierre de Caussade, SJ, *The Sacrament of the Present Moment* (trans. Kitty Muggeridge from the original text of the treatise on Self-Abandonment to Divine Providence; London: Collins Fount Paperbacks, 1981), pp. 85–6.
47 Andrew Louth, 'Light, Vision and Religious Experience in Byzantium', in *The Presence of Light: Divine Radiance and Religious Experience* (ed. Matthew K. Kapstein; Chicago: University of Chicago Press, 2004), pp. 85–103.
48 John Anthony McGuckin, *Standing in God's Holy Fire: The Byzantine Tradition* (London: Darton Longman and Todd, 2001), p. 127.
49 Kallistos Ware, 'Light and Darkness in the Mystical Theology of the Greek Fathers', in O'Collins and Myers, *Light from Light*, pp. 131–59 (135–7).
50 Tomaš Špidlík, *The Spirituality of the Christian East, vol. 2: Prayer: The Spirituality of the Christian East* (Kalamazoo, MI: Cistercian Publications, 2005), p. 248.
51 For example, Rowan D. Williams, 'The Philosophical Structures of Palamism', *Eastern Churches Review* 9.1–2 (1977), pp. 27–44.
52 Andreas Andreopoulos, *Metamorphosis: The Transfiguration in Byzantine Theology and Iconography* (Crestwood, NY: St Vladimir's Seminary Press, 2005), pp. 166–7.
53 This reserve is evident in a 1985 document of the Congregation for the Doctrine of the Faith on meditation techniques: 'Some physical exercises automatically produce a feeling of quiet and relaxation, pleasing sensations, perhaps even phenomena of light and of warmth, which resemble spiritual well-being.' Congregation for the Doctrine of the Faith, *Orationis Formas*: 'Letter to the Bishops of the Catholic Church on Some Aspects of Christian Meditation' 28. Available online: Http://www.vatican.va/roman_curia/congregations/cfaith/documents/rc_con_cfaith_doc_19891015_meditazione-cristiana_en.html (accessed 27 April 2020).
54 Tom Wright, *Paul: A Biography* (London: SPCK, 2018), p. 224.
55 'The altar should, moreover, be so placed as to be truly the centre toward which the attention of the whole congregation of the faithful naturally turns.' Catholic Church, Roman Rite, 'The General Instruction of the Roman Missal', no. 299, in *The Roman Missal. Renewed by Decree of the Most Holy Second Ecumenical Council of the Vatican, Promulgated by Authority of Pope Paul VI and Revised at the Direction of Pope John Paul II, English Translation According to the Third Typical Edition* (London: The Catholic Truth Society, 2011), pp. 21–122 (96).

Chapter 9

LIGHT, SUN AND LITURGY

We now turn to light and sun symbolism in the liturgical cycles celebrating the mysteries of the incarnation and of Christ's death and resurrection, and then in the texts of the Roman Missal and the Liturgy of the Hours. We see how solar imagery marked the development of the liturgical season of Christmas and the celebration of Holy Week, and how the overall symbolic balance of light and sun language in the New Testament is replicated in the Roman liturgy.

The incarnation

Epiphany: A feast of light

It is often presumed in the English-speaking world that Christmas, the feast of Christ's Nativity, started as a Christianized pagan light-festival bringing cheer in the bleak midwinter. In fact, the origin was more complex and more Mediterranean, involving two feasts of Christ's coming. The earlier feast, the Epiphany (literally Manifestation) of Christ in his birth and baptism, was celebrated on 6 January, and had its origins in the East, later spreading in the West.[1] It was always a feast associated with light, and there is no evidence of pagan antecedents. Suggestions, for example, that it was a replacement for pagan winter solstice celebrations in Egypt and elsewhere have not been substantiated. The most probable background for this early celebration of Christ's birth is in Christian solar symbolism. As early as the third century, links were made between the birth of the new sun and the birth of Christ without any link to a particular date.[2] As regards Epiphany as a celebration of Christ's baptism, according to Gabrielle Winkler this probably goes back to the earliest history of Christianity, and may have had an association with light from the beginning.[3] By the late second or early third century in Egypt, there was a single feast of the birth and baptism of Jesus celebrated on 6 January. In Cappadocia, the name of the feast translates as 'The Lights',[4] and in Syria as 'Dawn of the Light'. Ephrem of Syria (306–76) linked the Epiphany as the celebration of the birthday of Christ with the creation of the sun on the fourth day in the creation narrative in Genesis. For Ephrem, the manifestation of Jesus at his birth marked the end of pagan sun worship.[5]

When the feast of the Epiphany was taken up in the Roman tradition, it came to be associated principally with the adoration of the Magi. The manifestation of light remains central, with the star of Bethlehem leading the Magi to Christ who is proclaimed as the 'light for revelation to the Gentiles, and for glory to your people Israel' (Lk. 2.32).[6] The first reading of the current Mass of the day for the Epiphany starts: 'Arise, shine; for your light has come,/and the glory of the Lord has risen upon you'. (Isa. 60.1).

Christmas and the winter solstice

The feast of the Nativity of Christ on 25 December was celebrated in Rome by 336, and later spread to the East, while the Epiphany started in the East, only later spreading westwards. Both East and West ended up with two feasts, Christmas and Epiphany, celebrating the coming of Christ, with the focus of each narrowing as time went on. The origin of Christmas continues to be debated. One school of thought, often referred to as the History of Religions approach, emphasizes the influence of the surrounding religious culture of late antiquity. The feast on 25 December (the date Julius Caesar had determined to mark the winter solstice) is seen as a replacement of the celebration of the imperial cult of the Unconquered Sun instituted by the Emperor Aurelian in 274. A second school, emphasizing factors within the Christian church itself, points out that Christians had celebrated Christmas in North Africa prior to 274, and that Christians had been calculating the date of Christ's birth based on suppositions about the date of the Annunciation.[7] The debate goes on and there would seem to be something in both approaches.[8] Perhaps Roman Christians felt the need for a celebration of the coming of Christ analogous to that of the Epiphany in the Eastern churches.[9] Probably the long-established tradition of calling Christ the Sun of Justice and the Rising Sun as well as earlier efforts to determine the date of Christ's birth fed into the evolution of a celebration.[10] That being said, the solar character of the Christian feast of Christmas did not come from the gospel accounts of the Nativity. Pagan celebrations were certainly in the background. From its inception, the feast of Christ's Nativity was in competition with alternative festivities at the turn of the year such as Saturnalia which began on 17 December and Lupercalia in February. There was, moreover, a pastoral need to counteract the temptation to sun worship among the recently Christianized population of Rome. Whatever the precise process of development, the result was a feast of the Nativity of Christ on 25 December, around the time of the winter solstice, as the Light and True Sun of the world.

The Christian celebration of the Nativity continued to have an attention to light, and a link with the motif of the rising sun. The Advent O Antiphons at vespers date from the seventh century or earlier and are still in use today. The antiphon for 21 December, the winter solstice, echoes Luke 1.78–9:

> O Rising Sun, you are the splendour of eternal light and sun of justice. O come and enlighten those who sit in darkness and in the shadow of death.[11]

The paschal mystery

Baptism

From the second century, baptism, when the new Christian is initiated into the paschal mystery of Christ's death and resurrection, was also referred to as *photismos* – illumination – and for both Ambrose and Augustine the white garments worn by the newly baptized symbolized light.[12] The *Physiologus*, the Egyptian bestiary we saw in Chapter 2, gives a solar fable of the sacrament. The eagle finds in the sun the source of eternal youth (see Ps 103.5):

> Physiologus says of the eagle that, when he grows old, his wings grow heavy and his eyes grow dim. What does he do then? He seeks out a fountain and then flies up into the atmosphere of the sun, and he burns away his wings and the dimness of his eyes, and descends into the fountain and bathes himself three times and is restored and made new again.
>
> … As you fly into the height of the sun of justice [Mal. 4:2] who is Christ as the Apostle says, he himself will burn off your old clothing which is the devil's … Be baptized in the everlasting fountain.[13]

In northern Italy, three sermons of Zeno of Verona (died *c.* 370) illustrate a rich cosmic symbolism of baptism. The first sermon, despite being entitled a sermon on the birth of Christ, was probably preached at Easter. The four animals refer to the four-horse chariot which was a traditional part of solar symbolism:

> This is our sun, the true sun, which with the abundance of its brightness lights the dazzling fires of the world and the sisters, the fires of the shining stars of the heavens. This is the one which set once for all and rose again, never to repeat its setting. This, I say, is the one crowned with a crown of twelve rays, that is the twelve apostles, the one who is drawn along its course around the world not by four dumb animals, but by the four Gospels with their proclamation of salvation.[14]

Zeno now addresses the Easter congregation in a second sermon. The catechumens have yet to be baptized, and he compares their imminent immersion in the baptismal pool to sinking down with the sun into the ocean to rise again at dawn. The sunset invites them so that:

> immersed in the milky depth of the sacred ocean, and rising from there, new with the new day, and, radiant with their own light, they may come with us in a safe course on the heavenly path of immortality to the time of promise where one rises for ever.[15]

In a third sermon, Zeno addresses the newly baptized. After the disciplines of Lent, they have participated in the light ceremony, and then been baptized. He now invites them to the eucharist:

After the chaste fast of holy expiation has been most devoutly accomplished, after the sweet vigils of the night dazzling with its own sun, after your souls grew in the hope of immortality by the life-giving bath of the milky font ... I urge you to celebrate the feast of such a great birth with a joyful banquet.[16]

Good Friday

Various solar metaphors were used from an early date to describe Christ's death. In a comparison that would become standard, Ignatius of Antioch, writing probably in the middle of the second century, has death and resurrection symbolized as the setting and rising of the sun.[17] The darkness that came over the whole land at noon in the synoptic accounts of the crucifixion came to be seen as expressing sorrow or shame, as physical creation reacts to what is happening to the Divine Sun on the cross.[18] John Chrysostom (c. 349–407) linked the eclipse with the Johannine theme of the cross as the manifestation of Christ's glory: the visible sun hid its rays when it saw the Sun of Justice shining from the cross.[19] According to John Damascene (676–749), 'for this reason the sun was darkened, since it could not bear to see the intelligible sun of righteousness undergoing violence'.[20] In some mediaeval images, the sun is red-faced hanging its head in shame.[21] In another metaphor, Christ is radiant or shining on the cross as a light on a lampstand.[22] Just as a householder places a lamp on high to lighten up the whole house, so the Sun of Justice shines out from the top of the lampstand that is the cross.[23]

Architecture, too, employed the symbol of the sun, to place the crucifixion at the centre of time and space. In the sixth century, Golgotha remained in the open between two churches in Jerusalem, not because of any construction requirement but to express the cosmic dimension of the crucifixion. Only in 614 was it covered.[24] The idea that at the crucifixion the sun stood over the cross at its zenith, at midday, was linked to the notion that Jerusalem was the centre of the world.[25] An anonymous Benedictine pilgrim from the Icelandic monastery of Thingeyrar visited the church on the feast of the Nativity of John the Baptist, 24 June, the summer solstice, sometime between 1151 and 1154. He came from the 'ends of the earth' to Jerusalem. When the sun stood directly over the circular window at the summit of the dome, he was conscious, he said, of being at the centre of the world.[26]

These solar themes did not die out and for Thomas Traherne, in the seventeenth century, the cross is the pillar of fire at the Exodus and the rising sun at dawn: 'This Body is not the cloud, but the pillar assumed to manifest His love unto us. In these shades doth this sun break forth most oriently. In this death is His love painted in most lively colours.'[27]

Holy Saturday

In his second-century *Dialogue with Trypho*, Justin Martyr insists that the Lord God remembered his dead people of Israel who lay in their graves, and he descended to preach salvation to them.[28] This descent, which figures in the Apostle's Creed and the fourth eucharistic prayer of the current liturgy, was expressed in solar terms. In the late second century, Melito of Sardis (died *c.* 180) applies the image of a sun rising from on high (Lk. 1.78) to Christ in the underworld: 'King of Heaven, Prince of creation, sun of the eastern sky who appeared both to the dead in Hades and to mortals upon earth, he, the only true Helios [sun], arose for us out of the highest summits of heaven.'[29] According to Clement of Alexandria, Christ, the 'Sun of the Resurrection', shines into the darkness of the underworld and raises fallen humanity from the dead,[30] while, for both John Chrysostom and John Damascene, this descent turned Hades into heaven.[31] The descent of Christ among the dead came to be celebrated liturgically on Holy Saturday, as we first see in Amphilochius of Iconium (*c.* 340–*c.* 400):

> Today we celebrate the feast of our Savior's burial. He, with the dead below, is loosing the bonds of death and filling Hades with light and awakening the sleepers …
>
> Yesterday the crucified one darkened the sun, and night fell in the middle of the day; today Death is undone because he swallowed up a dead man who was not his. Yesterday the creation was in mourning, seeing the frenzy of the Jews, and it put on darkness as a mourning garment; today 'the people who sat in darkness have seen a great light'.[32]

Sometimes the symbol of Christ's descent was expressed in graphic narratives. In a Holy Saturday homily of Pseudo-Epiphanius, the 'God-Sun-Christ' has gone under the earth bringing salvation to the invisible world: Receive the great light![33] The fourth-century apocryphal *Acts of Pilate*, which would influence the medieval mystery plays of the Harrowing of Hell, has a group of Jewish chief priests including Annas, Caiphas and Gamaliel interrogating men raised from the dead by Jesus. The men call for pen and paper and write:

> We then were in Hades with all those who had fallen asleep from the beginning. But when it was middle of the night, into that darkness there arose as it were the light of the sun, and it shone and enlightened everyone; and we saw one another.[34]

The symbol of Christ's descent was also given visual expression. A floor mosaic in a villa from around 350 in Hinton St Mary in England has the earliest image of Christ found in Britain. Pagan mythology is harnessed to express Christian beliefs. Christ is flanked by two pomegranates which evoked the myth of Persephone/Proserpina being rescued from the underworld and pointed to Christ's descent among the dead. In later centuries, the Byzantine icon of Christ descending into Hades to liberate those in darkness and the shadow of death is called the *Anastasis* icon – the 'resurrection' icon.[35] Christ is usually surrounded by a mandorla or halo, both solar symbols, and his vivid white garments, symbolizing light, can sometimes contrast with the less vivid whitish clothing of Adam, who is receiving light. The figure of Jesus displays power and energy, sometimes in contrast with the listless posture of Adam and his companions sitting in darkness and the shadow of death. When this Eastern tradition is taken alongside the depictions of the Harrowing of Hell in the West, for example, in the mediaeval English mystery plays, it points to a *sensus fidelium* that the descent of Christ into the underworld is 'more the beginning of the glory of Easter Day than the continuation of the suffering of Good Friday'.[36] For Joseph Ratzinger, the Holy Saturday liturgy is a liturgy of the cross that shines with the light of the resurrection:

> Thus this liturgy proceeds like the sunrise, the first light of Easter morning shines into it. If Good Friday places before our eyes the buffeted figure of the pierced one, Holy Saturday's liturgy is as much reminiscent of the early Church's view of the cross, surrounded by beams of light, as much symbol of resurrection as of death.[37]

In his sermon at the Easter vigil of 2007, Pope Benedict exploits the *Anastasis* icon to express Christ's entry into the darkness, the sunlessness we could say, of contemporary life: 'By his death he now clasps the hand of Adam, of every man and woman who awaits him and brings them to the light.' The homily ends with a prayer, in which Benedict asks the risen Lord to descend into our 'dark nights':

> On this night, then, let us pray: Lord, show us that love is stronger than hatred, that love is stronger than death. Descend into the darkness and the abyss of our modern age, and take by the hand those who await you. Bring them to the light! In my own dark nights, be with me to bring me forth![38]

Easter

In the New Testament, Christ's resurrection is a non-metaphorical dateable event known through the discovery of an empty tomb and a series of appearances of the risen Jesus. In a second step, the resurrection is described using metaphors of light just as his disciples are said metaphorically to die and rise with him in baptism or to shine with resurrected light.[39] The feast termed Easter in English did not start as a feast of light or sun as such but developed out of a single feast of the Pasch which focused on Christ's sufferings as well as his resurrection. The unitary feast developed into the present celebration of the final three days of Holy Week, the sacred triduum. The Pasch evoked the creation of light in Genesis, as well as the pillar of fire lighting up the path of the Israelites in Exodus, and readings from Genesis and Exodus figure still in the readings of the Roman Rite Easter Vigil today.

Solar motifs were applied to the resurrection in the late second century and became more common subsequently. In the fourth century, Easter came to be celebrated as a feast of light, as it still is in the current Easter Vigil. In an Easter homily, Hesychius of Jerusalem cries out: 'Let us celebrate this holy night with sacred torches, let us sing a divine melody, a heavenly hymn. The Sun of Justice, Our Lord Jesus Christ, has illumined this day for the whole world. He has risen through the cross and saved those who believe.'[40] Practices such as the use of torches were taken from the pagan mystery cults, and the ceremony seems to have sometimes been conducted in competition with rival rites – Apuleius, for example, recounts how, when he was being initiated into the mysteries of Isis, 'I came to the boundary of death … In the middle of the night I saw the sun flashing with bright light'.[41] The Easter candle itself, standing for the Easter Light of Christ, developed from the Christian evening prayer at the lighting of the lamps, the *Lucernarium*. In the Eastern churches, by the fourth century this evening celebration became the climax of the ceremony just before the celebration of eucharist. In the West, it is at the beginning.[42]

As we have emphasized in earlier chapters, past generations distinguished between light and sun, but associated them more closely than we do today, and gave them more attention. People in the ancient world were fascinated by the purity of light, with various forms of a popular saying going back at least to the philosopher Diogenes (fifth to fourth century BCE), to the effect that, even if it shines into filth, sunlight retains its pristine purity. Echoing this, Tertullian says that the sun can shine into a sewer without being made filthy.[43] At the same time, associations with the freshness of early morning flowed naturally from the gospel narrative of Mary Magdalene and other women going to the tomb 'very early on the first day of the week, when the sun had risen' (Mark 16.2). In the words of Maximus of Turin, 'As the world's sun was growing bright she alone, before anyone else, recognised the rising of the sun of justice, and with the coming of the dawn she rejoiced in the return of day, but still more she rejoiced in Christ risen from the dead.'[44]

Natural sunlight could even seem brighter at Easter, and the light of springtime, the European season of Easter, was particularly evocative: 'The sky is transparent, the sun radiant, the moon brilliant, and the choirs of stars bright. The springs of water are clear and the rivers full, for these are now freed from the fetters of ice. The fields emit sweet scents, green plants sprout, and lambs bound in green pastures.'[45] Once more, we see that these motifs did not die out. The same sentiments are expressed in John McGahern's *That They May Face the Rising Sun*:

> On such an Easter morning, as we were setting out for Mass, we were always shown the sun; Look how the molten globe and all the glittering rays are dancing. The whole of heaven is dancing in its joy that Christ has risen.[46]
>
> The sun was now high above the lake. There wasn't a wisp of cloud. Everywhere the water sparkled. A child could easily believe that the whole of heaven was dancing.[47]

Light and sun in the current liturgy

The Roman Missal

In the Latin text of the current Roman Missal there is abundant vocabulary of light but virtually none of it refers to the sun or to the east.[48] The two Latin words for light, *lux* and *lumen*, in their different cases, occur 160 times. *Sol,* the word for sun, in its different cases, occurs only six times. Three of these occurrences are in the fixed expression *sol iustitiae*, the Sun of Justice, and three in the expression 'from the rising of the sun to its setting', which is not focused on the sun itself. The Latin equivalent of the Greek *anatole*, signifying the rising sun/dawn/east, is *oriens*. This noun occurs once the missal, in the expression *ad orientem*, referring not to the rising sun but to the star of Bethlehem, in the vigil mass of the Epiphany. In the eucharistic prayers and prefaces, the vocabulary of light highlights the eternal God 'dwelling in unapproachable light' (preface of the fourth eucharistic prayer) and yet at the same time the hope of eternal life in 'the light of your face' (second eucharistic prayer). An examination of the liturgical texts confirms what we saw in the last chapter. The idea that the eucharist should be celebrated literally or symbolically facing the rising sun in the east has no basis in the texts of the current missal, nor in the missal used up the Second Vatican Council where the expression *ad orientem* was not used at all, and where solar vocabulary was even more sparse.[49] The eucharist is not linked to diurnal solar rhythms, in marked contrast with the Liturgy of the Hours.

Taken together, the eucharist and the Liturgy of the Hours reflect the pattern of vocabulary in the New Testament: light symbolism is paramount, and solar imagery secondary. In the eucharist, the language directs the worshippers not eastwards towards the sun but upwards towards light. Attention is not to be given, either, to inward-looking private devotions, but to the altar where the direction of prayer is upwards. As we saw, this was current in the early church and has a warrant in scripture (e.g. at the prayer of Jesus at the miracle of the loaves and fishes). It is another area where, in John McGahern's expression that we saw in the Introduction, 'you never lost it, Patrick.' The ancient custom of praying with outstretched hands and directing attention upwards, the *orans* position, has continued with the celebrant at the eucharist praying in this posture. In the Roman Canon, just prior to the consecration of the bread Christ is described as praying 'with eyes raised to heaven' – *elevatis oculis in coelum* – and the celebrant looks upwards when speaking these words. The eucharistic prayer is a vertical offering of sacrifice, 'to your altar on high' – *in sublime altare tuum*.[50] The faithful, too, are invited to direct their attention upwards when, before the eucharistic prayer, they are urged to 'lift up your hearts' – *sursum corda*. This directs participants not towards the presiding priest, nor towards the physical sun, but upwards to the heavenly world of 'unapproachable light', a light that is located, in Pope Francis's expression in *Laudato si*, 'beyond the sun.'[51]

The most dramatic celebration of light in the liturgy is, of course, the Easter Vigil. In the missal overall, however, the language of light is most prominent in the liturgy of Advent and Christmastide. This harks back to the Christmas and Epiphany liturgies from their inception. In the prayers of the Masses for Christmastide, light is variously described as true light, brilliant light, eternal light, kindly light and new light. The way the missal employs this imagery of light exemplifies the catholic character of the Roman rite. The Mass texts are not specific to the Mediterranean area where they largely originated, and they can be used with equal ease anywhere from the North to the South Pole. Australian liturgist Tom Elich insists that though the winter solstice may well have played a role in the development of the feast of Christmas, this process has not marked the texts of the current Roman Missal. The Roman liturgical books 'display an admirable and helpful reticence in their specificity to a particular time and place'.[52] These universal texts apply readily to a country where, for Elich, the Invincible Sun at Christmas evokes the salty smell of the sea and the heat of the Australian summer. We can add that they apply as readily to northern climes like the England described by T. S. Eliot where 'the short day is brightest, with frost and fire' ('Little Gidding').

The Liturgy of the Hours

In the Latin text of the Liturgy of the Hours of the Roman Rite, occurrences of light vocabulary, principally *lux* and *lumen* in their different cases, number in the thousands. Solar symbolism is more prominent than in the Missal with expressions related to sun and east numbering in the hundreds. *Sol* appears over three hundred times, *oriens* (including the expression *sol oriens*) over forty times. *Ad orientem* appears nineteen times and *sol justitiae* over thirty times.[53] On the feast of Christ the King, we read: 'Behold a man whose name is "The Rising Sun"; he will sit on the throne and rule overall; he will speak of peace to the peoples.'[54] This prominence of solar motifs is due to the origins and development of the Divine Office, and to its place in an overall pattern of Christian prayer. Another reason for their prominence is a deliberate *ressourcement* with patristic symbolism by the experts who worked on the revision of liturgical texts after Vatican II. The hymn '*Sol, ecce, lentus occidens*', for instance, which is markedly solar in its symbolism, was composed on patristic models by Anselmo Lentini, a Benedictine Latinist from the Abbey of Monte Cassino.[55]

The origins of the public prayer of the church are to be found in the need of the Christian to pray, alone or with others, at the beginning of the day and in the evening. There is a spontaneous need for a sort of morning offering looking to what is ahead as the day begins, and for an examination of conscience and an act of contrition as the day is drawing to a close.[56] From early centuries, efforts were also made to give St Paul's injunction to pray always (1 Thess. 5.17) concrete expression in a variety of prayer forms at different times of the day. A pattern of public morning, midday and afternoon or evening prayer developed, as did a twofold pattern of personal prayer at morning and night. As they shaped their prayers, Christians were influenced by scripture, nature and the human cycles of waking and sleeping. As is often the case, the practice is older than the different forms of theological rationale given for it.[57] The cycle of the rising and setting of the sun, and the alternation of night and day, provided a cosmic matrix for the rites and texts that developed in cathedral offices, and then in various forms of monastic offices. In the breviary, the compendious editions in use in modern times prior to the Second Vatican Council, there was less emphasis on the contrast of light and darkness and on the natural symbols of sunrise and sunset than there had been in earlier eras.[58]

The present form of the Roman Liturgy of the Hours is the fruit of changes introduced by the Second Vatican Council.[59] The commission that worked on the changes aimed to produce a flexible work to be used for public and private prayer by monastics and religious, priests and laypeople.[60] The final product, however, is more a contemplative prayer book that can be recited privately than a resource for popular devotional services,[61] but, in an unforeseen contribution of technology, mobile devices and computer software are making the Liturgy of the Hours more accessible. Perhaps there is a parallel with the Books of Hours, digests of the Divine Office for lay people, the most popular books of the Late Middle Ages.[62] People now have easy access to texts for daily prayer that are rich in biblical and patristic symbolism, including the symbolism of light and sun.[63] Praying the Liturgy of the Hours can be a means of living a more integrated life in a contemporary world that can be disjointed and scattered, and of re-appropriating the cosmic rhythms of day and night.[64] The traditional links of sunset and sleep with death and sunrise with resurrection can help us reintegrate the reality of death in a balanced and wholesome spirituality: 'Yours is the day and yours the night, Lord God:/let the Sun of Justice shine so steadily in our hearts,/that we may come at length/to that light where you dwell eternally.'[65]

Conclusion

The rich imagery of light and sun used traditionally to articulate the mysteries of the incarnation and the paschal mystery receives insufficient attention, and its potential for linking the mysteries of the faith with cosmic realities is largely unexploited. In the eucharist, the language is typically one of light and not of sun, replicating the pattern of imagery in the New Testament. The best option for giving this language physical expression is to have the altar and apse bathed in natural light, a symbol of God's presence. Despite the label *ad orientem*, a celebrant facing the altar from the same side as the congregation is not a solar symbol. The postural expression of prayer direction in the eucharist with the deepest roots in tradition is the *orans* position depicted in the catacombs, and still adopted by the celebrant during the eucharistic prayer. Its direction is not sunwards, but upwards to heavenly light, beyond the sun. More promising as strategies to revive traditional Christian solar symbolism are attention to natural light and sun, and daily morning and evening prayer. The Liturgy of the Hours, especially, with its abundant traditional solar imagery, is a rich resource.

Notes

1   In the calendar of the Armenian Apostolic Church there is still no Christmas feast on 25 December.
2   Wallraff, *Christus Verus Sol*, p. 193.

3   Gabrielle Winkler, 'The Appearance of the Light at the Baptism of Jesus and the Origins of the Feast of Epiphany: An Investigation of Greek, Syriac, Armenian, and Latin Sources', in *Between Memory and Hope: Readings on the Liturgical Year* (ed. Maxwell E. Johnson; Collegeville, MN: The Liturgical Press, 2000), pp. 291–347 (344, 347). The association of the Baptism of Jesus with light continued: '"I have need to be baptized by you", says the lamp to the Sun, the voice to the Word, the friend to the Bridegroom.' Gregory of Nazianzen, *Oratio* 39.15. PG 36. 352. ET *Divine Office,* vol. 1, p. 379.
4   Paul F. Bradshaw and Maxwell E. Johnson, *The Origins of Feasts, Fasts and Seasons in Early Christianity* (Collegeville, MN: Liturgical Press, 2011), p. 145.
5   Wallraff, *Christus Verus Sol*, pp. 192–3.
6   Bradshaw and Johnson, *The Origins of Feasts*, p. 156.
7   For example, Bryan D. Spinks, 'The Growth of Liturgy and the Church Year', in *The Cambridge History of Christianity*, vol. 2: *Constantine to c. 600* (ed. Augustine Casiday and Frederick W. Norris; Cambridge: Cambridge University Press, 2007), pp. 601–17 (615).
8   Susan K. Roll, 'The Origins of Christmas: The State of the Question', in Johnson, *Between Memory and Hope*, pp. 273–90 (290).
9   See Bradshaw and Johnson, *Origins of Feasts*, p. 127.
10 The *De Pascha Computus*, written in 243, has Christ's birth on the spring equinox, 25 March in the Roman calendar. Wallraff, *Christus Verus Sol*, p. 185.
11 Magnificat antiphon at Evening Prayer, 21 December, *Divine Office*, vol. 1, p. 153.
12 Martin Walraff, 'Licht', in *Reallexikon für Antike und Christentum, vol. 23* (ed. Georg Schöllgen; Stuttgart: Anton Hiersemann, 2010), pp. 100–37 (111).
13 *Physiologus*, pp. 12–13.
14 Zeno of Verona, *Tractatus* 2.12.2. ET Gordon P. Jeanes, *The Day Has Come! Easter and Baptism in Zeno of Verona* (Alcuin Club Collection, 73; Collegeville, MN: The Liturgical Press, 1995), pp. 89, 114–16.
15 Zeno of Verona, *Tractatus* 1.44.1. ET Jeanes, *The Day Has Come*, pp. 73, 109.
16 Zeno of Verona, *Tractatus* 1.24.1. ET Jeanes, *The Day Has Come*, pp. 63, 130–2.
17 Ignatius, *Romans* 2.2. PG 5. 688. See Wallraff, *Christus Verus Sol*, p. 111.
18 Mk 15.33; Mt. 27.45; Lk. 23.44. Stefan Heid, *Kreuz, Jerusalem, Kosmos: Aspekte frühchristlicher Staurologie* (Münster: Aschendorff, 2001), pp. 189–94.
19 John Chrysostom, *Instruction to Catechumens* 3.4. Jean Chrysostome, *Trois catéchèses baptismales* (ed. and trans. Auguste Piédagnel and Louis Doutreleau; SC, 366; Paris: Cerf, 1990), pp. 228–9.
20 John Damascene, *Homilia in Sabbatum Sanctum* 21. PG 96. 620. ET Tikhon Alexander Pino, 'St John Damascene: Homily on Holy Saturday', in *The Orthodox Word* 52.4 (2016), pp. 157–97 (178).
21 Hugo Rahner, *Greek Myths and Christian Mystery*, p. 117.
22 Ibid., pp. 194–202.
23 John Chrysostom, *De Coemeterio et de Cruce* 2. PG 49. 397.
24 Heid, *Kreuz, Jerusalem, Kosmos*, p. 220.
25 Ibid., p. 105.
26 Ibid., p. 193
27 Traherne, *Centuries*, 1.90, p. 46.
28 Justin Martyr, *Dialogue with Trypho* 72.4. ET *St Justin Martyr Dialogue with Trypho* (ed. Michael Slusser; trans. Thomas B. Falls; revised by Thomas P. Halton; FC, 3; Washington, DC: Catholic University of America Press, 2003), p. 112.

29 Melito of Sardis, *Fragment* 8b. Méliton de Sardis, *Sur la Pâque et fragments* (ed. and trans. Othmar Perler; SC, 123; Paris: Cerf, 1966), p. 232. ET Melito of Sardis, *On Pascha with the Fragments of Melito and Other Material Related to the Quartodecimans* (trans. Alastair Stewart-Sykes; Crestwood, NY: St Vladimir's Seminary Press, 2001), p. 75. Despite questions about authorship, this text is to be dated to the second or third century: Wallraff, *Christus Verus Sol*, p. 123, n. 55.

30 Clement of Alexandria, *Protrepticus* 9. PG 8. 196.

31 John Chrysostom, *De Coemeterio et de Cruce* 2. PG 49. 395. John Damascene, *Homilia in Sabbatum Sanctum* 22. PG 96. 622.

32 Amphilochius of Iconium, *Oratio V In diem Sabbati sancti* 1. PG 39. 89. ET Raniero Cantalamessa, *Easter in the Early Church: An Anthology of Jewish and Early Christian Texts* (Collegeville, MN: The Liturgical Press, 1993), p. 77.

33 Pseudo-Epiphanius, *Homilia in Sancto Sabbato*. PG 43. 440.

34 'The Gospel of Nicodemus (The Acts of Pilate) B (Including the Descent into Hades)' 18. ET Bart D. Ehrman and Zlatko Pleše (eds and trans.), *The Apocryphal Gospels: Texts and Translations* (New York: Oxford University Press, 2011), p. 477.

35 Alyssa Lyra Pitstick, *Light in Darkness: Hans Urs von Balthasar and the Catholic Doctrine of Christ's Descent into Hell* (Grand Rapids, MI and Cambridge, UK: William B. Eerdmans, 2007), pp. 77–9.

36 Ibid., p. 84.

37 Joseph Ratzinger, 'Five Meditations', in Joseph Ratzinger and William Congdon, *The Sabbath of History* (Washington, DC: William G. Congdon Foundation, 2000), pp. 15–57 (47).

38 Pope Benedict XVI, Homily Easter Vigil 2007. Available online: http://w2.vatican.va/content/benedict-xvi/en/homilies/2007/documents/hf_ben-xvi_hom_20070407_veglia-pasquale.html (accessed 28 April 2020).

39 Wright and Bird, *The New Testament and Its World*, pp. 301, 306, 309.

40 Hesychius of Jerusalem, *Paschal Homily* 1.1. Hésychius de Jérusalem, Basile de Séleucie, Jean de Béryte, Pseudo-Chrysostome, Léonce de Constantinople, *Homélies paschales (cinq homélies inédites)* (ed. and trans, Michel Aubineau; SC, 187; Paris: Cerf, 1972), p. 63. Author's translation.

41 Apuleius, *Metamorphoses* 11.23. ET Apuleius, *Metamorphoses, vol. 2* (trans. J. Arthur Hanson; Cambridge, MA and London: Harvard University Press, 1989), p. 341.

42 Bradshaw and Johnson, *The Origins of Feasts*, p. 67.

43 Tertullian, *De Spectaculis* 20.2. PL 1. 652. Alexandre Olivar, 'L'image du soleil non souillé dans la littérature patristique', *Didaskalia* 5.1 (1975), pp. 3–20.

44 Maximus of Turin, Sermon 29.1 (on Psalm 21). CCL 23, p. 113. ET *The Sermons of St Maximus of Turin*, trans. Boniface Ramsey, pp. 70–1.

45 Gregory of Nazianzen, *In Novam Dominicam*. PG 36. 617. ET Anscar J. Chupungco, OSB, *Shaping the Easter Feast* (Washington, DC: The Pastoral Press, 1992), p. 29.

46 John McGahern, *That They May Face the Rising Sun*, p. 251.

47 Ibid., p. 261.

48 Catholic Church, Roman Rite, *Missale Romanum Ex Decreto Sacrosancti Œcumenici Concilii Vaticani II Instauratum, Auctoritate Pauli PP. VI Promulgatum, Ioannis Pauli PP. II Cura Recognitum, Editio Typica Tertia* (Vatican City: Typis Vaticanis, 2002).

49 André Pflieger, *Liturgicae Orationis Concordantia Verbalis, Prima Pars: Missale Romanum* (Rome: Herder, 1964), p. 639.

50 Angelo Lameri, 'L'orientamento nei testi liturgici', in *Spazio liturgico e orientamento: atti del IV convegno liturgico internazionale Bose, 1–3 giugno 2006* (ed. Goffredo Boselli; Magnano: Edizioni Qiqajon, 2007), pp. 189–201 (195–7).
51 *Laudato sì* 243.
52 Tom Elich, 'A View from the Antipodes. The Invincible Summer Sun', *Studia Liturgica* 40.1–2 (2010), pp. 85–93 (91).
53 Catholic Church, Roman Rite, *Divinum Officium ex Decreto Oecumenici Concilii Vaticani II Instauratum Auctoritate Pauli PP VI Promulgatum: Liturgia Horarum Iuxta Ritum Romanum Editio Typica Altera* (4 vols; Vatican City: Libreria Editrice Vaticana, 1985).
54 Solemnity of Christ the King, Morning Prayer, Antiphon 1, *Divine Office*, vol. 3, p. 797.
55 Anselmo Lentini, *Te Decet Hymnus: L'innario della 'Liturgia Horarum'* (Vatican City: Typis Polyglottis Vaticanis, 1984), p. 55.
56 Robert Taft, 'The Divine Office: Monastic Choir, Prayer Book, or Liturgy of the People of God? An Evaluation of the New Liturgy of the Hours in Its Historical Context', in *Vatican II Assessment and Perspectives: Twenty-five Years After (1962–1967), vol. 2* (ed. René Latourelle; New York and Mahwah: Paulist Press, 1989), pp. 27–46 (39).
57 McGowan, *Ancient Christian Worship*, pp. 188–9, 202–3.
58 Gregory W. Woolfenden, *Daily Liturgical Prayer: Origins and Theology* (Aldershot: Ashgate, 2004), p. 294.
59 Second Vatican Council, Constitution *Sacrosanctum Concilium* 83–101. Available online: http://www.vatican.va/archive/hist_councils/ii_vatican_council/documents/vat-ii_const_19631204_sacrosanctum-concilium_en.html (accessed 29 April 2020).
60 Stanislaus Campbell, FSC, *From Breviary to Liturgy of the Hours: The Structural Reform of the Roman Office 1964–1971* (Collegeville, MN: The Liturgical Press, 1995), pp. 282–5.
61 'In spite of the Council, the private Office is more predominant than before.' Lazló Dobzay, 'The Divine Office in History', in *T&T Clark Companion to Liturgy* (ed. Alcuin Reid; London: Bloomsbury, 2016), pp. 207–37 (234).
62 Eamon Duffy, *Marking the Hours: English People and Their Prayers 1240–1570* (New Haven and London: Yale University Press, 2011), p. 4.
63 'The Sun of Justice' (Malachi 4.2) rising from on high (Luke 1.78) is evoked explicitly in the introduction to the *Divine Office*: Catholic Church, Roman Rite, 'The General Instruction on the Liturgy of the Hours', no. 38, in *The Divine Office*, vol. 1, pp. xix–xcii (xl).
64 Arnaud Join-Lambert, *La Liturgie des heures pour tous les baptisés: l'expérience quotidienne du mystère pascal* (London, Paris and Dudley, MA: Peeters, 2009), pp. 236–47, 300.
65 The Concluding Prayer of Vespers, Tuesday, Week 2, with which Join-Lambert ends his book. Ibid., p. 300.

Chapter 10

JESUS THE SUN OF JUSTICE IN A SUNLESS AGE

We have seen that a rich heritage of solar symbolism has not disappeared. It is, however, neglected in contemporary theology and spirituality. In the first section of this chapter, I suggest that sunlessness – the metaphor of the sun not shining – captures something in the recent religious experience of believers and non-believers alike. In a second section, I propose the revival of the ancient Christological title 'Sun of Justice'.

A sunless age

Friedrich Nietzsche and Thérèse of Lisieux

In 1882, nine years after the birth of Thérèse of Lisieux, Friedrich Nietzsche announced the death of God. They seem to have lodged simultaneously in the same Parisian hotel when she was travelling as a girl with her father. More significantly, there are surprising parallels in thought and feeling between the pioneering atheist and the enclosed Carmelite nun.[1] Nietzsche and 'The Little Flower' are hugely different, but they both portrayed atheism as sunlessness.[2]

Thérèse gives an original twist to Christian solar tradition: she would like to soar in the heights like the eagles, the great saints who can stare directly at the Divine Sun, but she is a weak little bird – *un faible petit oiseau* – soaked and bedraggled, with weak wings. She cannot fly majestically upwards, but she can keep her gaze fixed in faith on the Sun of Love who she knows shines behind the clouds. Sometimes not a single ray is visible. She asks Jesus, the Divine Eagle, that she may take off into the upper regions, with his wings.[3] In the final lines of *Thus Spoke Zarathustra*, Nietzsche proclaims a radical alternative. Zarathustra is the new pagan rising sun, an eternally recurring dawn that is also a recurring noon, a recurring sunset and midnight: '"This is *my* morning, *my* day begins: *rise up now, rise up, great noontide!*" / Thus spoke Zarathustra and left his cave, glowing and strong, like a morning sun emerging from behind dark mountains.'[4] At the same time, for Nietzsche, the death of God means no more sun:

> Have you not heard of that madman who lit a lantern in the bright morning hours, ran to the market-place and cried incessantly: 'I am looking for God, I am looking for God! ... Where has God gone? he cried. 'I shall tell you. *We have killed him* – you and I. We are all his murderers. ... What did we do when we unchained this earth from its sun? Whither is it moving now? Whither are we moving now? Away from all suns? ... Is more and more night not coming on all the time? Must not lanterns be lit in the morning?'[5]

Paradoxically, Thérèse had similar thoughts. As a girl, in 1887, she spent forty-five minutes in total darkness in a tunnel, travelling by train through the Gothard Pass. Three years later, she was convinced that Jesus was leading her to an underground place where the sun does not shine.[6] Her brief life would end with two years of darkness and doubt. In the official edition of her Autobiography, her accounts of these experiences were softened and relocated earlier in her life. It emerges that she was gripped by what she described as the strangest thoughts. She saw herself in solidarity with her brother atheists, a remarkable stance for a young woman from her religious background. A Discalced Carmelite, she follows John of the Cross, referring to a 'night of faith',[7] but expresses a solidarity with atheists that is original. She expressed her experience of sunlessness in a document in the archives of the Lisieux Carmel:

> He permitted my soul to be invaded by the thickest darkness, and that the thought of heaven, up until then so sweet to me, be no longer anything but the cause of struggle and torment. ... One would have to travel through this dark tunnel to understand its darkness. I will try to explain it by a comparison.
>
> I imagine I was born in a country that is covered in thick fog. I never had the experience of contemplating the joyful appearance of nature flooded and transformed by the brilliance of the sun. It is true that from childhood I heard people speak of these marvels, and I know the country I am living in is not really my true fatherland, and there is another I must long for without ceasing. This is not simply a story invented by someone living in the sad country where I am, but it is a reality, for the King of the fatherland of the bright sun actually came and lived for thirty-three years in the land of darkness.[8]

We turn now to another, quite different, fellow traveller of Thérèse, a university librarian in the north of England.

Philip Larkin

Philip Larkin (1922–85), who described himself as agnostic, gave the fear of death bleak expression in a poem about a sunless dawn, entitled with heavy irony 'Aubade' – a dawn love-song. Waking at four, he is a day nearer death: 'Waking at four to soundless dark, I stare. / In time the curtain-edges will grow light. / Till then I see what's really always there: / Unresting death, a whole day nearer now.'[9] Larkin wrote 'Aubade' in 1977, expressing a lifelong obsession with living in the shadow of death. In an earlier poem 'High Windows', he contemplates 'the sun-comprehending glass, / And beyond it, the deep blue air, that shows / Nothing, and is nowhere, and is endless'.[10] In 'Aubade', he changed an earlier draft 'the open emptiness for ever' to 'the total emptiness for ever'. Any possibility of further vistas or salvific possibilities is ruthlessly cut out.[11] The line 'The sky is white as clay, with no sun' evokes a bloodless corpse and the clay typically dug out of graves in Hull, the city where Larkin spent most of his adult life.

Some of his other poems help us appreciate the full bleakness of the monosyllables: 'with no sun'. In 'Toads Revisited', he imagines himself in the shoes of the unemployed, the old and the destitute, who use a local park during the day: clouds obscure the sun as they watch bread being delivered.[12] In 'Aubade' we find once more deliveries – now the postman – and the same heavy Hull cloud cover. By contrast, 'Solar' from the sixties has been called 'a pagan incantation: a hymn to the sun'.[13] It is a celebration of a generous and life-giving natural force. The sun is luxuriant, majestic and fiery, with rays like the petals of a flower, and it even has a face, that of a lion. It is golden, like the precious metal, or like honey. Five years after 'Aubade', he wrote '1982', evoking the joy of noon on a hot summer day.[14] There is the same blazing abundance as in 'Solar', the botanical imagery and even the lion: 'Whatever conceived / Now fully leaved, / Abounding, ablaze – / O long lion days!' A year before he wrote 'Aubade' he had penned a versified Valentine's Day note to his secretary: 'You are fine as summer weather, / May to August all in one, / And the clocks, when we're together, / Count no shadows. Only sun.'[15] In 'Aubade', at four in the morning with death approaching, 'the sky is white as clay, with no sun.'

'A wintry season'

Thérèse is representative of wider currents. Teresa of Calcutta also goes down into a sunless tunnel. She spoke of darkness, loss and loneliness, and strange suffering. 'Our Lord thought it better for me to be in the tunnel – so He is gone again – leaving me alone.'[16] She saw her suffering as on behalf of others, but without Thérèse's characteristic identification with them: 'If I ever become a saint – I will be surely one of "darkness." I will continually be absent from heaven – to light the light of those in darkness on earth.'[17] Again, a Carthusian novice master rehearses for his charges some of the realities of the Dark Night: monks can pity those without the light of faith, he says, until one day the Lord extinguishes it and launches them into a painful process of purification. In a sense, one day a contemplative has to lose the faith to find it. He describes impenetrable darkness and disorientation reminiscent of Nietzsche's description of the death of God. Only on emerging from these trials do monks realize that 'the sun is shining, the sky is above us, the earth beneath our feet'.[18] John of the Cross's words 'These are the ones who go down into hell alive' would seem to apply here.[19] This 'descent into hell' is not, however, resurrection light shining into the darkness, as in the *Anastasis* icon, but entering Sheol with those still sitting in darkness and the shadow of death awaiting liberation.

There are parallels in the experience of non-believers. In the wider Western culture, the impossibility of looking directly at the sun continued into the modern era not as referring to God but to the difficulty of contemplating death. The best-known saying to this effect is a maxim of the seventeenth-century essayist La Rochefoucauld: 'Neither the sun nor death can be looked at steadily.'[20] Singer David Bowie does try to face dying in his last album released shortly before his death in 2016 and entitled 'Blackstar', echoing an Elvis Presley song that linked the image of a black star and imminent death.[21] The video portrays a surreal, dark, sunless world. Three scarecrow figures writhe in agony as they are crucified. As one critic put it, 'here's melancholy as a form of exhilaration, ghosts of other songs and characters, a weakness for the sensational, glimmers of the supernatural, daydream, trance, faith and passion all existing on the borders of waking thought'.[22] A recurring refrain speaks of 'a solitary candle' at the centre of everything. Wallace Stevens's poem 'Final Soliloquy of the Interior Paramour' describes a different scene, a genteel evening gathering: 'How high that highest candle lights the dark. / Out of this same light, out of the central mind, / We make a dwelling in the evening air, / In which being there together is enough.'[23] We can see Bowie's video as a sort of visual *Tenebrae* and Good Friday, and Stevens's evening ceremony as an Easter Vigil but neither Bowie's solitary candle nor Stevens's highest candle is the paschal candle, and the Sun of Resurrection does not shine for them. In this, they share common traits with the believing and non-believing voices we have briefly listened to.

In a similar vein, for Karl Rahner, we live in a 'wintry season' and the devotional life of Christians does not have the luxuriant forms of past eras with their 'devotions and pious practices'.[24] He probably has the Baroque in mind. Elsewhere he talks of the 'cheerful brightness' of Baroque church interiors, and of an artistic creativity that built 'Baroque churches with the joyous exuberance of the shining transfiguration of the world'.[25] The Baroque era as Rahner sees it is a time of light. Winter, on the other hand, is a time when the light and warmth of the sun are limited. This season captures something of late modern spiritual experience in the West, of believers and unbelievers alike. In contrast with the Baroque age that had John of the Cross's Dark Night but also a joyful shining transfiguration of the world, we have a distorted light-deficient pattern of imagery that is less faithful to the balance of light and darkness in the Bible. All the same, just as winter involves looking forward to spring and the return of the sun, perhaps what Pope Francis describes as a change of epoch and not just an epoch of change will involve a new experience of light.[26]

The Sun of Justice

> But for you who revere my name the Sun of Justice shall rise, with healing in its wings. You shall go out leaping like calves from the stall.
>
> (Malachi: 4.2, slightly modified)

Dusk and dawn

Hegel's oft-quoted statement at the end of the Preface to his *Philosophy of Right* that the Owl of Minerva takes flight only at dusk – a historical epoch can only be understood as it is ending – fits perfectly John McGahern's dusk graveyard scene that we saw in the Introduction.[27] McGahern describes a rural Catholic culture, bound up with a cosmic symbolism of light and sun, just as that way of life was coming to an end. The situation now in the Western world is largely urban, technological and secular. In some respects, it is like that of Israel at the time of Malachi.[28] Israel was a small outpost of the Persian Empire. Jews were asking whether it was worthwhile distinguishing themselves from their neighbours, and whether God did indeed reward those who faithfully practise the Law. That did not seem to be the case. Today, with Christians increasingly a minority, with scandals of clerical sexual abuse and cover-ups, and many women saying they are not heard in the church, people inevitably ask analogous questions to those of the Jews of Malachi's day. Do the moral teachings and religious practices of the church make for flourishing human beings? And are these teachings and practices God-given?

Malachi's 'Sun of Justice' promised cosmic, social, and personal healing in an image of dawn.[29] Perhaps the verse from Malachi that so captivated early Christians can speak today. The Sun of Justice is the man whose name is Rising Sun, Dawn, East (Zech. 3.8) and who is described as a great light dawning on a people who sat in darkness and the shadow of death (Mt. 4.12-25). He calls to conversion and heals people suffering from every form of sickness. When, in the Eastern *Anastasis* icon, the Risen Christ breaks open the gates of Sheol or Hades to bring Adam and Eve out into the light, the whole of humanity is represented in them.[30] Christ in the icon is a figure of light and energy, he who rises from on high to shine on those in darkness and the shadow of death (Lk. 1.78-9): 'Almighty, ever-living God, / shed the light of your glory / on the peoples who are living in the shadow of death, / as you did long ago, / when our Lord Jesus Christ, the Sun of Justice, / came among us from on high.'[31]

When he spoke at the consistory where he was elected pope, Francis alluded to the patristic metaphor of the church as moon that we saw in Origen.[32] He returned to it in a homily on the feast of the Epiphany in 2016:

> The Church cannot illude herself into thinking that she shines with her own light. Saint Ambrose expresses this nicely by presenting the moon as a metaphor for the Church: 'The moon is in fact the Church ... [she] shines not with her own light, but with the light of Christ. She draws her brightness from the Sun of Justice, and so she can say: "It is no longer I who live, but Christ who lives in me."' (*Hexaemeron*, IV, 8, 32)[33]

Jesus and the sun

The metaphor of Jesus as the Sun of Justice invites us to attend to both poles of the comparison: to Jesus Christ the Just One (Acts 22.14) and to the sun. To understand what it is for him to come with healing in his wings, we turn most particularly to the gospel accounts of his ministry, as well as to the other pole of the metaphor, the physical reality of the sun. In the words of Ambrose of Milan, 'when you behold it, reflect on its Author. When you admire it, give praise to its Creator. If the sun as consort of and participant in nature is so pleasing, how much goodness is there to be found in that "Sun of Justice"'.[34] For poet Patrick Kavanagh, a shaft of sunlight can be a place where God gives teaching.[35]

We cannot look at the sun directly, given the danger of retinopathy, and we perceive it as it illumines objects of our attention. In 1911 the poet Rupert Brooke asked Virginia Woolf, 'Virginia, what is the brightest thing you can think of?' 'A leaf with the light on it', she replied.[36] Cultivating an awareness of sunlight in daily life can become a simple spiritual practice. Seen obliquely or indirectly, sunlight gives a hint of the splendour of the all-seeing and invisible God who, since Old Testament times, has been described as shining like the sun. Aquinas spells out some of the import of the metaphor in characteristically clear terms. God is continuously at work in the life of each person, causing them to be 'justified', just as the sun causes the air to be lit during the day.[37] The Sun of Justice is always active – it is never night for him – but we are not always able to receive his grace because of the obstacles put in its way.[38]

Holistic justice

With poverty, inequality and environmental degradation increasingly obvious, there is a widespread desire for justice and healing. The Christological symbol of the Sun of Justice coming with healing in his wings could not be timelier. The Hebrew word for justice was translated into Greek and Latin sometimes as justice, sometimes as mercy. For John Milton, humankind will find grace 'in mercy and in justice both, / Through heaven and earth, so shall my glory excel, / But mercy first and last shall brightest shine'.[39] In church Latin, the word *iustitia* is always closely linked with the idea of salvation[40] and the *Sol Iustitiae* is also the Sun of Salvation where salvation is to be understood broadly as embracing the physical, the cosmic and the eschatological, as well as the spiritual. At the same time, Pope Francis suggests that 'while it is true that the word "justice" can be a synonym for faithfulness to God's will in every aspect of our life, if we give the word too general a meaning, we forget that it is shown especially in justice towards those who are most vulnerable: "Seek justice, correct oppression; defend the fatherless, plead for the widow" (Isa. 1.17).'[41] This emphasis favours opting for the wording 'Sun of Justice' rather than 'Sun of Righteousness'.

Justice in the church

We saw how, for Ambrose of Milan, the soul of the Christian should be like a church building – a single undivided space without internal walls, with a window to the east so that, symbolized as the sun, God could look in.[42] Perhaps this metaphor of the Sun of Justice streaming into an open space that fills with light could also be an image of a church renewed in addressing the crisis of sexual abuse and cover-ups, seeking justice and healing through transparency and accountability.

When it comes to the injustice of women's voicelessness in the church, however, there is a particular difficulty. Insofar as solar symbolism is gendered, it is usually in terms of male metaphors (the use of Aztec solar warrior symbolism to express Christ's saving work would be a good example).[43] The *mysterium lunae*, the ecclesial lunar symbolism referred to by Pope Francis, can be called feminine in character, but applies to the whole church, and not to women as such. While solar symbolism can be combined with unquestionably feminine imagery such as that of Christ compared to a hen gathering her chickens, as we saw in Hippolytus,[44] sun motifs do not provide resources for directly addressing the voicelessness of women. A more promising strategy is to look to gospel narratives where women have a voice and bring about the shining of the light. In the Fourth Gospel, it is Mary Magdalene who, at dawn, is the first to see and speak with the risen Lord. Subsequently, 'Mary Magdalene went and announced to the disciples, "I have seen the Lord"; and she told them that he had said these things to her' (Jn 20.18) – hence, her traditional title *Apostola Apostolorum*. Earlier in the Gospel, in Chapter 4, a Samaritan woman has a robust exchange with Jesus: 'How is it that you, a Jew, ask a drink of me, a woman of Samaria?' 'Are you greater than our ancestor Jacob, who gave us the well, and with his sons and his flocks drank from it?' Returning to the city, she recounts what Jesus has said and asks, 'He cannot be the Messiah, can he?' Other Samaritans come to faith because of her testimony, and, in the Greek Orthodox Church, she is celebrated as a saint with the name *Photine* (luminous one) *and Equal to the Apostles*.[45] Her exchange with Christ in a public place under the bright midday sun contrasts with Nicodemus, in Chapter 3, who speaks in private under the cover of night. However, the most effective utterances at the service of light on the part of a woman in John's Gospel are in Chapter 2, at the wedding feast in Cana of Galilee. Mary, the mother of Jesus, induces him to perform his first sign, and his glory shines forth: 'They have no wine.' / 'Woman, what concern is that to you and to me? My hour has not yet come.' / 'Do whatever he tells you.'

Restoring cosmic order

The spiritual, the social and the cosmic are often unconnected in our individualistic and relatively acosmic Western Christian culture. The concept of *ma'at* or justice that Israel absorbed from other religions and integrated into the cult of Yahweh is the opposite of such uncoupling. Jürgen Moltmann describes the Mesopotamian god Shamash dispensing *ma'at*:

> This righteousness is the cosmic order of the world and life, like the light of the sun. In the morning the divine righteousness rises with the sun and leads the country and the people along right paths. The person is righteous who guides justly; what is righteous is what is healthy; the person is righteous if he lives rightly. To live rightly can be said of plants, animals and human beings in the rhythm of the sun's light.[46]

This holistic notion of justice includes promoting justice and peace in the world and protecting the environment of our common home on earth, whether in political or social activity or in choices made as a voter or a consumer. The notion of justice as restoring right order – restorative justice – is also to be linked to the traditional spiritual concept of reparation. Working for justice can take distinctive forms in the lives of people who have limited direct impact on society and the environment. According to an anonymous Carthusian monk, the prayer of solitary contemplatives and the suffering of the sick can be works of justice. Prayer is efficacious and 'for us monks, prayer for others is a sacred duty of charity, and something that we owe in justice to the poor who are our brothers (St Thomas speaks of "spiritual alms"; I would rather say "justice").'[47] The prayer and fasting of monks make reparation – 'to restore an order that has been disrupted by sin (our own sin**,** or the sin of those for whom we are praying). In this way, prayer becomes something more total, that engages our whole person, and takes on a greater existential weight'.[48] The Carthusian author gives the example of a sick person who has been to Lourdes several times and has not been cured. They continue praying, with increasing openness to the will of God, and 'what begins as a request for healing, can gradually become, through patience, a life offered in reparation'.[49]

Healing and conversion

The Sun of Justice comes with healing in his wings. In the ancient Mediterranean world, sun was associated with health. At the beginning of the Christian era, the poet Ovid has Apollo, god of the sun, declare to Daphne: 'The art of medicine I gave the world. / And all men call me "healer".'[50] There was a Roman saying about health that could be translated 'You can't beat sun and salt!'[51] In the contemporary world, the dangers of excessive sun-exposure have often obscured the importance of natural light and sunshine, and the associated circadian rhythms, for human health and flourishing.[52] Overall, the sun is both a resource for health and a potential threat. Malachi is read today in a time of ecological crisis when the sun is a matter of life and death. Unless human beings take care of their common home on earth, the sun and its heat will be a curse bringing life-threatening global warming. On the other hand, solar power could be a blessing. In his novel *Klara and the Sun*, Kazuo Ishiguro depicts a futuristic dystopia where perennial questions about loneliness and love play out in a world of constricted emotions where intelligence is boosted artificially with life-threatening procedures. For Klara, pollution is evil and the sun a nourishing healer. She is a solar-powered android capable of childlike love and of self-sacrifice. When she prays to the sun to heal her sickly human charge Josie who could be paying with her life for her artificially enhanced intelligence, it seems that perhaps the prayer is being answered. The sick-bed scene where the sun shines on Josie and she recovers is central to the novel like McGahern's graveyard scene in *That They May Face the Rising Sun*: 'So, for the next few moments, we all remained in our fixed positions as the Sun focused ever more brightly on Josie. We watched and waited, and even when at one point the orange half-disc looked as if it might catch alight, none of us did anything. Then Josie stirred, and with squinting eyes, held a hand up in the air. "Hey. What's with this light anyway?" she said.'[53] Rather like John Quinn in McGahern's burial scene who concludes that it would almost make you think, Josie's mother has the final word: 'Okay, let's assume nothing.'[54]

The image of solar healing in Christian symbolism has roots in the Bible. For Isaiah, 'the light of the sun will be sevenfold, like the light of seven days, on the day when the Lord binds up the injuries of his people and heals the wounds inflicted by his blow' (Isa. 30.26). The culmination of Christ's work to bring healing and justice was on the Cross:

> He could not launch God's kingdom of justice, truth, and peace unless injustice, lies, and violence had done their worst and, like a hurricane, had blown themselves out, exhausting their force on this one spot. He could not begin the work of healing the world unless he provided the antidote to the infection that would otherwise destroy the project from within. This is how the early work of Jesus' public career, the healings, the celebrations, the forgiveness, the changed hearts, all look forward to this moment.[55]

We saw in the last chapter how the paschal mystery, in its different dimensions, is described with metaphors of light and sun. In the fifth century, Theodoret of Cyr describes the saving effects of the resurrection: Christ 'rose like a kind of sun for us who were seated in darkness and shadow, freed us from sin, gave us a share in righteousness, covered us with spiritual gifts like wings, and provided healing for our souls'.[56]

Returning to our key verse, Mal. 4.2, with its promise of solar healing, the fact that it is sandwiched between two verses, 4.1 and 4.3, can only 'provoke a disturbing uneasiness in the modern reader'[57]:

> 4.1 See, the day is coming, burning like an oven, when all the arrogant and all evildoers will be stubble; the day that comes shall burn them up, says the Lord of hosts, so that it will leave them neither root nor branch.

> 4.3 And you shall tread down the wicked, for they will be ashes under the soles of your feet, on the day when I act, says the Lord of hosts.

What are we to make of these verses? Disconcertingly, the text contrasts the lot of Malachi's readers and that of evildoers whose fate is spelled out in verses 1 and 3. How are we to read the entirety of 4.1-3? I suggest that the curse of being burnt to a frazzle and trodden underfoot is not to be applied exclusively to others as retribution for their faults but is to be read as the other side of the coin of the promise made in 4.2. 'See, I am setting before you today a blessing and a curse' (Deut. 11.26). A divine judge is a consuming fire, and there is no healing without conversion. Just as Francis of Assisi's *Canticle of Brother Sun* was sung to effect a change of heart among the warring factions of Assisi as well as to console Francis himself as he was dying, Mal. 4.2 is to be read as a challenge as well as a promise.

Conclusion

While the metaphor of sunlessness, of the sun not shining, captures a felt lack in the recent experience of believers and unbelievers alike, the ancient Christological title of the Sun of Justice crystallizes traditional solar symbolism with the promise of integrating the cosmic, the ecological and the spiritual in a sustained focus on the person of Jesus Christ, the Light of the World.

Notes

1. Noëlle Hausman, *Frédéric Nietzsche Thérèse de Lisieux: deux poétiques de la modernité* (Paris: Beauchesne, 1984). Michael Paul Gallagher, *Dive Deeper: The Human Poetry of Faith* (London: Darton, Longman and Todd, 2001), pp. 65–76. Bridget Edman, OCD, *St Thérèse of Lisieux: Nietzsche is My Brother* (Washington, DC: ICS Publications, 2010).
2. Tomáš Halík, *Patience with God: The Story of Zacchaeus Continuing in Us* (New York: Doubleday, 2009), pp. 24–36.
3. Sainte Thérèse de l'Enfant Jésus, *Manuscrits autobiographiques* (Lisieux: Carmel de Lisieux, 1957), pp. 233–7.
4. Friedrich Nietzsche, *Thus Spoke Zarathustra* (trans. R. J. Hollingdale; Harmondsworth: Penguin, 1969), p. 336.
5. Friedrich Nietzsche, 'The Gay Science', no. 125, in *A Nietzsche Reader* (ed. and trans. R. J. Hollingdale; Harmondsworth: Penguin, 1977), pp. 202–3.
6. Thomas R. Nevin, *The Last Years of Saint Thérèse: Doubt and Darkness, 1895–1897* (New York: Oxford University Press, 2013), p. 148.
7. Ibid., p. 36.
8. Thérèse of Lisieux, *Manuscript C 05v–6v*. Available online: http://www.archives-carmel-lisieux.fr/english/carmel/index.php/c01-10/c05/c05v (accessed 29 April 2020).
9. Philip Larkin, *The Complete Poems* (ed. Archie Burnett; London: Faber and Faber, 2018), p. 115.
10. Ibid., p. 80.
11. James Booth, *Philip Larkin: Life, Art and Love* (London: Bloomsbury, 2014), p. 417.
12. Larkin, *Complete Poems*, p. 55.
13. Ibid., pp. 89–90. Booth, *Philip Larkin*, p. 300.
14. Larkin, *Complete Poems*, p. 323; Booth, *Philip Larkin*, p. 435.
15. 'Be My Valentine this Monday.' Larkin, *Complete Poems*, p. 316.
16. Mother Teresa, *Come Be My Light: The Revealing Private Writings of the Nobel Peace Prize Winner* (ed. with commentary Brian Kolodiejchuk, MC; London: Rider, 2008), p. 177.
17. Ibid., p. 230.
18. A Carthusian, *Interior Prayer: Carthusian Novice Conferences* (trans. Sister Maureen Scrine; Leominster: Gracewing, 2006), p. 157.
19. John of the Cross, *The Dark Night* 2.6.6. *Collected Works*, p. 406.
20. François de La Rochefoucauld, *Maxim 26*. ET *La Rochefoucauld Collected Maxims and Other Reflections. New Translation with Parallel French Text* (trans. E. H. Blackmore, A. M. Blackmore and Francine Giguère; Oxford: Oxford University

Press, 2007), p. 11. During the Covid-19 pandemic, BBC Home Editor Mark Easton compared the difficulty of thinking about death to looking directly at the sun. *News* 5.15pm, [TV programme] BBC 1, 25 April 2020.
21 David Bowie, *Blackstar* [video]. Available online: https://www.youtube.com/watch?v=kszLwBaC4Sw (accessed 5 April 2021).
22 Paul Morley, *The Age of Bowie: How David Bowie Made a World of Difference* (London, New York, etc.: Simon and Schuster, 2016), p. 458.
23 Wallace Stevens, *Selected Poems* (London: Faber and Faber, 2010), p. 128.
24 Karl Rahner, 'Christian Living Formerly and Today', in *Theological Investigations, vol. 7: Further Theology of the Spiritual Life 1* (trans. David Bourke; New York: Herder and Herder and London: Darton, Longman and Todd, 1971), pp. 3–24 (13).
25 Karl Rahner, 'The Ignatian Mysticism of Joy in the World', in *Theological Investigations, vol. 3: The Theology of the Spiritual Life* (trans. Karl-H. Kruger; London: Darton Longman and Todd and New York: The Seabury Press, 1974), pp. 277–93 (290).
26 'One could say that today we are not living an epoch of change so much as an epochal change.' Pope Francis, Meeting with the Participants in the Fifth Convention of the Italian Church. Available online: http://w2.vatican.va/content/francesco/en/speeches/2015/november/documents/papa-francesco_20151110_firenze-convegno-chiesa-italiana.html (accessed 29 April 2020). See also Pope Francis in Conversation with Austen Ivereigh, *Let Us Dream: The Path to a Better Future* (London: Simon and Schuster UK, 2020), p. 54.
27 Georg Wilhelm Friedrich Hegel, *Hegel's Philosophy of Right* (trans. and notes T. M. Knox; London, Oxford and New York: Oxford University Press, 1967), p. 13.
28 Elie Assis, 'Structure and Meaning in the Book of Malachi', in *Prophecy and Prophets in Ancient Israel: Proceedings of the Oxford Old Testament Seminar* (ed. John Day; New York and London: T&T Clark, 2010), pp. 354–69 (366).
29 See above, pp. 7–9.
30 Joseph Ratzinger, *Daughter Sion: Meditation on the Church's Marian Belief* (San Francisco: Ignatius Press, 1983), p. 66.
31 Final Prayer, Morning Prayer, Thursday, Week 3, *Divine Office* vol. 3, p. [338].
32 O'Connell, *The Election of Pope Francis*, p. 154.
33 Pope Francis, Homily Epiphany 2016. Available online: http://w2.vatican.va/content/francesco/en/homilies/2016/documents/papa-francesco_20160106_omelia-epifania.html (accessed 29 April 2020).
34 Saint Ambrose, *Hexameron* 4.1.2. CSEL 32.1, p. 111. ET *Saint Ambrose, Hexameron, Paradise and Cain and Abel* (trans. John. J. Savage; FC, 42; New York: Fathers of the Church, 1961), p. 127.
35 Patrick Kavanagh, 'The Great Hunger', in *Collected Poems*, p. 76.
36 Cohen, *Chasing the Sun*, p. 245.
37 Thomas Aquinas, ST 2.2. q.4. a.4. ad 3. Thomas Aquinas, *Summa Theologiae, vol. 31: (2a2ae. 1–7) Faith* (ed. Thomas Gilby, OP, trans. T. C. O'Brien; repr., Cambridge: Cambridge University Press, 2006), p. 131.
38 Thomas Aquinas, Commentary on John 9.1.1306. Saint Thomas Aquinas, *Commentary on the Gospel of John Chapters 9–21* (ed. The Aquinas Institute; trans. Fr. Fabian R. Larcher, OP; Latin/English Edition of the Works of St. Thomas Aquinas, 36; Lander, Wyoming: The Aquinas Institute for the Study of Sacred Doctrine, 2013), p. 6.
39 John Milton, *Paradise Lost* bk 3, lines 132–4.

40 Alister E. McGrath, *Iustitia Dei: A History of the Christian Doctrine of Justification* (Cambridge: Cambridge University Press, 1986), pp. 10–12.
41 Pope Francis, Apostolic Exhortation *Gaudete et Exsultate* 79. Available online: http://w2.vatican.va/content/francesco/en/apost_exhortations/documents/papa-francesco_esortazione-ap_20180319_gaudete-et-exsultate.html (accessed 29 April 2020).
42 See above, p. 25.
43 Susan K. Roll, 'Christ as Sun/King: The Historical Roots of a Perduring Dualism', *Journal of the European Society of Women in Theological Research* 6 (1998), pp. 133–42.
44 See above, p. 15.
45 'Photine of Samaria', *Orthodoxwiki*. Available online: https://orthodoxwiki.org/Photine_of_Samaria (accessed 12 December 2020).
46 Jürgen Moltmann, *Sun of Righteousness, Arise! God's Future for Humanity and the Earth* (London: SCM, 2010), p. 127.
47 A Carthusian, *Interior Prayer*, p. 47.
48 Ibid., p. 49.
49 Ibid., p. 50.
50 Ovid, *Metamorphoses* Bk. 1, lines 521–2. ET Ovid, *Metamorphoses* (trans. A. D. Melville; Oxford: Oxford University Press, 1998), p. 16.
51 Franz Joseph Dölger, *Sol Salutis: Gebet und Gesang im christlichen Altertum mit besonderer Rücksicht auf die Ostung in Gebet und Liturgie* (Münster: Aschendorff, 1925), p. 383.
52 For a panoramic view of sun and health, see Richard Hobday, *The Healing Sun: Sunlight and Health in the 21st Century* (Forres: Findhorn Press, 1999).
53 Kazuo Ishiguro, *Klara and the Sun* (London: Faber and Faber, 2021), p. 284.
54 Ibid., p. 285.
55 Wright and Bird, *The New Testament in Its World*, p. 259.
56 Theodoret of Cyr, *Interpretatio Malachiae Prophetae* 4.2. PG 81.1984. ET Alberto Ferreiro and Thomas C. Oden (eds), *The Twelve Prophets* (Ancient Christian Commentary on Scripture, Old Testament, 14; Downers Grove, IL: InterVarsity Press, 2003), p. 311.
57 Andrew E. Hill, *Haggai, Zechariah and Malachi: An Introduction and Commentary* (Downers Grove, IL: InterVarsity Press, 2012), p. 360.

CONCLUSIONS

Christian solar symbolism

Where it came from

We return to the questions raised in the Introduction. First, where did Christian solar symbolism come from? It had its origin in biblical themes, such as an invisible God who shines, mediated particularly by expressions freighted with meaning, such as *Anatole/Oriens* (the Rising Sun, the Dawn, the East) and 'Sun of Justice', and in the natural phenomena of light and sun. It was not a simple transfer of pagan mythology or imperial ideology. In the first centuries of the Christian era, the gospel entered a culture that was markedly solar in its interests and provided fertile ground for Christian light and sun motifs. Symbols and images from Greco-Roman culture such as the halo or the mandorla were applied to Christ, just as features of the sun god Shamash were taken over and applied to Yahweh in the Old Testament.

Why it weakened

Our second question was: why did the impact of this symbolism weaken? When Christianity spread widely in the late Roman Empire, the church took measures to guard against a perceived danger of sun worship. We can think of the fifth-century Pope Leo berating the Christians of Rome for reverencing the sun on entering St Peter's. Charles Taylor remarks that even with necessary reform movements, a price is paid, and they can end up crushing or side-lining 'important facets of spiritual life, which had in fact flourished in earlier "paganisms", for all their faults'.[1] What was sidelined was a link between faith experience and the cosmic reality of the sun and its light. This process of loss continued in various ways in the Latin West, with a decline of symbolic sensitivity and the development of an 'acosmic humanism'. In the modern era, technological developments such as electric light contributed to a detachment from natural cosmic cycles of light and darkness, with spirituality often taking an introspective turn.

In the modern Western church, there has been a marked interest in darkness, cloud and night, describing aspects of inner experience. Darkness and cloud have a prominence that is disproportionate, when put alongside the pattern of light, darkness and sun imagery in the Bible. This is partly due to the poetic genius of John of the Cross and his fascinating symbol of the Dark Night, even if his focus on night seems to have been part of a wider cultural shift in the early modern era. In a later development, the metaphor of sunlessness employed by people as diverse as Friedrich Nietzsche, Thérèse of Lisieux and Philip Larkin captures aspects of an age Karl Rahner termed a wintry season. The image of sunlessness points to a need for something new symbolized in the coming of the sun. Christian sun symbolism is still accessible. As Jamesie says to Patrick Ryan in the graveyard scene in John McGahern's *That They May Face the Rising Sun* that we saw at the beginning of this book, 'You never lost it, Patrick.'

How it can be revived

As to our third question, how to revive the symbolism, we need to think and make choices – in the words of John Quinn, another of the characters in John McGahern's graveyard scene, 'It'd nearly make you start to think.' Introspection, esoteric practices and personal or liturgical orientation do not offer a way forward. But there are strategies to retrieve the freshness and force of patristic and early medieval sun symbolism, and to find a symbolic balance of light and darkness, day and night, that is closer to that found in the Bible. I suggest five strategies centring on: (1) the Book of Scripture; (2) the Book of Nature; (3) liturgy and prayer; (4) natural light as a theological resource; and (5) the Christological title Sun of Justice.

Five strategies for revival

The Book of Scripture

Light and sun in the Bible are not synonyms, but they are closely linked, as we see in the first pages of Genesis. In the Bible as a whole, light is a primary symbol for God, and the sun is a secondary ancillary symbol. The two senses of darkness we examined are also secondary symbols. In the relative dualism of the New Testament (as distinct from absolute dualism such as those of Zoroastrianism or Manicheism), articulated most particularly in the Johannine writings, anti-divine darkness is sin and ignorance and the opposite of the divine light. In Exodus, however, there is a divine darkness that is effectively an aspect of the divine light as dazzling or blinding. This second sense of darkness, what we can term good darkness, was not taken up in the New Testament as a major theme but was explored by Origen, Gregory of Nyssa and Dionysius the Areopagite. It went on to feed into the symbolism of darkness, cloud and night so prominent in the modern West, but without a countervailing attention to the secondary symbol of the sun. In a nutshell, if we want to do justice to the overall biblical teaching on light and darkness, we need to give the sun and its light the attention it merits.

The visual culture of the ancient world two millennia before Thomas Edison's lightbulbs is a hermeneutical key that helps us understand what the biblical authors meant when they spoke about light. People lived in more intimate connection with the realities of sunlight and daylight. The sun was such an awe-inspiring phenomenon that a resounding No to sun worship was necessary. It was created by God and fulfils his purposes, providing light and serving humans by determining the rhythms of night and day – 'By him', as Francis of Assisi puts it, 'you give us light'. The sun, especially as it rises at dawn, is presented as a symbol for Christ, and sunlight is a divinely revealed image of the God who cannot be seen and yet 'shines', most particularly in the face of Christ. The title Sun of Justice from the Prophet Malachi expresses how God brings justice, right order and healing. Taken up in the early church and still occupying a significant, but unnoticed, place in the prayer of the church, it is ripe for revival.

The Book of Nature

Traditionally the Book of Scripture is read alongside the Book of Nature. The Bible helps us 'read' the physical sun differently, and attention to the natural phenomenon of the sun and its light can help us appreciate, for instance, what it means to say in Lk. 1.78 that the Rising Sun has come to visit us. Gertrude the Great and Thomas Traherne point to the potential of simple exercises of observation and awareness. We look at a few concrete examples. The bright shining light of the sun, which no human being can view directly, gives a hint of the inaccessible light where God dwells. Sunlit scenery and spaces, and the sun shining on plants or buildings afford contemplative opportunities in ordinary life. Light shining through a crevice or chink is a natural symbol of the God of the Old Testament who cannot be seen but who 'shines'. Moreover, our natural response to the warmth and beauty of sunlight is at once spiritual and biological. Physical light, whether presently experienced, remembered or anticipated, is a natural symbol of the divine. As Francis of Assisi put it, 'Of you it is the sign.'

Whereas for fifth-century Romans the sun could represent a temptation to idolatry, today it could be an antidote to the technologically fuelled polytheism analysed by Pope Benedict. The physical phenomena of sun and light are divinely revealed symbols of the divine, and our gaze is to be directed outwards towards them. We might see this as part of a wider strategy of extroversion advocated by Pope Francis. Recollection and self-examination in 'discernment' are harnessed in an orientation outward to other human beings and to creation. 'High' culture, such as Dante's Divine Comedy or Hagia Sophia, is there to be exploited but the principal place to access the symbol of light is universal, everyday experience. In a perspective of faith, the sun also shines even when it is absent. Physical darkness and gloom and the various forms of urban darkness indicated by Carlos María

Galli point to the Sun of Justice at work despite all appearances, in a way accessible only in faith.

Liturgy and prayer

The texts of the eucharist direct us upwards to the heavenly world, beyond the sun. There are frequent references to light but little solar imagery in the Mass texts. The extra-biblical idea of praying to the east, to the rising sun – *ad orientem* – is not in the Roman Missal, never having attained a secure place in Western practice. We are directed, rather, upwards to where God dwells in unapproachable light. In the texts of the Liturgy of the Hours, on the other hand, there is abundant sun imagery. This is where biblical and traditional solar motifs are presented to nourish the Christian life. Technological developments such as dedicated computer software make a form of prayer that was largely the preserve of priests and religious readily accessible to all. Adoration of the Blessed Sacrament with the sunburst monstrance is also a point of insertion into the traditions we have been studying. In daily life, the simple practice of saying morning and evening prayers has been an essential part of Christian life for two millennia, anchoring the person in the rhythm of night and day. Given the role that natural light has played in the construction of Christian churches, it would be wise to give sunshine and natural light, divinely revealed symbols of God as they are, their rightful place in the design of churches. La Sagrada Familia Cathedral in Barcelona shows that epiphanic architecture of light need not be the preserve of past eras.

The natural theology of sunlight

In the words of Mircea Eliade, 'it is of the greatest importance, we believe, to rediscover a whole mythology, if not a theology, still concealed in the most ordinary, everyday life of contemporary man'.[2] As we see for instance in hymns of Ambrose of Milan, the bodily experience of the light of the sun can itself be an experience of Christ. This opens new avenues for a theology that is more concrete and contemplative, along the lines of the 'natural theology' described by Alister McGrath.

The metaphorical character of most Christian light and solar language is theologically significant, helping us avoid confusions and cul-de-sacs, such as searching in introspection for light phenomena, or looking to esoteric practices to see what would otherwise be invisible. Rather, we should emulate the creativity shown in the design of Irish and Anglo-Saxon high crosses, with Pierre de Bérulle and his spiritual appropriation of Copernican cosmology, or in the successful inculturation of Christianity in the world of the Aztecs. A creative recasting of solar symbolism in the light of scientific developments, in a new cultural situation, is called for. Contemporary chronobiology underpins the physiological and psychological importance of sunlight for human life. Contemporary cosmology reveals a universe of unimaginable expanses of time and space, and the extraordinary phenomenon of our common home on the planet earth, with its anthropic ecosystem, revolving around its sun. New theological and devotional possibilities open. The earth's sun and its light – local, temporary and anthropic in an unimaginably vast expanse of time and space – is a distinct *locus theologicus*, a place to look for theological data.

Jesus Christ the Sun of Justice

In the visual culture that produced the light imagery of the Bible and within which this imagery was understood in the premodern world, there was a distinction between light and sun, but they were more closely associated than is the case today. The physical reality of sunlight is a hermeneutical key for appreciating Christian light symbolism, rich but largely dormant solar metaphors, and neglected christological titles such as New Sun, Spiritual Sun and True Sun. Among these titles, Christ the Rising Sun (Luke 1.78) and the Sun of Justice (Mal 4.2) have the clearest biblical warrant. If we want to select a single title as a focus for a revival of solar symbolism, I suggest the Sun of Justice because of its threefold personal, social and cosmic/ecological reference.

On our 'common home' on earth, the sun has always inspired awe, but in the perspective of Christian faith it takes on a domestic character, so to speak. It is awe-inspiring ('Sir') but a member of a local family of creatures ('Brother'). The sun is 'Sir Brother Sun'. Francis of Assisi's Canticle beginning with the words '*Laudato si*' was a call to repentance and conversion. We are invited to attend anew to 'Sir Brother Sun' who is there for us but who, unlike water or air or earth, does not need our care, and to biblical voices such as that of Malachi that so captivated early Christians. This may help us negotiate in faith a wintry time in Christianity in the 'developed' Western world, beset by numerical decline, divisions and scandals, in the confident hope that spring will come. Such a spring can only be a renewed encounter with the person of Jesus Christ who is depicted in the Eastern *Anastasis* icon coming in radiant light to those in darkness and the shadow of death:

> But for you who revere my name the Sun of Justice shall rise, with healing in his wings. You shall go out leaping like calves from the stall.

Notes

1. Charles Taylor, *A Secular Age* (Cambridge, MA and London: The Belknap Press of Harvard University Press, 2007), p. 771.
2. Mircea Eliade, *Images and Symbols: Studies in Religious Symbolism* (London: Harvill, 1961), p. 18.

BIBLIOGRAPHY

Achtemeier, Elizabeth R., 'Jesus Christ, the Light of the World: The Biblical Understanding of Light and Darkness', *Interpretation* 7.4 (1963), pp. 439–49.

Adrych, Philippa, et al., *Images of Mithra* (Oxford: Oxford University Press, 2017).

Ambrose of Milan, *Saint Ambrose, Hexameron, Paradise, and Cain and Abel* (trans. John J. Savage; FC, 42; New York: Fathers of the Church, 1961).

Ambrose of Milan, *Homilies of Saint Ambrose on Psalm 118 (119)* (trans. Íde Ní Riain; Dublin: Halcyon Press, 1998).

Anderson, Paul N., Felix Just, SJ and Tom Thatcher (eds), *John, Jesus, and History, vol. 2: Aspects of Historicity in the Fourth Gospel* (Atlanta: Society of Biblical Literature, 2009).

Andreopoulos, Andreas, *Metamorphosis: The Transfiguration in Byzantine Theology and Iconography* (Crestwood, NY: St Vladimir's Seminary Press, 2005).

Anglo, Sydney, 'The London Pageants for the Reception of Katharine of Aragon: November 1501', *Journal of the Warburg and Courtauld Institutes* 26.1/2 (1963), pp. 53–89.

Anselm, St., *St Anselm's Proslogion with* A Reply on Behalf of the Fool by Gaunilo *and* The Author's Reply to Gaunilo (trans. M.J. Charlesworth; Notre Dame, IN: University of Notre Dame Press, 1979).

Apuleius, *Metamorphoses, vol. 2* (trans. J. Arthur Hanson; Cambridge, MA and London: Harvard University Press, 1989).

Arbuckle, Gerald A., *Culture, Inculturation, and Theologians: A Post-modern Critique* (Collegeville, MN: Liturgical Press, 2010).

Ashton, John, *Understanding the Fourth Gospel* (Oxford: Clarendon Press, 1993).

Assis, Elie, 'Structure and Meaning in the Book of Malachi', in *Prophecy and Prophets in Ancient Israel: Proceedings of the Oxford Old Testament Seminar* (ed. John Day; New York and London: T&T Clark, 2010), pp. 354–69.

Atkinson, T. D., 'Points of the Compass', in *Encyclopaedia of Religion and Ethics, vol. 10* (ed. James Hastings; Edinburgh: Clark, 1908–1926), pp. 73–88.

Augustine, 'Augustine of Hippo Sermon on Psalm 41 (Vulgate)' (trans. Bernard McGinn), in *The Essential Writings of Christian Mysticism* (ed. Bernard McGinn; New York: Random House, 2006), pp. 21–6.

Augustine, *Confessions* (ed. Michael P. Foley; trans. F. J. Sheed; introduction Peter Brown; repr., Indianapolis and Cambridge: Hackett Publishing Company, 2nd edn, 2006).

Augustine, *Expositions of the Psalms 33–50 (III/6)* (ed. John E. Rotelle, OSA; trans. and notes Maria Boulding, OSB; Hyde Park, NY: New City Press, 2000).

Augustine, *Expositions of the Psalms (Enarrationes in Psalmos) 99–120, III/19* (ed. Boniface Ramsay; trans. Maria Boulding, OSB; Hyde Park, NY: New City Press, 2003).

Augustine, 'The Lord's Sermon on the Mount' (trans. Michael G. Campbell, OSA; introduced and annotated by Boniface Ramsay), in *New Testament I and II* (ed. Boniface Ramsay; The Works of St Augustine, vols 15–16; Hyde Park, NY: New City Press, 2014), pp. 9–129.

Augustine, *New Testament I and II* (ed. Boniface Ramsay; The Works of St Augustine, vols 15–16; Hyde Park, NY: New City Press, 2014).
Augustine, *Sermons 1 (1–19) on the Old Testament* (ed. John E. Rotelle, OSA; trans. and notes Edmund Hill, OP; Brooklyn, New York: New City Press, 1990).
Bärnreuther, Andrea (ed.), *Sonne: Brennpunkt der Kulturen der Welt* (Neu-Isenburg: Edition Minerva, 2009).
Beeley, Christopher A., *The Unity of Christ: Continuity and Conflict in Patristic Tradition* (New Haven and London: Yale University Press, 2012).
Bentley, G. E., Jr. (ed.), *Blake Records: Documents (1741–1841) Concerning the Life of William Blake and His Family* (New Haven and London: Yale University Press, 2nd edn, 2004).
Bernard of Clairvaux, *Cistercians and Cluniacs: St Bernard's* Apologia *to Abbot William* (trans. Michael Casey, OCSO and introduction by Jean Leclercq, OSB; Athens, OH: Cistercian Publications, 1970).
Bernard of Clairvaux, *Bernard of Clairvaux: Sermons for Advent and the Christmas Season* (ed. John Leinenweber; trans. Irene Edmonds, Wendy Mary Beckett and Conrad Greenia, OCSO; Cistercian Fathers, 51; Collegeville, MN: Liturgical Press, 2008).
Bernard of Clairvaux, *Sermons on the Song of Songs, vol. 4* (trans. Irene M. Edmonds; Cistercian Fathers, 40; Collegeville, MN: Liturgical Press, 1980).
Bérulle, Pierre de, *Bérulle and the French School: Selected Writings* (ed. William M. Thompson; trans. Lowell L. Glendon, SS; New York and Mahwah: Paulist, 1989).
Blocher, Felix, 'Sonne und Sonnengottheiten im alten Vorderasien', in *Sonne: Brennpunkt der Kulturen der Welt* (ed. Andrea Bärnreuther; Neu-Isenburg: Edition Minerva, 2009), pp. 40–53.
Bonamente, Giorgio, et al. (eds), *Costantino prima e dopo Costantino Constantine before and after Constantine* (Bari: Edipuglia, 2012).
Bonhoeffer, Dietrich, *Works, vol. 5: Life Together: Prayerbook of the Bible* (ed. Geffrey B. Kelly; trans. Daniel W. Bloesch and James H. Burtness; Minneapolis: Fortress Press, 1996).
Booth, James, *Philip Larkin: Life, Art and Love* (London: Bloomsbury, 2014).
Boselli, Goffredo (ed.), *Spazio liturgico e orientamento: atti del IV convegno liturgico internazionale Bose, 1 – 3 giugno 2006* (Magnano: Edizioni Qiqajon, 2007).
Bowes, Kim, *Private Worship, Public Values, and Religious Change in Late Antiquity* (New York: Cambridge University Press, 2011).
Bowie, David, *Blackstar* [video]. Available online: https://www.youtube.com/watch?v=kszLwBaC4Sw (accessed 5 April 2021).
Bradbury, Ray, *Fahrenheit 451* (repr., New York: Simon and Schuster, 2012).
Bradshaw, Paul F. and Maxwell E. Johnson, *The Origins of Feasts, Fasts and Seasons in Early Christianity* (Collegeville, MN: Liturgical Press, 2011).
Brittenham, Claudia, 'Quetzalcoatl and Mithra', in *Images of Mithra* (Philippa Adrych, et al.; Oxford: Oxford University Press, 2017), pp. 173–82.
Brown, Peter, *Augustine of Hippo: A Biography* (Berkeley and Los Angeles: University of California Press, 2000).
Brown, Raymond E., *An Introduction to the Gospel of John* (ed., updated, introduced and concluded by Francis J. Moloney, SDB; New York: Doubleday, 2003).
Brown, Raymond E., *An Introduction to the New Testament* (New York: Doubleday, 1997).
Brown, Raymond E., *The Gospel According to John (i–xii)* (London: Geoffrey Chapman, 1971).

Brown, William P. (ed.), *Oxford Handbook of the Psalms* (New York: Oxford University Press, 2014).
Bunyan, John, *The Pilgrim's Progress* (ed. N. H. Keeble; Oxford: Oxford University Press, 1998).
Burkhart, Louise M., 'The Solar Christ in Nahuatl Doctrinal Texts of Early Colonial Mexico', *Ethnohistory* 35.3 (1998), pp. 234–56.
Butler, Dom Cuthbert, *Western Mysticism: The Teaching of Augustine, Gregory and Bernard on Contemplation and the Contemplative Life* (London: Constable, 3rd edn, 1967).
Butterfield, Herbert, *The Origins of Modern Science: 1300–1800* (London: Bell and Hyman, 1957).
Caesarius of Arles, *Sermons, vol. 3 (187–238)* (trans. Sister Mary Magdeleine Mueller, OSF; FC, 66; Washington, DC: Catholic University of America Press, 1973).
Calvin, John, *Commentary on the Book of Psalms, vol. 6* (trans. James Anderson; repr., Grand Rapids, MI: Baker Book House, 1989).
Cambe, Michel, *Avenir solaire et angélique des justes: le psaume 19 (18) commenté par Clément d'Alexandrie* (Strasbourg: Université de Strasbourg, 2009).
Campanella, Tommaso, *La città del sole: dialogo poetico = The City of the Sun: A Poetical Dialogue* (trans. Daniel J. Donno; Berkeley, Los Angeles and London: University of California Press, 1981).
Campbell, Roy, *Mithraic Emblems* (London: Boriswood, 1936).
Campbell, Stanislaus, FSC, *From Breviary to Liturgy of the Hours: The Structural Reform of the Roman Office 1964–1971* (Collegeville, MN: The Liturgical Press, 1995).
Cantalamessa, Raniero, *Easter in the Early Church: An Anthology of Jewish and Early Christian Texts* (Collegeville, MN: The Liturgical Press, 1993).
Caraman, Philip, *Tibet: The Jesuit Century* (Tiverton: Halsgrove, 1998).
Carthusian Spirituality: The Writings of Hugh of Balma and Guigo de Ponte (trans. Dennis D. Martin; New York and Mahwah: Paulist Press, 1997).
A Carthusian, *Interior Prayer: Carthusian Novice Conferences* (trans. Sister Maureen Scrine; Leominster: Gracewing, 2006).
Casiday, Augustine and Frederick W. Norris (eds), *The Cambridge History of Christianity, vol. 2: Constantine to c. 600* (Cambridge: Cambridge University Press, 2007).
Catholic Church, Roman Rite, *The Divine Office: The Liturgy of the Hours According to the Roman Rite* (3 vols; London: Collins, 1974).
Catholic Church, Roman Rite, *Divinum Officium ex Decreto Oecumenici Concilii Vaticani II Instauratum Auctoritate Pauli PP VI Promulgatum: Liturgia Horarum Iuxta Ritum Romanum Editio Typica Altera* (4 vols; Vatican City: Libreria Editrice Vaticana, 1985).
Catholic Church, Roman Rite, 'The General Instruction on the Liturgy of the Hours', in *The Divine Office: The Liturgy of the Hours According to the Roman Rite, vol. 1: Advent, Christmastide & Weeks 1–9 of the Year* (London: Collins, 1974), pp. xix–xcii.
Catholic Church, Roman Rite, 'The General Instruction of the Roman Missal', in *The Roman Missal. Renewed by Decree of the Most Holy Second Ecumenical Council of the Vatican, Promulgated by Authority of Pope Paul VI and Revised at the Direction of Pope John Paul II, English Translation According to the Third Typical Edition* (London: The Catholic Truth Society, 2011), pp. 21–122.
Catholic Church, Roman Rite, *Missale Romanum Ex Decreto Sacrosancti Œcumenici Concilii Vaticani II Instauratum, Auctoritate Pauli PP. VI Promulgatum, Ioannis*

Pauli PP. II Cura Recognitum, Editio Typica Tertia (Vatican City: Typis Vaticanis, 2002).

Caussade, Jean-Pierre de, SJ, *The Sacrament of the Present Moment* (trans. Kitty Muggeridge from the original text of the treatise on Self-Abandonment to Divine Providence; London: Collins Fount Paperbacks, 1981).

Cavadini, John C. (ed.), *Gregory the Great: A Symposium* (Notre Dame and London: University of Notre Dame Press, 1995).

Certeau, Michel de, *The Practice of Everyday Life* (Berkeley and Los Angeles: University of California Press, 1984).

Cervantes, Fernando, *Conquistadores: A New History* (London: Allen Lane, 2020).

Chantal, Jeanne-Françoise Frémyot de, *Sa vie et ses œuvres, vol. 4: lettres* (Paris: E. Plon, 1877).

Charlesworth, James Hamilton (ed. and trans.), *The Odes of Solomon* (Oxford: Clarendon Press, 1973).

Chenu, M. D., *Nature, Man and Society in the Twelfth Century: Essays on New Theological Perspectives in the Latin West* (eds and trans. Jerome Taylor and Lester K. Little; Chicago and London: University of Chicago Press, 1968).

Chenu, M. D., *Toward Understanding St Thomas* (eds and trans. A.M. Landry and D. Hughes; Chicago: Henry Regnery Company, 1963).

Chryssavgis, John, *Light through Darkness: The Orthodox Tradition* (London: Darton, Longman and Todd, 2004).

Chupungco, Anscar J., OSB, *Shaping the Easter Feast* (Washington, DC: The Pastoral Press, 1992).

Clément, Olivier, *The Roots of Christian Mysticism: Text and Commentary* (Welwyn Garden City: New City, 2015).

Coakley, Sarah (ed.), *Religion and the Body* (Cambridge: Cambridge University Press, 1997).

Cohen, Richard, *Chasing the Sun: The Epic Story of the Star That Gives Us Life* (London: Simon and Schuster, 2011).

Collins, Raymond F., *The Thessalonian Correspondence* (Leuven: Leuven University Press, 1990).

Congregation for the Doctrine of the Faith, *Orationis Formas*: 'Letter to the Bishops of the Catholic Church on Some Aspects of Christian Meditation'. Available online: http://www.vatican.va/roman_curia/congregations/cfaith/documents/rc_con_cfaith_doc_19891015_meditazione-cristiana_en.html (accessed 27 April 2020).

Coolman, Boyd Taylor, *The Theology of Hugh of St Victor: An Interpretation* (Cambridge: Cambridge University Press, 2010).

Corpus Christianorum, Series Latina (Turnhout: Brepols, 1953–).

Corpus Scriptorum Ecclesiasticorum Latinorum (Vienna: Hoelder-Pichler-Tempsky, 1866–).

Cox, Brian and Andrew Cohen, *Human Universe* (London: William Collins, 2015).

Coupe, Lawrence (ed.), *The Green Studies Reader: From Romanticism to Ecocriticism* (London and New York: Routledge, 2000).

Cross, Richard, 'Thomas Aquinas', in *The Spiritual Senses: Perceiving God in Western Christianity* (eds Paul L. Gavrilyuk and Sarah Coakley; Cambridge and New York: Cambridge University Press, 2012), pp.174–89.

Crotty, Patrick (ed.), *The Penguin Book of Irish Poetry* (London: Penguin, 2010).

Cupitt, Don, *The Last Testament* (London: SCM, 2012).

Cyprian of Carthage, *Saint Cyprian Treatises* (ed. and trans. Roy J. Deferrari; FC, 36; repr., Washington, DC: Catholic University of America Press, 1981).

Dalarun, Jacques, *The Canticle of Brother Sun: Francis of Assisi Reconciled* (trans. Philippe Yates; New York: Franciscan Institute Publications, 2016).

Dante Alighieri, *The Divine Comedy* (ed. and trans. Robin Kirkpatrick; repr., London: Penguin, 2012).
Dawkins, Richard, *The Magic of Reality: How We Know What's Really True* (London: Black Swan, 2012).
Day, John (ed.), *Prophecy and Prophets in Ancient Israel: Proceedings of the Oxford Old Testament Seminar* (New York and London: T&T Clark, 2010).
Day, John, 'Psalm 104 and Akhenaten's Hymn to the Sun', in *Jewish and Christian Approaches to the Psalms: Conflict and Convergence* (ed. Susan Gillingham; Oxford: Oxford University Press, 2013), pp. 211–28.
Day, John, *Yahweh and the Gods and Goddesses of Canaan* (Sheffield: Sheffield Academic Press, 2000).
De Blaauw, Sible, 'In vista della luce: un principio dimenticato nell'orientamento dell'edificio di culto paleocristiano', in *Arte medievale: le vie dello spazio liturgico* (ed. Paolo Piva; Milan: Jaca Book, 2012), pp. 19–48.
De Blaauw, Sible, 'Innovazioni nello spazio di culto fra basso medioevo e cinquecento: la perdita dell'orientamento liturgico e la liberazione della navata', in *Lo spazio e il culto: relazioni tra edificio ecclesiale e uso liturgico dal xv al xvi secolo* (ed. Jörg Strabenow; Venice: Marsilio, 2006), pp. 25–51.
De Bruyne, Edgar, *Études d'esthétique médiévale III. Le XIII siècle* (Bruges: De Tempel, 1946).
The Dead Sea Scrolls Translated: The Qumran Texts in English (ed. Florentino García Martínez; trans. Wilfred G. E. Watson; Leiden, New York and Cologne: E. J. Brill and Grand Rapids, MI: William B. Eerdmans, 2nd edn, 1996).
Deckers, Johannes G., 'Constantine the Great and Early Christian Art', in *Picturing the Bible: The Earliest Christian Art* (ed. Jeffrey Spier, with contributions by Herbert L. Kessler, et al.; New Haven and London: Yale University Press, 2008), pp. 87–109.
The Didascalia Apostolorum in English (ed. and trans. Margaret Dunlop Gibson; repr., Cambridge: Cambridge University Press, 2011).
Dionysius the Areopagite, Pseudo-Dionysius, *The Complete Works* (trans. Colm Luibheid; New York and Mahwah: Paulist Press, 1987).
Dobzay, Lazló, 'The Divine Office in History', in *T&T Clark Companion to Liturgy* (ed. Alcuin Reid; London: Bloomsbury, 2016), pp. 207–37.
Dodaro, Robert, OSA, 'Light in the Thought of St Augustine', in *Light from Light: Scientists and Theologians in Dialogue* (eds Gerald O'Collins, SJ and Mary Ann Myers; Grand Rapids, MI and Cambridge, UK: Eerdmans, 2012), pp. 195–207.
Dölger, Franz Joseph, *Sol Salutis: Gebet und Gesang im christlichen Altertum mit besonderer Rücksicht auf die Ostung in Gebet und Liturgie* (Münster: Aschendorff, 1925).
Dozeman, Thomas B., *Exodus* (Grand Rapids, MI and Cambridge, UK: Eerdmans, 2009).
Druzbicki, Gaspar, SJ, *Meta Cordium Cor Jesu* (repr. Lviv: Ludova, 1875).
Duffy, Eamon, *Marking the Hours: English People and Their Prayers 1240–1570* (New Haven and London: Yale University Press, 2011).
Duffy, Kevin, 'Change, Suffering and Surprise in God: Von Balthasar's Use of Metaphor', *Irish Theological Quarterly* 76.4 (2011), pp. 370–87.
Dunkle, Brian P., SJ, *Enchantment and Creed in the Hymns of Ambrose of Milan* (Oxford: Oxford University Press, 2016).
Dupré, Louis, *Passage to Modernity: An Essay in the Hermeneutics of Nature and Culture* (New Haven and London: Yale University Press, 1993).
Durandus, Guillelmus, *Rationale Divinorum Officiorum, vol.1* (ed. A. Davril, OSB and T.M. Thibodeau; Corpus Christianorum Continuatio Mediaevalis, 140; Turnhout: Brepols, 1995).

Easton, Mark, *News* 5.15pm, [TV programme] BBC 1, 25 April 2020.
Eco, Umberto, *Art and Beauty in the Middle Ages* (New Haven and London: Yale University Press, 2002).
Edman, Bridget, OCD, *St Thérèse of Lisieux: Nietzsche Is My Brother* (Washington, DC: ICS Publications, 2010).
Edwards, Denis, '"Sublime Communion": The Theology of the Natural World in *Laudato si*', *Theological Studies* 77.2 (2016), pp. 377–91.
Ehrman, Bart D. and Zlatko Pleše (eds and trans.), *The Apocryphal Gospels: Texts and Translations* (New York: Oxford University Press, 2011).
Eliade, Mircea, *Images and Symbols: Studies in Religious Symbolism* (London: Harvill, 1961).
Eliade, Mircea, *The Sacred and the Profane: The Nature of Religion* (New York: Harper & Row, 1961).
Elich, Tom, 'A View from the Antipodes. The Invincible Summer Sun', *Studia Liturgica* 40.1–2 (2010), pp. 85–93.
Elizabeth of the Trinity, *I Have Found God: The Complete Works, vol. 2: Letters from Carmel* (trans. Anne Englund Nash; Washington, DC: ISC Publications, 1995).
Endean, Philip, 'The Ignatian Prayer of the Senses', *Heythrop Journal* 31.4 (1990), pp. 391–418.
English Heritage, *Carrawburgh Roman Fort and Temple of Mithras – Hadrian's Wall*. Available online: http://www.English-Heritage.Org.Uk/Visit/Places/Temple-Of-Mithras-Carrawburgh-Hadrians-Wall/ (accessed 16 April 2020).
Ernst, Cornelius, OP, *Multiple Echo: Explorations in Theology* (ed. Fergus Kerr, OP and Timothy Radcliffe, OP; London: Darton, Longman and Todd, 1979).
Erskine Stuart, Mother Janet, *Prayer in Faith: Thoughts for Liturgical Seasons and Feasts, vol. 2* (ed. L. Kepple; London: Longmans, Green and Co., 1936).
Eucherius of Lyons, *The Formulae of St. Eucherius of Lyons* (trans. Karen Rae Keck; Grand Rapids, MI: Christian Classics Ethereal Library, 2000). Available online: http://www.ccel.org/ccel/eucherius/formulae.html (accessed 11 December 2020).
Evagrius of Pontus, Évagre le Pontique, *Traité pratique ou le moine* (trad., commentary and tables by Antoine Guillaumont and Claire Guillaumont; SC, 171; Paris: Cerf, 1971).
Evans, G. R., *The Thought of Gregory the Great* (Cambridge: Cambridge University Press, 1986).
Eymard, Pierre-Julien, *La sainte eucharistie: la présence réelle, vol. 1* (Paris: Librarie Eucharistique, 1950). ET 'Eucharist: sacrament of life'. Available online: http://www.ssscongregatio.org/index.php/en/about-us/the-founder/feast-day-liturgy (accessed 22 December 2020).
Falk, Seb, *The Light Ages: A Medieval Journey of Discovery* (London: Allen Lane, 2020).
Ferreiro, Alberto and Thomas C. Oden (eds), *The Twelve Prophets* (Ancient Christian Commentary on Scripture, Old Testament, 14; Downers Grove, IL: InterVarsity Press, 2003).
Ficino, Marsilio, *Opera, vol. 1* (Basel: Henric Petrina, 1576).
Finan, Thomas and Vincent Twomey (eds), *Scriptural Interpretation in the Fathers: Letter and Spirit* (Dublin: Four Courts Press, 1995).
Flechner, Roy, *Saint Patrick Retold: The Legend and History of Ireland's Patron Saint* (Princeton and Oxford: Princeton University Press, 2019).
Flynn, Gillian, *Gone Girl* (London: Phoenix, 2013).
Focant, Camille, 'Les fils du jour (1 Thes 5,5)', in *The Thessalonian Correspondence* (ed. Raymond F. Collins; Leuven: Leuven University Press, 1990), pp. 348–55.

Fontaine, Jacques, et al. (eds), *Ambroise de Milan: hymnes* (repr., Paris: Cerf, 2008).
Francis of Assisi, 'Canticle of Brother Sun', in André Vauchez, *Francis of Assisi: The Life and Afterlife of a Mediaeval Saint* (New Haven and London: Yale University Press, 2012), p. 277.
Francis, Mark R., CSV, *Local Worship, Global Church: Popular Religion and the Liturgy* (Collegeville, MN: Liturgical Press, 2014).
Fries, Heinrich (ed.), *Handbuch der theologischen Grundbegriffe* (Munich: Kösel, 1963).
Frye, Northrop, *The Great Code: The Bible and Literature* (Cambridge, MA: Harvard University Press, 1982).
Gabrieli, Francesco (ed.) and E. J. Costello (trans.), *Arab Historians of the Crusades* (London: Routledge, 2010).
Gallagher, Michael Paul, *Dive Deeper: The Human Poetry of Faith* (London: Darton, Longman and Todd, 2001).
Galli, Carlos María, *Dio vive in città: verso una nuova pastorale urbana* (Vatican City: Libreria Editrice Vaticana, 2014).
García Martínez, Florentino (ed.), *The Dead Sea Scrolls Translated: The Qumran Texts in English* (trans. Wilfred G. E. Watson; Leiden, New York and Cologne: E. J. Brill and Grand Rapids, MI: William B. Eerdmans, 2nd edn, 1996).
Gathercole, Simon J., 'The Heavenly ἀνατολή (Luke: 78–9)', *Journal of Theological Studies* NS, 56.2 (2005), pp. 47–88.
Gaus, Joachim, 'Die Lichtsymbolik in der mittelalterlichen Kunst', *Symbolon: Jahrbuch für Symbolforschung*, Neue Folge 12 (1995) pp. 107–18.
Gavrilyuk, Paul L. and Sarah Coakley (eds), *The Spiritual Senses: Perceiving God in Western Christianity* (Cambridge and New York: Cambridge University Press, 2012).
Geddes, Linda, *Chasing the Sun: The New Science of Sunlight and How It Shapes Our Bodies and Minds* (London: Profile Books, 2019).
Gertrude the Great of Helfta, *Spiritual Exercises* (trans. Gertrud Jaron Lewis and Jack Lewis; Cistercian Fathers Series, 49; Kalamazoo, MI: Cistercian Publications, 1989).
Gibson, Margaret Dunlop (ed. and trans.), *The Didascalia Apostolorum in English* (repr., Cambridge: Cambridge University Press, 2011).
Gildas, *The Works of Gildas Surnamed 'Sapiens', or The Wise* (trans. J. A. Giles; London: 1842). Available online: http://www.gutenberg.org/cache/epub/1949/pg1949-images.html (accessed 21 April 2020).
Gillingham, Susan (ed.), *Jewish and Christian Approaches to the Psalms: Conflict and Convergence* (Oxford: Oxford University Press, 2013).
Giuffo, John, 'The Power of Light in La Sagrada Familia', *Forbes*, 13 May 2011. Available online: https://www.forbes.com/sites/johngiuffo/2011/05/13/the-power-of-light-in-la-sagrada-familia/#774b356f603d (accessed 22 April 2020).
Goizueta, Roberto S., 'The Symbolic Realism of U.S. Latino/a Popular Catholicism', *Theological Studies* 65.2 (2004), pp. 255–74.
González, Justo L., *A Brief History of Sunday: From the New Testament to the New Creation* (Grand Rapids, MI: Eerdmans, 2017).
Grabar, Ernst, *Christian Iconography: A Study of Its Origins* (repr., Princeton, NJ: Princeton University Press, 1981).
Green, Bernard, *The Soteriology of Leo the Great* (Oxford: Oxford University Press, 2008).
Gregory of Nyssa, *The Life of Moses* (trans. Abraham J. Malherbe and Everett Ferguson; New York, Ramsey and Toronto: Paulist Press, 1978).
Gronchi, Maurizio, *La cristologia di S. Bernardino da Siena: l'imago Christi nella predicazione in volgare* (Bologna: Marietti, 1992).

Grossberg, Daniel, 'The Dual Glow/Grow Motif', *Biblica* 67.4 (1986), pp. 547–54.
Halík, Tomáš, *Patience with God: The Story of Zacchaeus Continuing in Us* (New York: Doubleday, 2009).
Hallo, William W. (ed.), *The Context of Scripture, vol.1: Canonical Compositions from the Biblical World* (Leiden, New York and Cologne: Brill, 1997).
Hamburger, Jeffrey F. and Anne-Marie Bouché (eds), *The Mind's Eye: Art and Theological Argument in the Middle Ages* (Princeton, NJ: Princeton University Press, 2006).
Hausman, Noëlle, *Frédéric Nietzsche Thérèse de Lisieux: deux poétiques de la modernité* (Paris: Beauchesne, 1984).
Heaney, Seamus, *New Selected Poems 1966–1987* (London: Faber and Faber, 1990).
Heaney, Seamus, *Preoccupations: Selected Prose 1968–1978* (London: Faber and Faber, 1980).
Hegel, Georg Wilhelm Friedrich, *Hegel's Philosophy of Right* (trans. and notes T. M. Knox; London, Oxford and New York: Oxford University Press, 1967).
Heid, Stefan, 'Gebetshaltung und Ostung in frühchristlicher Zeit', *Rivista di Archeologia Cristiana* 82 (2006), pp. 347–404.
Heid, Stefan, *Kreuz, Jerusalem, Kosmos: Aspekte frühchristlicher Staurologie* (Münster: Aschendorff, 2001).
Heilbron, J. L., *The Sun in the Church: Cathedrals as Solar Observatories* (Cambridge, MA and London: Harvard University Press, 1999).
Herren, Michael W. and Shirley Ann Brown, *Christ in Celtic Christianity: Britain and Ireland from the Fifth to the Tenth Century* (Woodbridge: The Boydell Press, 2002).
Hesychius of Jerusalem, Hésychius de Jérusalem, Basile de Séleicie, Jean de Béryte, Pseudo-Chrysostome, Léonce de Constantinople, *Homélies paschales (cinq homélies inédites)* (ed. and trans. Michel Aubineau; SC, 187; Paris: Cerf, 1972).
Hildegard of Bingen, *Hildegard of Bingen: An Anthology* (eds Fiona Bowie and Oliver Davies; London: SPCK, 1990).
Hildegard of Bingen, *The Letters of Hildegard of Bingen* (trans. Joseph L. Baird and Radd K. Ehrman; 3 vols; New York and Oxford: Oxford University Press, 1994, 1998, 2004).
Hildegard of Bingen, *Saint Hildegard of Bingen*, Symphonia: *A Critical Edition of the* Symphonia armonie celestium revelationum *[Symphony of the Harmony of Celestial Revelations]* (ed. and trans. Barbara Newman; Ithaca and London: Cornell University Press, 1998).
Hildegard of Bingen, *Scivias* (trans. Mother Columba Hart and Jane Bishop; New York and Mahwah: Paulist Press, 1990).
Hildegard of Bingen, *Hildegard of Bingen: Selected Writings* (trans. with introduction and notes Mark Atherton; London: Penguin, 2001).
Hill, Andrew E., *Haggai, Zechariah and Malachi: An Introduction and Commentary* (Downers Grove, IL: InterVarsity Press, 2012).
Hoare, Peter G. and Hans Ketel, 'English Medieval Churches, "Festival Orientation" and William Wordsworth, SEAC 2011 Stars and Stones: Voyages in Archaeoastronomy and Cultural Astronomy, Proceedings of a conference held 19–22 September 2011', in *Archaeopress/British Archaeological Reports (2015)*, pp. 286–92. Available online: http://adsabs.harvard.edu/abs/2015ssva.conf.286H (accessed 27 April 2020).
Hobday, Richard, *The Healing Sun: Sunlight and Health in the 21st Century* (Forres: Findhorn Press, 1999).
Hoffmeier, James K., *Akhenaten and the Origins of Monotheism* (Oxford: Oxford University Press, 2015).
Holford-Strevens, Leofranc, *The History of Time: A Very Short Introduction* (New York: Oxford University Press, 2005).

Hurtado, Larry W., *Destroyer of the Gods: Early Christian Distinctiveness in the Roman World* (Waco, TX: Baylor University Press, 2016).

Ignatius of Loyola, *Saint Ignatius of Loyola, Personal Writings: Reminiscences, Spiritual Diary, Select Letters, Including the texts of The Spiritual Exercises* (trans. with introductions and notes Joseph A. Munitiz and Philip Endean; London: Penguin, 1996).

Incerti, Manuela, *Il disegno della luce nell'architettura cistercense: allineamenti astronomici nelle abbazie di Chiaravalle della Colomba, Fontevivo e San Martino de' Bocci* (Firenze: Certosa Cultura, 1999).

Inge, Denise (ed.), *Happiness and Wholeness: Thomas Traherne and His Writings* (Norwich: Canterbury Press, 2008).

Isidore of Seville, San Isidoro de Sevilla, *Etimologiás, edición Bilingüe* (eds and trans. José Oroz Reta and Manuel-A. Marcos Casquero; Madrid: Biblioteca de Autores Cristianos, 2004).

Jackson, Kenneth Hurlstone, *A Celtic Miscellany: Translations from the Celtic Literatures* (Harmondsworth: Penguin, 1971).

John Scotus Eriugena, *Iohannis Scotti Eriugenae Carmina* (trans. Michael W. Herren; Scriptores Latini Hiberniae, 12; Dublin: School of Celtic Studies, Dublin Institute for Advanced Studies, 1993).

John Scotus Eriugena, *Iohannis Scotti Eriugenae Periphyseon (De Divisione Naturae), Liber Tertius* (ed. and trans. I.P. Sheldon-Williams, with the collaboration of Ludwig Bieler; Scriptores Latini Hiberniae, 11; Dublin: Dublin Institute for Advanced Studies, 1981).

Jabi, Wassim and Iakonos Potamianos, 'Geometry, Light, and Cosmology in the Church of Hagia Sophia', *International Journal of Architectural Computing* 5.2 (2007), pp. 303–19.

Jackson, Kenneth, *Studies in Early Celtic Nature Poetry* (Cambridge: Cambridge University Press, 1935).

Janowski, Bernd, *Konfliktgespräche mit Gott: Eine Anthropologie der Psalmen* (Neukirchen: Neukirchener Theologie, 2013).

Jeanes, Gordon P., *The Day Has Come! Easter and Baptism in Zeno of Verona* (Alcuin Club Collection, 73; Collegeville, MN: The Liturgical Press, 1995).

Jensen, Robin M., 'Recovering Ancient Ecclesiology: The Place of the Altar and the Orientation of Prayer in the Early Latin Church', *Worship* 89.2 (2015), pp. 99–124.

Jensen, Robin M., *The Substance of Things Seen: Art, Faith, and the Christian Community* (Grand Rapids, MI and Cambridge, UK: Eerdmans, 2004).

Jensen, Robin M., 'Towards a Christian Material Culture', in *The Cambridge History of Christianity, vol. 1: Origins to Constantine* (eds Margaret M. Mitchell and Frances M. Young; Cambridge: Cambridge University Press, 2006), pp. 568–85.

John Chrysostom, Jean Chrysostome, *Trois catéchèses baptismales* (ed. and trans. Auguste Piédagnel and Louis Doutreleau; SC, 366; Paris: Cerf, 1990).

John Damascene, *Die Schriften des Johannes von Damaskos, vol. 2* (ed. Bonifatius Kotter; Berlin and New York: Walter De Gruyter, 1973).

John Damascene, 'St John Damascene: Homily on Holy Saturday' (trans. Tikhon Alexander Pino), *The Orthodox Word* 52.4 (2016), pp. 157–97.

John of the Cross, *The Collected Works of Saint John of the Cross* (trans. Kieran Kavanagh, OCD and Ottilio Rodriguez, OCD; Washington, DC: ICS Publications, 1991).

Johnson, Andy, *1 and 2 Thessalonians* (Grand Rapids, MI: Eerdmans, 2016).

Johnson, Maxwell E. (ed.), *Between Memory and Hope* (Collegeville, MN: Liturgical Press, 2000).

Join-Lambert, Arnaud, *La Liturgie des heures pour tous les baptisés: l'expérience quotidienne du mystère pascal* (London, Paris and Dudley, MA: Peeters, 2009).

Jordan, D.K. (trans.), *Readings in Classical Nahuatl: Nican Mopohua: Here It Is Told* (University of California San Diego, n.d.). Available online: https://pages.ucsd.edu/~dkjordan/nahuatl/nican/NicanMopohua.html (accessed 24 April 2020).

Judge, Philip, *The Sun: A Very Short Introduction* (Oxford: Oxford University Press, 2020).

Julian, Emperor, *The Works of the Emperor Julian, vol. 1* (trans. Wilmer Cave Wright, Loeb Classical Library; London: Heinemann and New York: Macmillan, 1913).

Justin Martyr, *St Justin Martyr Dialogue with Trypho* (ed. Michael Slusser; trans. Thomas B. Falls; revised by Thomas P. Halton; FC, 3; Washington, DC: Catholic University of America Press, 2003).

Kantorowicz, Ernst H., 'Oriens Augusti – Lever du Roi', *Dumbarton Oak Papers* 17 (1963), pp. 117–77.

Kantorowicz, Ernst H., *The King's Two Bodies* (repr., Princeton, NJ: Princeton University Press, 2016).

Kapstein, Matthew K. (ed.), *The Presence of Light: Divine Radiance and Religious Experience* (Chicago: University of Chicago Press, 2004).

Kavanagh, Patrick, *Collected Poems* (ed. Antoinette Quinn; London: Penguin, 2005).

Keener, Craig S., '"We Beheld His Glory!" (John:4)', in *John, Jesus, and History, vol. 2: Aspects of Historicity in the Fourth Gospel* (eds Paul N. Anderson, Felix Just, SJ and Tom Thatcher; Atlanta: Society of Biblical Literature, 2009), pp. 5–25.

Kelly, J. F., 'Eucherius of Lyons: Harbinger of the Middle Ages', *Studia Patristica* 23 (1989), pp. 138–42.

Kent, Hannah, *Burial Rites* (Sydney: Picador Pan Macmillan, 2013).

Kerlouégan, François, 'Gildas', in *Oxford Dictionary of National Biography, in Association with the British Academy: From the Earliest Times to the Year 2000, vol. 22* (eds H.C.G. Matthew and Brian Harrison; Oxford: Oxford University Press, 2004), pp. 223–4.

Kinzig, Wolfram, et al. (eds.), *Liturgie und Ritual in der alten Kirche. Patristische Beiträge zum Studium der gottesdienstlichen Quellen in der alten Kirche* (Leuven: Peeters, 2011).

Knowles, Murray and Rosamund Moon, *Introducing Metaphor* (London: Routledge, 2006).

Kidson, Peter, 'Panofsky, Suger and St Denis', *Journal of the Warburg and Courtauld Institutes* 50 (1987), pp. 1–17.

Koslofsky, Craig, *Evening's Empire: A History of the Night in Early Modern Europe* (Cambridge: Cambridge University Press, 2011).

Kuhn, Thomas S., *The Copernican Revolution: Planetary Astronomy in the Development of Western Thought* (Cambridge, MA: Harvard University Press, 1996).

Laird, Andrew, 'Nahua Humanism and Political Identity in Sixteenth-Century Mexico: A Latin Letter from Antonio Cortés Totoquihuatzin, Native Ruler of Tlacopan, to Emperor Charles V (1552)', *Renaissance Forum* 10 (2016), pp. 127–72 (158). Available online: http://www.renaessanceforum.dk/10_2016/06_laird_nahua_humanism.pdf (accessed 23 April 2020).

Lameri, Angelo, 'L'orientamento nei testi liturgici', in *Spazio liturgico e orientamento: atti del IV convegno liturgico internazionale Bose, 1 – 3 giugno 2006* (ed. Goffredo Boselli; Magnano: Edizioni Qiqajon, 2007), pp. 189–201.

Lane, Belden C., 'Thomas Traherne and the Awakening of Want', *Anglican Theological Review* 81.4 (1975), pp. 651–64.

Lane Fox, Robin, *Augustine: Conversions and Confessions* (London: Penguin, 2015).

Lang, Uwe Michael, 'Benedict XVI and the Theological Foundations of Church Architecture', in *Benedict XVI and Beauty in Sacred Art and Architecture* (ed. D. Vincent Twomey, SVD and Janet E. Rutherford; Dublin: Four Courts Press, 2011), pp. 112–21.

Lang, Uwe Michael, *Turning towards the Lord: Orientation in Liturgical Prayer* (San Francisco: Ignatius Press, 2009).

Lara, Jaime, *Christian Texts for Aztecs: Art and Liturgy in Colonial Mexico* (Notre Dame, IN: University of Notre Dame Press, 2008).
Lara, Jaime, 'A Meaty Incarnation: Making Sense of Divine Flesh for Aztec Christians', in *Image and Incarnation: The Early Modern Doctrine of the Pictorial Image* (eds Walter S. Melion and Lee Palmer Wandel; Leiden: Brill, 2015), pp. 109–36.
La Rochefoucauld, François de, *La Rochefoucauld Collected Maxims and Other Reflections. New Translation with Parallel French Text* (trans. E. H. Blackmore, A. M. Blackmore and Francine Giguère; Oxford: Oxford University Press, 2007).
Larkin, Philip, *The Complete Poems* (ed. Archie Burnett; London: Faber and Faber, 2018).
Latourelle, René (ed.), *Vatican II Assessment and Perspectives: Twenty-five Years after (1962–1967), vol. 2* (New York and Mahwah: Paulist Press, 1989).
Lawrence, D. H., *Phoenix: The Posthumous Papers of D. H. Lawrence* (ed. Edward D. McDonald; London: William Heineman, 1936).
LeMon, Joel M., *Yahweh's Winged Form in the Psalms: Exploring Congruent Iconography and Texts* (Fribourg: Academic Press and Göttingen: Vandenhoeck and Ruprecht, 2010).
Lentini, Anselmo, *Te Decet Hymnus: L'innario della 'Liturgia Horarum'* (Vatican City: Typis Polyglottis Vaticanis, 1984).
Leo the Great, *St Leo the Great: Sermons* (trans. Jane Patricia Freeland, CSJB, and Agnes Josephine Conway, SSJ; FC, 93; Washington, DC: Catholic University of America Press, 1996).
Lewis, C. S., *They Stand Together: The Letters of C. S. Lewis to Arthur Greeves (1914–1963)* (ed. Walter Hooper; London: Collins, 1979).
Lincoln, Andrew T., *The Gospel According to St John* (Grand Rapids, MI: Baker Academic, 2003).
Lockley, Steven W. and Russell G. Foster, *Sleep: A Very Short Introduction* (Oxford: Oxford University Press, 2012).
Lossky, Vladimir, *In the Image and Likeness of God* (Crestwood, NY: St Vladimir's Seminary Press, 1974).
Louth, Andrew, 'The Body in Western Catholic Christianity', in *Religion and the Body* (ed. Sarah Coakley; Cambridge: Cambridge University Press, 1997), pp. 111–30.
Louth, Andrew, 'Light, Vision and Religious Experience in Byzantium', in *The Presence of Light: Divine Radiance and Religious Experience* (ed. Matthew K. Kapstein; Chicago: University of Chicago Press, 2004), pp. 85–103.
Louth, Andrew, *The Origins of the Christian Mystical Tradition: From Plato to Denys* (Oxford: Clarendon Press, 1981).
Lubac, Henri de, *Corpus Mysticum: The Eucharist and the Church in the Middle Ages* (ed. Laurence Paul Hemming and Susan Frank Parsons; trans. Gemma Symmonds, CJ with Richard Price and Christopher Stephens; London: SCM, 2006).
MacGregor, A. J., *Fire and Light in the Western Triduum: Their Use at Tenebrae and at the Paschal Vigil* (Collegeville, MN: The Liturgical Press, 1992).
Macmillan, D., *The Life of George Matheson* (London: Hodder and Stoughton, 1910).
Madigan, Kevin, *Medieval Christianity: A New History* (New Haven and London: Yale University Press, 2015).
Magli, Giulio, *Architecture, Astronomy and Sacred Landscape in Ancient Egypt* (Cambridge: Cambridge University Press, 2013).
Mâle, Emile, *The Gothic Image: Religious Art in France of the Thirteenth Century* (trans. Dora Nussey; London: Collins, 1961).
Markus, R. A., *The End of Ancient Christianity* (Cambridge: Cambridge University Press, 1998).

Matheson, George, *Sacred Songs* (Edinburgh and London: William Blackwood and Sons, 1904).
Matheson, George, *Searchings in the Silence: A Series of Devotional Meditations* (London: Cassell, 1895).
Mathews, Thomas F., *The Clash of Gods: A Reinterpretation of Early Christian Art* (Princeton, NJ: Princeton University Press, 1993).
Maximus of Turin, *The Sermons of St. Maximus of Turin* (trans. Boniface Ramsey, OP; New York and Mahwah: Newman Press, 1989).
McCabe, Herbert, *God Matters* (London: Chapman, 1987).
McDermott, John M., 'Soleil', in *Dictionnaire de spiritualité ascétique et mystique, doctrine et histoire, vol. 14* (eds M. Viller, et al.; Paris: Beauchesne, 1990), pp. 981–99.
McGahern, John, 'The Church and Its Spire', in *Love of the World: Essays* (London: Faber and Faber, 2009), pp. 133–48.
McGahern, John, *Collected Stories* (London: Faber and Faber, 2014).
McGahern, John, *Love of the World: Essays* (London: Faber and Faber, 2009).
McGahern, John, *Memoir* (London: Faber and Faber, 2005).
McGahern, John, *That They May Face the Rising Sun* (London: Faber and Faber, 2009).
McGinn, Bernard, 'Contemplation in Gregory the Great', in *Gregory the Great: A Symposium* (ed. John C. Cavadini; Notre Dame and London: University of Notre Dame Press, 1995), pp. 146–67.
McGinn, Bernard, *The Essential Writings of Christian Mysticism* (New York: Random House, 2006).
McGowan, Andrew B., *Ancient Christian Worship: Early Church Practices in Social, Historical, and Theological Perspective* (Grand Rapids, MI: Baker Academic, 2014).
McGrath, Alister E., *Iustitia Dei: A History of the Christian Doctrine of Justification* (Cambridge: Cambridge University Press, 1986).
McGrath, Alister E., *Re-imagining Nature: The Promise of a Christian Natural Theology* (Oxford: Wiley Blackwell, 2017).
McGuckin, John Anthony, *Standing in God's Holy Fire: The Byzantine Tradition* (London: Darton Longman and Todd, 2001).
McInroy, Mark, *Balthasar on the Spiritual Senses: Perceiving Splendour* (Oxford: Oxford University Press, 2014).
Mechtild of Magdeburg, *The Flowing Light of the Godhead* (trans. and introduced Frank Tobin; preface Margot Schmidt; New York and Mahwah: Paulist Press, 1998).
Melito of Sardis, *On Pascha with the Fragments of Melito and Other Material Related to the Quartodecimans* (trans. Alastair Stewart-Sykes; Crestwood, NY: St Vladimir's Seminary Press, 2001).
Melito of Sardis, Méliton de Sardis, *Sur la Pâque et fragments* (ed. and trans. Othmar Perler; SC, 123; Paris: Cerf, 1966).
Merkt, Andreas, *Maximus I. von Turin: Die Verkündigung eines Bischofs der frühen Reichskirche im zeitgeschichtlichen, gesellschaftlichen und liturgischen Kontext* (Leiden, New York and Cologne: Brill, 1997).
Merton, Thomas, *Conjectures of a Guilty Bystander* (London: Burns and Oates, 1968).
Merton, Thomas, *The Seven Storey Mountain* (London: Sheldon Press, 1975).
Migne, J.-P. (ed.), *Patrologiae Cursus Completus, Series Graeca* (166 vols; Paris: J.-P. Migne, 1857–83).
Migne, J.-P. (ed.), *Patrologiae Cursus Completus, Series Latina* (221 vols; Paris: J.-P. Migne, 1844–65).
Miller, Dean A., *Imperial Constantinople* (New York: John Wiley and Sons, 1969).
Mitchell, Margaret M. and Frances M. Young (eds), *The Cambridge History of Christianity, vol. 1: Origins to Constantine* (Cambridge: Cambridge University Press, 2006).

Miziolek, Jerzy, '*Transfiguratio Domini* in the apse at Mount Sinai and the Symbolism of Light', *Journal of the Warburg and Courtauld Institutes* 53 (1990), pp. 42–60.
Miziolek, Jerzy, 'When Our Sun Is Risen: Observations on Eschatological Visions in the Art of the First Millennium – II', *Arte Christiana* 83.766 (1995), pp. 3–22.
Moltmann, Jürgen, *Sun of Righteousness, Arise! God's Future for Humanity and the Earth* (London: SCM, 2010).
Mongrain, Kevin, *The Systematic Thought of Hans Urs von Balthasar: An Irenaean Retrieval* (New York: Crossroad, 2002).
Morley, Paul, *The Age of Bowie: How David Bowie Made a World of Difference* (London, New York, etc.: Simon and Schuster, 2016).
Mother Teresa, *Come Be My Light: The Revealing Private Writings of the Nobel Peace Prize Winner* (ed. with commentary Brian Kolodiejchuk, MC; London: Rider, 2008).
Murphy, Gerald (ed. and trans.), *Early Irish Lyrics: Eighth to Twelfth Century* (Oxford: Clarendon Press, 1956).
Murray, Paul, OP, *Aquinas at Prayer: The Bible, Mysticism and Poetry* (London: Bloomsbury, 2013).
Murray, Paul, OP, *Rites and Meditations* (Dublin: The Dolmen Press, 1982).
National Museum of Ireland, 'The Coggalbeg Hoard'. Available online: https://www.museum.ie/en-IE/Collections-Research/Collection/Resilience/Artefact/Test-7/3fa0198b-cee5-40dc-9649-76ef6725fa07 (accessed 23 March 2021).
Neil, Bronwen, 'Pagan Ritual and Christian Liturgy: Leo the Great's Preaching on Sun-Worship', in *Liturgie und Ritual in der alten Kirche. Patristische Beiträge zum Studium der gottesdienstlichen Quellen in der alten Kirche* (eds Wolfram Kinzig, et al.; Leuven: Peeters, 2011), pp. 127–40.
Nevin, Thomas R., *The Last Years of Saint Thérèse: Doubt and Darkness, 1895–1897* (New York: Oxford University Press, 2013).
Nican Mopohua, *Readings in Classical Nahuatl: Nican Mopohua: Here It Is Told* (trans, D.K. Jordan; University of California San Diego, n.d.). Available online: https://pages.ucsd.edu/~dkjordan/nahuatl/nican/ NicanMopohua.html (accessed 24 April 2020).
Nicholls, Terence L., *The Sacred Cosmos: Christian Faith and the Challenge of Naturalism* (Eugene, OR: Wipf and Stock, 2009).
Nietzsche, Friedrich, *A Nietzsche Reader* (ed. and trans. R. J. Hollingdale; Harmondsworth: Penguin, 1977).
Nietzsche, Friedrich, *Thus Spoke Zarathustra* (trans. R. J. Hollingdale; Harmondsworth: Penguin, 1969).
Ó'Carragáin, Éamonn, 'Christian Inculturation in Eighth-Century Northumbria: The Bewcastle and Ruthwell Crosses', *Colloquium Journal* 4 (2007), n.p. Available online: https://ism.yale.edu/sites/default/files/files/Christian%20Inculturation%20in%20 Eighth.pdf (accessed 21 April 2020).
Ó'Carragáin, Éamonn, 'High Crosses, the Sun's Course, and Local Theologies at Kells and Monasterboice', in *Insular and Anglo-Saxon Art and Thought in the Early Medieval Period* (ed. Colum Hourihane; Princeton, NJ: Princeton University, in association with Pennsylvania University Press, 2011), pp. 149–73.
Ó'Carragáin, Tomás, *Churches in Early Medieval Ireland: Architecture, Ritual and Memory* (New Haven and London: Yale University Press, 2010).
O'Collins, Gerald, SJ, and Meyers, Mary Ann (eds), *Light from Light: Scientists and Theologians in Dialogue* (Grand Rapids, MI and Cambridge, UK: Eerdmans, 2012).
O'Connell, Gerard, *The Election of Pope Francis: An Inside Account of the Conclave That Changed History* (Maryknoll, NY: Orbis, 2019).

The Odes of Solomon (ed. and trans. James Hamilton Charlesworth; Oxford: Clarendon Press, 1973).
O'Donnell, James J., *Pagans: The End of Traditional Religion and the Rise of Christianity* (New York: Ecco HarperCollins, 2016).
Ó Fiannachta, Padraig (ed.) and Desmond Forristal (trans.), *Saltair Urnaithe Duchais: Prayers from the Irish Tradition* (Dublin: Columba, 1988).
Olivar, Alexandre, 'L'image du soleil non souillé dans la littérature patristique', *Didaskalia* 5.1 (1975), pp. 3–20.
O'Loughlin, Thomas, *Discovering St Patrick* (London: Darton Longman and Todd, 2005).
O'Loughlin, Thomas, *Gildas and the Scriptures: Observing the World through a Biblical Lens* (Turnhout: Brepols, 2012).
O'Loughlin, Thomas, 'The Symbol Gives Life: Eucherius of Lyons' Formula for Exegesis', in *Scriptural Interpretation in the Fathers: Letter and Spirit* (eds Thomas Finan and Vincent Twomey; Dublin: Four Courts Press, 1995), pp. 221–52.
O'Meara, Thomas F., OP, *Theology of Ministry* (Mahwah, NJ: Paulist Press, 1999).
O'Neill, Charles E., SJ, '*Acatamiento*: Ignatian Reverence in History and Contemporary Culture', *Studies in the Spirituality of Jesuits* 8.1 (1976), pp. 2–41.
Origen, *Commentary on the Gospel According to John Books 1–10* (trans. Ronald E. Heine; FC, 80; Washington, DC: Catholic University of America Press, 1989).
Origen, *Commentary on the Gospel According to John Books 13–32* (trans. Ronald E. Heine; FC, 89; Washington, DC: Catholic University of America Press, 1993).
Origen, *The Commentary of Origen on the Gospel of Matthew, vol. 2* (trans. Ronald E. Heine; Oxford: Oxford University Press, 2018).
Origen, *Homilies on Genesis and Exodus* (trans. Ronald E. Heine; FC, 71; Washington, DC: Catholic University of America Press, 1981).
Origen, *Homilies on Leviticus 1–16* (trans. Gary Wayne Barkley; FC, 83; Washington, DC: Catholic University of America Press, 1990).
Origen, Origène, *Homélies sur les Nombres I, homélies I–X* (ed. Louis Doutreleau; SC, 415; Paris: Cerf, 1996).
Origen, *Origen's Treatise on Prayer, Translation and Notes with an Account of the Practice and Doctrine of Prayer from the New Testament Times to Origen* (ed. Eric George Jay; London: SPCK, 1954).
Origo, Iris, *The World of San Bernardino* (London: Jonathan Cape, 1963).
Orthodoxprayer. Available online: https://www.orthodoxprayer.org/Facing%20East.html (accessed 30 March 2021).
Orthodoxwiki. Available online: https://orthodoxwiki.org/Photine_of_Samaria (accessed 12 December 2020).
Osbeck, Kenneth W., *101 Hymn Stories* (Grand Rapids, MI: Kregel Publications, 1982).
Ovid, *Metamorphoses* (trans. A. D. Melville; Oxford: Oxford University Press, 1998).
Pascal, Blaise, *Pensées and Other Writings* (trans. Honor Levi; Oxford: Oxford University Press, 2008).
Patrick, St., *My Name Is Patrick: St Patrick's* Confessio (trans. Pádraig McCarthy; Dublin: Royal Irish Academy, 2011).
Pelikan, Jaroslav, *The Light of the World: A Basic Image of Early Christian Thought* (New York: Harper, 1962).
Pénin, Marie-Christine, *Tombes et sepultures dans les cimitières et autres lieux. Loménie de Brienne Etienne Charles de (1727–16 février 1794) Eglise Saint-Savinien de Sens (Yonne)*. Available online: https://www.tombes-sepultures.com/crbst_1064.html (accessed 27 April 2020).

Pfeifer, H., 'Iconografia', in *Ignazio e l'arte dei gesuiti* (ed. Giovanni Sale, SJ; Rome: La Civiltà Cattolica, 2003), pp. 171–206.

Pflieger, André, *Liturgicae Orationis Concordantia Verbalis, Prima Pars: Missale Romanum* (Rome: Herder, 1964).

Physiologus (trans. Michael J. Curley; Austin and London: University of Texas Press, 1979).

Pino, Tikhon Alexander, 'St John Damascene: Homily on Holy Saturday', *The Orthodox Word* 52.4 (2016), pp. 157–97.

Pirandello, Luigi, *The Late Mattia Pascal* (trans. William Weaver; New York: The New York Review of Books, 2005).

Pitstick, Alyssa Lyra, *Light in Darkness: Hans Urs von Balthasar and the Catholic Doctrine of Christ's Descent into Hell* (Grand Rapids, MI and Cambridge, UK: William B. Eerdmans, 2007).

Piva, Paolo (ed.), *Arte medievale: le vie dello spazio liturgico* (Milan: Jaca Book, 2012).

Plank, Peter, *ΦΟΣ ΙΛΑΡΟΝ: Christushymnus und Lichtdanksagung der frühen Christenheit* (Bonn: Borengässer, 2001).

Pliny, *Letters*. Available online: Pliny: Letters – Book 10 (b) (attalus.org) (accessed 14 December 2020).

Pope Benedict, Angelus 21 December 2008. Available online: http://www.vatican.va/content/benedict-xvi/en/angelus/2008/documents/hf_ben-xvi_ang_20081221.html. (accessed 11 December 2020).

Pope Benedict, Homily Epiphany 2009. Available online: 6 January 2009: Solemnity of the Epiphany of the Lord | BENEDICT XVI (vatican.va) (accessed 10 December 2020).

Pope Benedict XVI, General Audience, 6 October 2010. Available online: http://w2.vatican.va/content/benedict-xvi/en/audiences/2010/documents/hf_ben-xvi_aud_20101006.html (accessed 23 April 2020).

Pope Benedict XVI, Homily Barcelona, 7 November 2010. Available online: http://w2.vatican.va/content/benedict-xvi/en/homilies/2010/documents/hf_ben-xvi_hom_20101107_barcelona.html (accessed 22 April 2020).

Pope Benedict XVI, Homily Easter Vigil 2007. Available online: http://w2.vatican.va/content/benedict-xvi/en/homilies/2007/documents/hf_ben-xvi_hom_20070407_veglia-pasquale.html (accessed 28 April 2020).

Pope Francis, *Address to Participants in the Fifth Convention of the Italian Church 2015*. Available online: http://w2.vatican.va/content/francesco/en/speeches/2015/november/documents/papa-francesco_20151110_firenze-convegno-chiesa-italiana.html (accessed 29 April 2020).

Pope Francis, Apostolic Exhortation *Gaudete et Exsultate*. Available online: http://w2.vatican.va/content/francesco/en/apost_exhortations/documents/papa-francesco_esortazione-ap_20180319_gaudete-et-exsultate.html (accessed 29 April 2020).

Pope Francis, Apostolic Letter *Evangelii Gaudium*. Available online: http://w2.vatican.va/content/francesco/en/apost_exhortations/documents/papa-francesco_esortazione-ap_20131124_evangelii-gaudium.html (accessed 26 April 2020).

Pope Francis, Encyclical Letter *Laudato sì* On Care for Our Common Home. Available online: http://www.vatican.va/content/francesco/en/encyclicals/documents/papa-francesco_20150524_enciclica-laudato-si.html (accessed 26 April 2020).

Pope Francis, Encyclical Letter *Lumen Fidei*. Available online: http://w2.vatican.va/content/francesco/en/encyclicals/documents/papa-francesco_20130629_enciclica-lumen-fidei.html (accessed 26 April 2020).

Pope Francis, Homily Chiapas, Mexico, 15 February 2016. Available online: https://w2.vatican.va/content/francesco/en/homilies/2016/documents/papa-francesco_20160215_omelia-messico-chiapas.html (accessed 23 April 2020).

Pope Francis, Homily Epiphany 2016. Available online: http://w2.vatican.va/content/francesco/en/homilies/2016/documents/papa-francesco_20160106_omelia-epifania.html (accessed 29 April 2020).
Pope Francis in Conversation with Austen Ivereigh, *Let Us Dream: The Path to a Better Future* (London: Simon and Schuster UK, 2020).
Pope St. John-Paul II, Encyclical Letter, *Ut unum sint*. Available online: http://www.vatican.va/content/john-paul-ii/en/encyclicals/documents/hf_jp-ii_enc_25051995_ut-unum-sint.html (accessed 29 August 2020).
Powell, Timothy E., 'Christianity or Solar Monotheism: The Early Religious Beliefs of St Patrick', *Journal of Ecclesiastical History* 43.4 (1992), pp. 531–40.
Rabelais, François, *The Complete Works of François Rabelais* (trans. Donald M. Frame; Oakland: University of California Press, 1992).
Rahner, Hugo, *Greek Myths and Christian Mystery* (New York: Harper and Row, 1963).
Rahner, Karl, 'Christian Living Formerly and Today', in *Theological Investigations, vol. 7: Further Theology of the Spiritual Life 1* (trans. David Bourke; New York: Herder and Herder and London: Darton, Longman and Todd, 1971), pp. 13–24.
Rahner, Karl, 'The Ignatian Mysticism of Joy in the World', in *Theological Investigations, vol. 3: The Theology of the Spiritual Life* (trans. Karl-H. Kruger; London: Darton Longman and Todd and New York: The Seabury Press, 1974), pp. 277–93.
Ramirez, Janina, *The Private Lives of the Saints: Power, Passion and Politics in Anglo-Saxon England* (London: W.H. Allen, 2016).
Ratzinger, Joseph, *Daughter Sion: Meditation on the Church's Marian Belief* (trans. John M. McDermott, SJ; San Francisco: Ignatius Press, 1983).
Ratzinger, Joseph, *The Feast of Faith: Approaches to a Theology of the Liturgy* (trans. Graham Harrison; San Francisco: Ignatius Press, 1986).
Ratzinger, Joseph, 'Five Meditations', in Joseph Ratzinger and William Congdon, *The Sabbath of History* (Washington, DC: William G. Congdon Foundation, 2000), pp. 15–57.
Ratzinger, Joseph, 'Licht', in *Handbuch der theologischen Grundbegriffe* (ed. Heinrich Fries; Munich: Kösel, 1963), pp. 44–54.
Ratzinger, Joseph, *The Spirit of the Liturgy* (trans. John Saward; San Francisco: Ignatius Press, 2000).
Ratzinger, Joseph and William Congdon, *The Sabbath of History* (Washington, DC: William G. Congdon Foundation, 2000).
Reid, Alcuin (ed.), *T&T Clark Companion to Liturgy* (London: Bloomsbury, 2016).
Resseguie, James L., *The Revelation of John: A Narrative Commentary* (Grand Rapids, MI: Baker Academic, 2009).
Revard, Stella P., 'Christ and Apollo in the Seventeenth-Century Religious Lyric', in *New Perspectives on the Seventeenth-Century English Religious Lyric* (ed. John R. Roberts; Colombia and London: University of Missouri Press, 1994), pp. 143–67.
Robert, Sylvie, *Les chemins de Dieu avec Ignace de Loyola* (Paris: Editions Facultés Jésuites de Paris, 2009).
Roberts, J.M., *The Penguin History of the World* (London: Penguin, 1997).
Roberts, Alexander and James Donaldson (eds), *Ante-Nicene Fathers: The Writings of the Fathers down to A.D. 325* (revised A. Cleveland Coxe; New York: Christian Literature Publishing Co., 1885).
Roberts, John R. (ed.), *New Perspectives on the Seventeenth-Century English Religious Lyric* (Colombia and London: University of Missouri Press, 1994).

Roll, Susan K., 'Christ as Sun/King: The Historical Roots of a Perduring Dualism', *Journal of the European Society of Women in Theological Research* 6 (1998), pp. 133–42.

Roll, Susan K., 'The Origins of Christmas: The State of the Question', in *Between Memory and Hope* (ed. Maxwell E. Johnson; Collegeville, MA: Liturgical Press, 2000), pp. 273–90.

Roll, Susan K., *Towards the Origins of Christmas* (Kampen: Kok Pharos, 1995).

Römer, Thomas, *The Invention of God* (trans. Raymond Guess; Cambridge, MA and London: Harvard University Press, 2015).

Rosenroth, Christian Knorr von, '*Morgenglanz der Ewigkeit*'. Available online: http://www.liederdatenbank.de/song/1671 (accessed 3 January 2020).

Ruffer, Tim, et al. (eds), *Ancient and Modern: Hymns and Songs for Refreshing Worship* (London: Hymns Ancient and Modern, 2013).

Sale, Giovanni, SJ (ed.), *Ignazio e l'arte dei gesuiti* (Rome: La Civiltà Cattolica, 2003).

Salin, Dominique, *L'expérience spirituelle et son langage: leçons sur la tradition mystique chrétienne* (Paris: Editions Facultés Jésuites de Paris, 2015).

Salin, Dominique, 'The Treatise on Abandonment to Divine Providence', *The Way* 46.2 (2007), pp. 21–36.

Savon, Henri, 'Zacharie, 6, 12, et les justifications patristiques de la prière vers l'orient', *Augustinianum* 20 (1980), pp. 319–33.

Schaff, Philip and Henry Wallace (eds), *Nicene and Post-Nicene Fathers* (Second Series; New York: The Christian Literature Company; Oxford and London: Parker and Company, 1893).

Schibelle, Nadine, *Hagia Sophia and the Byzantine Aesthetic Experience* (London: Routledge, 2016).

Schipper, Bernd U., 'Egyptian Background to the Psalms', in *Oxford Handbook of the Psalms* (ed. William P. Brown; New York: Oxford University Press, 2014), pp. 57–75.

Schönborn, Hans-Bernhard, '*Die Morgenröte*: Eine Naturerscheinung in Literatur und Kirchenlied', *Jahrbuch für Liturgik und Hymnologie* 23 (1979), pp. 145–57.

Schöllgen, Georg (ed.), *Reallexikon für Antike und Christentum, vol. 23* (Stuttgart: Anton Hiersemann, 2010).

Schröter, Elisabeth, 'Der Vatikan als Hügel Apollons und der Musen. Kunst und Panegyrik von Nikolaus V. bis Julius II.', *Römische Quartalschrift für christliche Altertumskunde und Kirchengeschichte* 74 (1979), pp. 208–40.

Schulte, Francisco Raymund, OSB, *A Mexican Spirituality of Divine Election for a Mission: Its Sources in Published Guadalupan Sermons, 1661–1821* (Rome: Gregorian University, 1994).

Schumacher, Lydia, *Divine Illumination: The History and Future of Augustine's Theory of Knowledge* (Chichester: Wiley-Blackwell, 2011).

Second Vatican Council, Constitution *Sacrosanctum Concilium*. Available online: http://www.vatican.va/archive/hist_councils/ii_vatican_council/documents/vat-ii_const_19631204_sacrosanctum-concilium_en.html (accessed 29 April 2020).

Seifrid, Mark A., *The Second Letter to the Corinthians* (Grand Rapids, MI and Cambridge, UK: Eerdmans, 2014).

Senior, Donald, CP, *Raymond E. Brown and the Catholic Biblical Renewal* (New York and Mahwah, NJ: Paulist Press, 2018).

Shaw, Prue, *Reading Dante: From Here to Eternity* (New York and London: Liveright, W. W. Norton & Company 2015).

Shea, Henry, SJ, 'Inculturation and the Guadalupana', *Lumen et Vita* 6.1 (2015). Available online: https://doi.org/10.6017/lv.v6i1.9146 (accessed 24 April 2020).

Shrimplin, Valerie, *Michelangelo, Copernicus and the Sistine Chapel: The Last Judgement Decoded* (Saarbrücken: Lap Lambert Academic Publishing, 2013).
Simon, Otto von, *The Gothic Cathedral: Origins of Gothic Architecture and the Mediaeval Concept of Order* (Princeton, NJ: Princeton University Press, 1988).
Sister Mary David, *The Joy of God: Collected Writings* (London: Bloomsbury Continuum, 2019).
Smith, Mark S., *The Early History of God: Yahweh and the Other Deities in Ancient Israel* (Grand Rapids, MI and Cambridge, UK: Eerdmans, 2002).
Smith, Mark S., 'The Near Eastern Background of Solar Language for Yahweh', *Journal of Biblical Literature* 109.1 (1990), pp. 29–39.
Smith, Steven D., *Pagans and Christians in the City: Culture Wars from the Tiber to the Potomac* (Grand Rapids, MI: Eerdmans, 2018).
Sor Juana Inés de la Cruz, *Sor Juana Inés de la Cruz, Selected Writings* (trans. and introduction Pamela Kirk Rappaport (Mahwah, NJ: Paulist Press, 2005).
Soskice, Janet Martin, *Metaphor and Religious Language* (Oxford: Clarendon Press, 1987).
Speer, Andreas, 'Is There a Theology of the Gothic Cathedral? A Re-reading of Abbot Suger's Writings on the Abbey Church of St.-Denis', in *The Mind's Eye: Art and Theological Argument in the Middle Ages* (eds Jeffrey F. Hamburger and Anne-Marie Bouché; Princeton, NJ: Princeton University Press, 2006), pp. 65–83.
Špidlík, Tomaš, *The Spirituality of the Christian East, vol. 2: Prayer: The Spirituality of the Christian East* (Kalamazoo, MI: Cistercian Publications, 2005).
Spier, Jeffrey (ed. with contributions by Herbert L. Kessler, et al.), *Picturing the Bible: The Earliest Christian Art* (New Haven and London: Yale University Press, 2008).
Spinks, Bryan D., 'The Growth of Liturgy and the Church Year', in *The Cambridge History of Christianity, vol. 2: Constantine to c. 600* (eds. Augustine Casiday and Frederick W. Norris; Cambridge: Cambridge University Press, 2007), pp. 601–17.
Stalley, Roger, *Early Irish Sculpture and the Art of the High Crosses* (New Haven and London: Paul Mellon Centre for Studies in British Art, Yale University Press, 2020).
Staniforth, Maxwell (trans.), *Early Christian Writings: The Apostolic Fathers* (Harmondsworth: Penguin, 1968).
'Stat Crux'. Available online: http://www.cartusiana.org/node/4943 (accessed 26 April 2020).
Steiner, Rudolf, *The Gospel of John* (Hudson, NY: Anthroposophic Press, 1984).
Steiner, Rudolf, *The Sun-Mystery in the Course of Human History: The Palladium, A Lecture by Rudolf Steiner, Dornach, 6 November 1921, GA 208'* (trans. D. S. Osmund; London: Rudolf Steiner Publishing Co., 1955). Available online: https://wn.rsarchive.org/GA/GA0208/19211106p01.html (accessed 25 April 2020).
Stevens, Wallace, *Selected Poems* (repr., London: Faber and Faber, 2010).
Strabenow, Jörg (ed.), *Lo spazio e il culto: relazioni tra edificio ecclesiale e uso liturgico dal xv al xvi secolo* (Venice: Marsilio, 2006).
Straw, Carole, *Gregory the Great: Perfection in Imperfection* (Berkeley, Los Angeles and London: University of California Press, 1988).
Suger, *Abbot Suger on the Abbey Church of St.-Denis and Its Art Treasures* (ed. and trans. Erwin Panofsky; Princeton, NJ: Princeton University Press, 1979).
Swan, William Declan, *The Experience of God in the Writings of Saint Patrick: Reworking a Faith Received* (Rome: Gregorian University, 2013).
Taft, Robert, *Beyond East and West: Problems in Liturgical Understanding* (Washington, DC: The Pastoral Press, 1984).
Taft, Robert, 'The Divine Office: Monastic Choir, Prayer Book, or Liturgy of the People of God? An Evaluation of the New Liturgy of the Hours in its Historical Context', in

Vatican II Assessment and Perspectives: Twenty-five Years After (1962–1967), vol. 2 (ed. René Latourelle; New York and Mahwah: Paulist Press, 1989), pp. 27–46.

Taft, Robert, *Liturgy of the Hours in East and West: The Origin of the Divine Office and Its Meaning for Today* (Collegeville: Liturgical Press,1993).

Taft, Robert, 'Spazio e orientamento nelle liturgie dell'oriente e dell'occidente: convergenze e divergenze', in *Spazio liturgico e orientamento: atti del IV convegno liturgico internazionale Bose, 1–3 giugno 2006* (ed. Goffredo Boselli; Magnano: Edizioni Qiqajon, 2007), pp. 217–39.

Tanner, Katheryn E., 'The Use of Perceived Properties of Light as a Theological Analogy', in *Light from Light: Scientists and Theologians in Dialogue* (ed. Gerald O'Collins, SJ and Mary Ann Myers (Grand Rapids, MI and Cambridge, UK: Eerdmans, 2012), pp. 122–30.

Tanzella-Nitti, Giuseppe, 'The Two Books Prior to the Scientific Revolution', *Annales Theologici* 18 (2004), pp. 51–83.

Taylor, Charles, *A Secular Age* (Cambridge, MA and London: The Belknap Press of Harvard University Press, 2007).

Taylor, J. Glen, *Yahweh and the Sun: Biblical and Archaeological Evidence for Sun Worship in Ancient Israel* (Sheffield: Sheffield Academic Press, 1993).

Teresa of Avila, 'The Interior Castle 7.1–2', in *The Essential Writings of Christian Mysticism* (ed. Bernard McGinn; New York: Random House, 2006), 451–9.

Thérèse of Lisieux, *Manuscript C*. Available online: http://www.archives-carmel-lisieux.fr/english/carmel/index.php/c01-10/c05/c05v (accessed 29 April 2020).

Thérèse of Lisieux, Sainte Thérèse de l'Enfant Jésus, *Manuscrits autobiographiques* (Lisieux: Carmel de Lisieux, 1957).

Thomas Aquinas, *Commentary on the Gospel of John Chapters 1–8* (ed. The Aquinas Institute; trans. Fr. Fabian R. Larcher, O.P.; Latin/English Edition of the Works of St. Thomas Aquinas, 35; Lander, WY: The Aquinas Institute for the Study of Sacred Doctrine, 2013).

Thomas Aquinas, *Commentary on the Gospel of John Chapters 9–21*(ed. The Aquinas Institute; trans. Fr. Fabian R. Larcher, O.P.; Latin/English Edition of the Works of St. Thomas Aquinas, 36; Lander, WY: The Aquinas Institute for the Study of Sacred Doctrine, 2013).

Thomas Aquinas, S. Tommaso d'Aquino, *Commento ai nomi divini di Dionigi e testo integrale di Dionigi, vol. 1, capitoli 1–4* (trans. Battista Mondin; Bologna: Edizioni Studio Domenicano, 2004).

Thomas Aquinas, *S. Thomae Aquinatis Scriptum Super Libros Sententiarum Magistri Petri Lombardi Episcopi Parisiensis, vol. 1* (ed. P. Mandonnet; Paris: P. Lethielleux, 1929).

Thomas Aquinas, *Summa Theologiae, vol. 3: (1a 12 – 13) Knowing and Naming God* (ed. Thomas Gilby, OP; trans. Herbert McCabe, OP; repr., Cambridge: Cambridge University Press, 2006).

Thomas Aquinas, *Summa Theologiae vol. 10: (1a 65 – 74) Cosmogony* (ed. Thomas Gilby, OP; trans. William A. Wallace; repr., Cambridge: Cambridge University Press, 2006).

Thomas Aquinas, *Summa Theologiae, vol. 31: (2a2ae. 1–7) Faith* (ed. Thomas Gilby, OP; trans. T. C. O'Brien; repr., Cambridge: Cambridge University Press, 2006).

Tixier, Frédéric, *La monstrance eucharistique: genèse, typologie et fonctions d'un objet d'orfèvrerie (xiii-xvi siècle)* (Rennes: Presses Universitaires de Renne, 2014).

Toynbee, Jocelyn and John Ward Perkins, *The Shrine of St Peter and the Vatican Excavations* (London: Longmans Green & Co, 1956).

Traherne, Thomas, *Centuries* (London and Oxford: Mowbray, 1960).

Traherne, Thomas *Christian Ethicks* (ed. George Robert Guffrey and general introduction and commentary by Carol L. Marks; Ithaca, NY: Cornell University Press, 1968).

Traherne, Thomas, 'Wonder'. Available online: https://www.poetryfoundation.org/poems/45418/wonder-56d22507c0b42. (accessed 24 April 2020).

Tripolitis, Antonia, 'ΦΟΣ ΙΛΑΡΟΝ: Ancient Hymn and Modern Enigma', *Vigiliae Christianae* 24 (1970), pp. 189–96.

Turner, Denys, *The Darkness of God: Negativity in Christian Mysticism* (Cambridge: Cambridge University Press, 1998).

Unesco, et al., *Starlight: Declaration in Defence of the Night Sky and the Right to Starlight* (La Palma: Starlight Institute, 2007). Available online: http://www.archeoastronomy.org/downloads/starlightdeclarationc.pdf (accessed 26 April 2020).

Vagaggini, Cyprian, OSB, *Theological Dimensions of the Liturgy: A General Treatise on the Theology of the Liturgy* (Collegeville, MN: The Liturgical Press, 1976).

Van der Sandt, Maximilian, SJ, *Pro Theologia Mystica Clavis Elucidarium, Onomasticon Vocabulorum et Loquutionum Obscurarum* (repr., Heverlee-Louvain: Éditions de la Bibliothèque SJ, 1963).

Vauchez, André, *Francis of Assisi: The Life and Afterlife of a Medieval Saint* (trans. Michael F. Cusato; New Haven and London: Yale University Press, 2012).

Vauchez, André, 'Lumières au moyen âge', in *Séance de rentrée des cinq académies sur le thème: « la lumière » mardi 27 octobre 2009 sous la coupole* (Paris: Institut de France, 2009). Available online: http://seance-cinq-academies-2010.institut-de-france.fr/discours/2009/vauchez.pdf (accessed 22 April 2020).

Verhoef, Pieter A., *The Books of Haggai and Malachi* (Grand Rapids, MI: Eerdmans, 1987).

Vitray-Meyerovitch, Evade de (ed.), *Anthologie du soufisme* (Paris: Sindbad, 1978).

Vitruvius Pollo, *The Ten Books on Architecture* (trans. Morris Hickey Morgan; Cambridge MA: Harvard University Press and London: Humphrey Milford, Oxford University Press, 1926).

Vogel, Cyrille, 'Sol aequinoctialis: problèmes et technique de l'orientation dans le culte chrétien', *Revue des Sciences Religieuses* 36.3 (1962), pp. 175–211.

Vogel, Cyrille, 'Versus ad Orientem: l'orientation dans les *Ordines Romani* du haut moyen âge', *Studi Medievali* 3.1 (1960), pp. 447–69.

Wallraff, Martin, *Christus Verus Sol: Sonnenverehrung und Christentum in der Spätantike* (Münster: Aschendorff, 2001).

Wallraff, Martin, 'Constantine's Devotion to the Sun after 324', *Studia Patristica* 34 (2001), pp. 256–69.

Wallraff, Martin, 'Die Ursprünge der christlichen Gebetsostung', *Zeitschrift für Kirchengeschichte* 111 (2000), pp. 169–84.

Wallraff, Martin, '*In Quo Signo Vicit?* Una Rilettura della visione e ascesa al potere di Costantino', in *Costantino prima e dopo Costantino Constantine before and after Constantine* (eds Giorgio Bonamente, et al.; Bari: Edipuglia, 2012), pp. 133–44.

Wallraff, Martin, 'Licht', in *Reallexikon für Antike und Christentum, vol. 23* (ed. Georg Schöllgen; Stuttgart: Anton Hiersemann, 2010), pp. 100–37.

Wallraff, Martin, 'Premesse', in *Spazio liturgico e orientamento: atti del IV convegno liturgico internazionale Bose, 1–3 giugno 2006* (ed. Goffredo Boselli; Magnano: Edizioni Qiqajon, 2007), pp. 155–65.

Wallraff, Martin, '"Sonne der Gerechtigkeit" Christus und die Sonne in der Spätantike', in *Sonne: Brennpunkt der Kulturen der Welt* (ed. Andrea Bärnreuther; Neu-Isenburg: Edition Minerva, 2009), pp. 75–85.

Wallraff, Martin, *Sonnenkönig der Spätantike: die Religionspolitik Konstantins des Grossen* (Freiburg im Breisgau: Herder, 2013).
Ware, Kallistos, 'Light and Darkness in the Mystical Theology of the Greek Fathers', in *Light from Light: Scientists and Theologians in Dialogue* (eds Gerald O'Collins, SJ and Mary Ann Myers; Grand Rapids, MI and Cambridge, UK: Eerdmans, 2012), pp. 131–59.
Warnke, Martin, et al. (eds), *Handbuch der politischen Ikonographie, vol. 2: Imperator bis Zwerg* (Munich: C. H. Beck, 2011).
Wesley, John and Charles Wesley, *Selected Prayers, Hymns, Journal Notes, Sermons, Letters and Treatises* (ed. Frank Whaling; London: SPCK, 1981).
Wessel, Susan, *Leo the Great and the Spiritual Rebuilding of a Universal Rome* (Leiden and Boston: Brill, 2008).
Where Silence Is Praise: From the Writings of a Carthusian (trans. A Monk of Parkminster; London: Darton, Longman and Todd, 1997).
Whidden, David L. III, *Christ the Light: The Theology of Light and Illumination in Thomas Aquinas* (Minneapolis: Fortress Press, 2014).
White, Roger M., *The Structure of Metaphor: The Way the Language of Metaphor Works* (Oxford: Blackwell, 1996).
Williams, Rowan D., 'The Philosophical Structures of Palamism', *Eastern Churches Review* 9.1–2 (1977), pp. 27–44.
Winkler, Gabrielle, 'The Appearance of the Light at the Baptism of Jesus and the Origins of the Feast of Epiphany: An Investigation of Greek, Syriac, Armenian, and Latin Sources', in *Between Memory and Hope: Readings on the Liturgical Year* (ed. Maxwell E. Johnson; Collegeville, MN: The Liturgical Press, 2000), pp. 291–347.
Woods, David, 'St Patrick and the "Sun" (*Conf.* 20)', *Studia Hibernica* 34 (2006–7), pp. 9–16.
Woolfenden, Gregory W., *Daily Liturgical Prayer: Origins and Theology* (Aldershot: Ashgate, 2004).
Wright, N.T. and Michael F. Bird, *The New Testament and Its World: An Introduction to the History, Literature and Theology of the First Christians* (London: SPCK, 2019).
Wright, Tom, *Paul: A Biography* (London: SPCK, 2018).
Zajonc, Arthur, *Catching the Light: The Entwined History of Light and Mind* (New York and Oxford: Oxford University Press, 1995).
Zander, Valentine, *St Seraphim of Sarov* (trans. Sister Gabriel Anne SSC; London: SPCK, 1975).
Ziegler, Hendrik, 'Sonne', in *Handbuch der politischen Ikonographie, vol. 2: Imperator bis Zwerg* (ed. Uwe Fleckner, et al.; Munich: C. H. Beck, 2011), pp. 358–65.

BIBLICAL REFERENCE INDEX

Old Testament

Genesis
1.1–5   5
1.16–19   5

Exodus
10.21   8
20.21   6
24   11
24.16   6
34   11

Numbers
6.24–26   11

Deuteronomy
4.19   7
11.26   136
33.2   7

Joshua
10.12–13   6

2 Samuel
23.3b–4   7

2 Kings
23.5   7
23.11   7

Job
31.26–27   7

Psalms
17   20
17.8   9
19.5   7
80.7   7
84.11   7
85.11–13   8

97.2   6
103.5   117
104.2   6
104.20–23   5
148.3   6

Proverbs
4.19   6

Ecclesiastes
2.14   6

Sirach
33.7   5

Wisdom
7.26   10
7.29–30   10
16.28   105

Isaiah
1.17   133
9.2   12
30.26   136
58.8   9
60.1   7, 116

Jeremiah
8.1–2   6

Ezekiel
8.16   7
8.16–18   7
43.2   10

Daniel
2.22   6
6.10   104

Habakkuk
3.4   6

Zechariah		20.18	134
3.8	10, 132		
6.12	10–11, 20, 105	Acts	
		10.9	105
Malachi		16.13	105
4.1	136	17.34	26
4.1–3	136	22.14	132
4.2	7–9, 15, 19–20, 49, 53, 66, 91, 95, 131, 136, 144		
		Romans	
4.3	136	13.12–13	10
		13.13	6

New Testament

		2 Corinthians	
Matthew		4.5–6	11
4.12–25	132		
4.16	12, 95	Ephesians	
13.43	12	5.14	6, 11, 19, 91
14.19	105		
17.1–2	11	1 Thessalonians	
17.1–9	11	5.4–5	20
23.37	15	5.5	5
		5.16–18	6
Mark		5.17	123
6.41	105		
7.34	105	1 Timothy	
9.2–8	11	6.16	6, 33
16.2	121		
		Hebrew	
Luke		1.3	20
1.78	119, 144	12.12	49
1.78–79	10, 11, 12, 116, 132		
2.32	116	James	
9.16	105	1.17	6, 66
9.28–36	11		
13.34	15	1 John	
		1	91
John		1.5	6, 91
1.14	10	5	91
4.14	80		
8.12	10	Revelation	
9.1–41	10	1.16b–17	12
9.5	10	7.16	12
11.41	104	21.23	12, 24, 93
12.35	10	22.4	12
13.30	20	22.5	12
17.1	104		

INDEX

Acts of Pilate 119
ad orientem 103, 108, 111, 122–4, 143
Aeschylus 19
Akhenaten 8, 9
Alan of Lille 77
Alexandria 9, 18, 25, 26, 46, 95, 105
Ambrose of Milan 16, 25, 32, 33, 40, 84, 117, 132–3, 143
Amphilochius of Iconium 119
Anastasis icon 119–20, 130, 132, 144
anatole 10–12, 15, 84, 85, 94, 106, 122, 140
Ancient and Modern 94–5
Annunciation 65, 116
Anselm of Canterbury 46
Apollo (sun god) 17, 21, 23, 24, 58–9, 84, 135
Apuleius 121
architecture 24, 47–9, 60–1, 78, 107–8, 118, 143
astronomy 10, 46, 60, 61, 89–90, 92, 99
Athanasius of Alexandria 17
Augustine of Hippo 22, 32–5, 40, 47, 77, 82, 91, 107, 117
Aurelian, Emperor 21, 116
Aztec 63–4, 69, 134, 143

Balthasar, Hans Urs von 78, 80–1
baptism 61, 115, 117–18, 120
basilica 24–5, 35–6, 47, 60–1, 105, 107, 111
Basil of Caesarea 16, 69, 105–6
Benedictus (Canticle, Lk.1.78–79) 10–11, 39
Benedictus male versus (church of) 108
Benedict XVI, Pope 49, 50, 78, 91–2, 100, 120, 142
Bernardine of Siena 62
Bernard of Clairvaux 46, 48, 49, 79
Bérulle, Pierre de 61, 69, 89, 143
Bewcastle Cross 39
Blake, William 84

Bonaventure of Bagnoregio 53, 93
Bonhoeffer, Dietrich 90–1
Book of Nature 59, 69, 77, 85, 93, 100, 142–3
Book of Scripture 77, 141–2
Bowie, David 131
Bradbury, Ray 90
Brooke, Rupert 133
Browne, Thomas 77
Bunyan, John 96
Butterfield, Herbert 60

Caesarius of Arles 24–5
Call of St Matthew, The (Caravaggio) 65
Campanella, Tommaso 59
Campbell, Roy 23
Canticle of Brother Sun (Francis of Assisi) 51–2, 92–3, 100, 136, 144
Cappadocia 115
Caravaggio 65
Carmelites 65–7, 128–9
Carthusians 97–8, 130, 135
Caussade, Jean-Pierre de 110
Centuries (Traherne) 67–9
Chantal, Jane Frances de 109
Chenu, M. D. 45, 53
Christ
   divinity of 17–18
   incarnation 35, 49, 61, 115–16, 124
   Pantokrator 23
   risen 6, 46, 79, 91, 93–4, 120–1, 132, 134
   Rising Sun (Luke 1.78) 10–11, 12, 83, 144. See also *anatole*
   shining face of 11–12
   as solar emperor 23–4
   and sun 10–12, 15, 17–18, 64, 83, 132–3
   'Sun of Christ' 94
   Sun of Justice 7–9, 12, 15, 18–20, 24, 26, 32–3, 35, 46, 49, 51–2, 53, 61–4, 79, 91–4, 96–8, 105–6, 116–18,

120–2, 124, 127 n.63, 131–7, 140, 142, 144
Christmas 17–18, 35, 46, 95, 115, 116, 122, 123
chronobiology 90, 99, 143
Chrysostom, John 82, 118, 119
churches
　Eastern 78–9, 85, 92, 110–11, 116, 121
　light in 24–5, 47–9
　orientation of 103–9
　Western 13, 32–40, 40, 54, 69–70, 78–80, 91, 106–11, 134, 141
Cistercians 48–9
Clement of Alexandria 15, 18–19, 24, 92, 109, 119
Clément, Olivier 78–9
Constantine 21–2, 24, 26–7, 81, 107
Constantinople 21–2, 24, 78, 111
Copernicus, Nicholaus 58–60, 89
cosmic order 8, 63, 134–5
Cosma e Damiano, Basilica of 24
cosmos, fading interest 36, 40
Council of Nicaea 17, 21
Cox, Brian 89
Cupitt, Don 84–5
Cyprian of Carthage 16

Daniel 104
Dante Alighieri 54, 58, 77, 92
darkness
　bad 6, 9–10, 20
　and cloud 13, 25, 26, 78, 141
　good 6, 11, 12, 20, 25–6, 65–6, 69, 91, 141
　and inwardness 109
　and light 5–6, 8–11, 13, 16, 25–7, 60, 78, 79, 82, 91, 131, 140–2
Dark Night (John of the Cross) 65–7, 69–70, 96, 98, 120, 130, 131, 141
Dawkins, Richard 89–90
Day of the Sun. *See* Sunday
De Blaauw, Sible 107
De Contemplatione (Guigo de Ponte) 97–8
Descartes, René 110
Dialogue with Trypho (Justin Martyr) 118
dies solis. See Sunday
Dionysius the Areopagite 6, 26–7, 38, 45, 48, 65, 67, 141
Divine Comedy (Dante Alighieri) 54, 77, 142
Donne, John 65, 106

Druzbicki, Gaspar 62
Durandus, Guillelmus 106

east 10, 20, 61, 103, 105–9
Easter 39, 45, 92, 93–4, 117–18, 120–1, 122, 131
Eastern church 78–9, 85, 92, 110–11, 116, 121
Easter Vigil 92, 120, 122, 131
Edict of Milan 21
Edison, Thomas 90, 142
Egeria 16
Egypt 7–9, 18–21, 26, 115
Eliade, Mircea 93, 143
Elich, Tom 122–3
Eliot, T. S. 123
Ephrem of Syria 115
Epiphany 46, 115–16, 122, 132
equinox 36, 39, 106
Eriugena, John Scotus 38, 45, 53
Ernst, Cornelius 53
esoteric practices 79, 81–2, 141, 143
eucharist 22, 62–4, 83, 91, 103, 105, 107, 111–12, 117, 119, 121, 122, 124, 143
Eucherius of Lyons 34–5
Eusebius of Caesarea 15–16, 21, 24
Evagrius of Pontus 77
Evangelii Gaudium (Pope Francis) 93
Eymard, Pierre-Julien 62

Fahrenheit 451 (Bradbury) 90
Ficino, Marsilio 59
Fontaine, Jacques 32
Francis de Sales 109–10
Francis of Assisi 48, 51–2, 54, 67, 92, 100, 104, 136, 142, 144
Francis, Pope 1, 21, 51, 62, 63, 77, 78, 89, 92–4, 100, 122, 131–4, 142

Galilei, Galileo 59–61, 77, 92
Galli, Carlos María 93–4, 142–3
Gertrude the Great of Helfta 50–1, 68, 142
Gildas 38
Giuffo, John 78
Good Friday 45, 106, 118, 120, 131
Grabar, André 23
graves 1, 103–4, 107
Gregory of Nazianzen 17
Gregory of Nyssa 25, 27, 104, 141

Gregory the Great, Pope 36–7, 72 n.49, 108, 109
Gregory XIII, Pope 92
Guadalupe, Virgin of 64
Guigo de Ponte 97–8

Hagia Sophia 25, 111, 142
Harrowing of Hell 119, 120
healing 9, 10, 12, 15, 33, 49, 66, 77, 105, 135–6
health 79, 90, 134, 135
Heaney, Seamus 40, 63
Herbert, George 85
Hesychius of Jerusalem 120
high crosses 38–9
    Bewcastle Cross 39
    Monasterboice 39
    Ruthwell Cross 39
Hildegard of Bingen 49–50, 54, 83
Hippolytus 15, 134
History of the World (Raleigh) 77
Holy Saturday 118–20
Holy Spirit 32, 50, 91, 103, 107
Homo sapiens 89
Hopkins, John Henry 96
Hugh of St Victor 77
hymns 7, 8, 11, 16, 19, 32, 40, 84, 94–7, 100, 123, 143

idolatry 5, 17, 62, 81–2, 92, 105, 142
Ignatius of Antioch 15, 118
Ignatius of Loyola 61–2
IHS 62
illumination 11, 12, 40, 47, 53, 61, 67, 117
imperial style theory 23
incarnation 35, 49, 61, 115–16, 124
inculturation 16–17, 26, 39, 63, 69, 143
Insular Christianity 37–40
interiority 34, 36, 109–11
Introduction to the Devout Life (Francis de Sales) 110
Ishiguro, Kazuo 135–6

Jane Frances de Chantal 109
Jennings, Elizabeth 69
Jesus. *See* Christ
John, Gospel of 9–10, 19, 134
John Damascene 1, 106, 118, 119

John of the Cross 6, 65–7, 69–70, 79, 96, 98, 110, 129, 130, 141
John XXIII, Pope 94
Joy of God, The (Sister Mary David) 79–80
Julian, Emperor 16
justice *See* Sun of Justice (Malachi 4.2)
Justin Martyr 15, 92, 118
Justinian 24

Kantorowicz, Ernst H. 23
Kavanagh, Patrick 63, 81, 133
Klara and the Sun (Ishiguro) 135–6

Larkin, Philip 129–30, 141
La Rochefoucauld, François de 131
Las Casas, Bartolomé de 64
Last Judgement, The (Michelangelo) 58
Late Mattia Pascal, The (Pirandello) 89
Laudato sì (Pope Francis) 51, 78, 92–3, 122, 144
Lawrence, D. H. 93
Lentini, Anselmo 123
Leo the Great, Pope 24, 35–6, 92, 107, 140
Leo X, Pope 58–9
Lewis, C. S. 67
light
    chinks of 21, 36–7, 81
    church 24–5, 47–9
    and darkness 5–6, 8–11, 13, 16, 25–7, 60, 78–9, 82, 91, 131, 140–2
    feasts of (Epiphany and Christmas) 115–16, 122–3
    interior 19, 34, 60–1, 79–80
    language of 53–4, 82
    Light Ages The (Falk) 46
    in Scripture 5–6, 9–10
    and the sun 5, 7, 10–12, 32, 45–6, 49, 54, 61, 77–80, 82, 85, 111, 115, 121–4, 132, 140, 141, 144
Liturgy of the Hours 123–4, 143
Lossky, Vladimir 82
Lubac, Henri de 46, 78
Lucernarium 121. *See also Phos Hilaron*
lumen 56 n.28, 121–3
Lumen Fidei (Pope Francis) 92
lux 47, 56 n.28, 88 n.53, 121–3

ma'at 8, 134
McCabe, Herbert 83

McGahern, John 1–2, 39–40, 48, 81, 93–4, 103–4, 121, 122, 132, 135–6, 141
McGrath, Alister 78, 143
McInroy, Mark 80
Manicheism 33, 35, 91, 141
Marco da Lisbona 104
Mary Magdalene 121, 134
Mary, Virgin 47, 64–5, 66, 84, 134
  Virgin of Guadalupe 64
Matheson, George 95–6
Mathews, Thomas F. 23
Maxentius, Basilica of 24
Maximus of Turin 17–18, 36, 121
Mechthild of Magdeburg 50
Melito of Sardis 119
Merton, Thomas 79, 98–9
Messiah 8, 10–11
metaphor 6, 7, 10, 12–13, 17–18, 33, 53, 79–85, 109–11, 118, 132–3, 144
Michelangelo 58
Middle Ages 18, 37, 45–54, 65, 92, 104, 106, 108, 124
Milky Way Galaxy 89
Milton, John 133
Missal, Roman 112, 121–3, 143
Mithras/Sol 22–3
Moltmann, Jürgen 134
Monasterboice 39
monstrance 62–3, 64, 143
moon 6–7, 19, 21, 22, 23, 50, 66, 77, 84, 88 n.55, 94, 132, 134
Murray, Paul 99

Nativity of Christ *See* Christmas
natural theology 78, 85, 111, 143–4
Newton, Isaac 60
Nicaea. *See* Council of Nicaea
Nietzsche, Friedrich 128–30, 141
night. *See also* Dark Night (John of the Cross)
  and darkness 20, 26
  and day 90, 143

O Antiphons 116
Odes of Solomon 15
On Architecture (Vitruvius) 107
oriens 35, 122, 123, 140
oriented prayer 105–9
Origen 6, 15, 19–21, 25–7, 80, 105, 141
Ovid 135

pagan 7, 18–19, 22–3, 25, 26, 32, 35–6, 40, 62, 63, 91, 92, 95, 99, 100, 104, 107, 108, 115, 116, 119, 121, 128, 130, 140
Palamas, Gregory 110
Palladius 108
Panofsky, Ervin 48
Pantokrator 23
paschal mystery 49, 117–21, 124, 136
Patrick, St 37–8
Paul IV, Pope 64
Paul, St 5–6, 10–12, 20, 26
Philosophy of Right (Hegel) 132
Phos Hilaron 16, 94
photismos 117
Physiologus 18, 83, 117
Pilgrim's Progress, The (Bunyan) 96
Pio of Pietrelcina 79
Pirandello, Luigi 89
Pliny 22
polytheism 6, 21, 92, 142
Pontificale Romanum 108
prayer
  daily 15–16, 124, 143
  evening 16, 51, 94, 121, 123–4, 143
  morning 16, 51, 90–1, 143
  oriented 105–6
  vertical 103–5, 112, 121–3
Protrepticus, or *Exhortation to the Heathen* (Clement of Alexandria) 19
Prudentius 25

Rabelais, François 59
Rahner, Karl 131, 141
Raleigh, Walter 77
Ratzinger, Joseph 26, 91, 120. *See also* Benedict XVI, Pope
Ravenna 24, 25, 38, 105
Reformation 38, 58–9, 60, 94–7
Renaissance 58–60, 67, 69
resurrection 15, 19, 98, 117–21, 124, 130, 136
rising sun 10–12, 17, 26, 33, 47, 63, 83, 84, 94, 98–9, 103, 116, 122
Roberts, J. M. 58
Rome 15, 23–5, 58, 60, 107, 108, 116, 140
Rosenroth, Christian Knorr von 96
Ruthwell Cross 39

sacred direction 103–12
Sacred Songs (Matheson) 95
Saint-Denis 47–8
Saint Peter, Basilica of 24, 25, 35–6, 58, 60, 107, 108, 140
Sales, Francis de 109, 110
Sant'Apollinare, Basilica of 25, 38, 105
Santa Prassede, Basilica of 47
Santa Pudenziana, Basilica of 24
science and technology 60, 89–91, 143
Self-Abandonment to Divine Providence 110
sense experience 80–2
Seraphim of Sarov 79
Seven Storey Mountain, The (Merton) 98
Shakespeare, William 8, 84, 104
Shamash 7, 134, 140
Shamash Hymn 7
Simon, Otto von 48
Sir Brother Sun 51–2, 93, 100, 144
Sister Mary David 79–80, 94
Society of Jesus 61–2
Sol Invictus 17–18, 21–3, 35, 92
solstice 18, 36, 37, 39, 64, 92, 106, 115, 116, 118, 123
Sor Juana Inés de la Cruz 64–5, 83
Soskice, Janet Martin 83
Spiritual Exercises (Ignatius) 61–2
spiritual senses 80–2
Stalley, Roger 39
Steiner, Rudolf 80, 81–2
Stevens, Wallace 78, 131
Suger, Abbot 47–9
sun
    and divine goodness 26, 52, 53
    interior 19, 82
    and justice 7–9. *See also* Sun of Justice (Malachi 4.2)
    and light 5, 7, 10–12, 32, 45–6, 49, 54, 61, 77–80, 82, 85, 111, 115, 121–4, 132, 140, 141, 144
    New Sun 17–18, 115, 144
    and night 20, 66–7
    Sacramented Sun 64
    setting sun 8, 16, 117, 118, 122, 123
    Spiritual Sun 19, 33, 84, 93, 144
    True Sun 33, 37, 38, 45, 51, 61, 64, 85, 92, 105, 116, 117

Unconquered Sun *See Sol Invictus*
    worship 6–7, 16, 63–4, 115
Sunday 22, 27
sunlessness 93–4, 120, 128–31, 137, 141
sunlight 6, 13, 33, 39–40, 81–2, 110, 111, 121, 142
    natural theology of 78, 143–4
    purity of 35, 121
Sun of Justice (Malachi 4.2) 7–9, 12, 15, 18–20, 24, 26, 32–3, 35, 46, 49, 51, 52, 53, 61–4, 79, 91, 94, 96–8, 105–6, 116–18, 120–2, 124, 127 n.63, 131–7, 140, 142, 144
    cosmic order 134–5
    healing and conversion 135–6
    justice in the church 133–4
Sun of Righteousness *See* Sun of Justice
sunrays 17, 20, 53, 61, 62, 64, 97
sunrise 19, 20, 24, 92, 98–9, 120, 123, 124
Symmachus, Pope 25

Taft, Robert 19, 109
Tanner, Katheryn 69
technology 11, 60, 65, 69, 89–92, 124, 132, 140, 142, 143
Teresa of Avila 82
Teresa of Calcutta 130
Tertullian 17, 105, 107, 121
That They May Face the Rising Sun (McGahern) 1–2, 39–40, 103–4, 121, 135, 141
theology, natural 78, 85, 111, 143–4
Theophilus of Antioch 16
Thérèse of Lisieux 79, 84, 128–9, 141
Thomas Aquinas 52–4, 80, 83, 106
Thus Spoke Zarathustra (Nietzsche) 128
Totah, Sister Mary David 79–80, 94
Traherne, Thomas 67–70, 118, 142

UNESCO La Palma Declaration 90
Urban VIII, Pope 60

Vatican II 94, 108, 122–4
Vaughan, Henry 65–6
Vitruvius Pollo 107

Wallraff, Martin 22
Ware, Kallistos 110

Wesley, Charles 94–5
Wesley, John 94–5
Western church 13, 32–40, 40, 54, 69–70, 78–80, 91, 106–11, 134, 141
'Wine Breath, The' (McGahern) 81
Winkler, Gabrielle 115
wintry season 130–1, 141

Wisdom personified 10, 50
Wright, Tom 111

Yahweh 6–9, 17, 134, 140

Zander, Valentine 79
Zeno of Verona 36, 117–18

www.ingramcontent.com/pod-product-compliance
Lightning Source LLC
Chambersburg PA
CBHW061836300426
44115CB00013B/2401